# SENIOR COUNSEL

## LEGAL AND FINANCIAL STRATEGIES
## FOR AGE 50 AND BEYOND

### CARL W. BATTLE
#### ATTORNEY AT LAW

With contributing authors: Reuben Brown, MBA;
Matthew Eldridge, Esq.; Valorie Jennings, Esq.;
Arnold Thibou, MBA; Leon Williams, Esq.

ALLWORTH PRESS, NEW YORK

To My Best Friend and Wife Extraordinary, Dyan Bryson Battle

and

To My Loving Mother, Ida M. Carter

Published by Allworth Press, an imprint of Allworth Communications, Inc., 10 East 23rd Street, New York, NY 10010.

Distributor to the trade in the United States:
Consortium Book Sales & Distribution, Inc.,
1045 Westgate Drive, Saint Paul, MN 55114-1065.

Book and Cover design by Douglas Design Associates, New York, NY.

ISBN: 1-880559-06-4

Library of Congress Catalog Card Number: 92-75526

This book is designed to provide accurate and authoritative information with respect to the subject matter covered. It is sold with the understanding that the publisher is not engaged in rendering legal or other professional services. If legal advice or other expert assistance is required, the services of a competent attorney or professional person should be sought. While every attempt is made to provide accurate information, the author or publisher cannot be held accountable for errors or omissions.

# TABLE OF CONTENTS

# PREFACE

America is growing older. There are more than 30 million Americans over the age of sixty-five and twice that figure for the number over fifty. By the year 2000, people age sixty-five and over will represent about 13 percent of the population, and will grow to about 22 percent, or 65 million. Senior America represents a nation within a nation.

In the past 200 years this country has seen the life expectancy of its population double. A child born today can expect to live to be at least seventy-five. The average age in our country has now reached thirty-two years and is expected to reach thirty-six by the end of the century. It should be easy to see that America is no longer a nation of youth.

Nevertheless, America in recent years has been youth-oriented. The focus of our lifestyles, fashion, and culture has been on being young. However, this is changing dramatically as America's baby boomers grow older. A lot of traditions are being and will continue to be revamped over the next twenty years.

This aging America offers a rich resource of talented workers, entrepreneurs, consultants, teachers, writers, mentors, and other professionals. Never before has such a vast pool of senior talent existed. But, ironically, this talent is virtually untapped.

As the country matures, new issues will face you and me. Our longer lives will present special requirements concerning health, independence, finances, retirement, leisure, housing, and many other issues. The normal life-cycle of 1) learning during youth, 2) working and raising a family during adulthood, and 3) retiring during old age will change with new options and opportunities during each stage. It is up to you to use these opportunities as you grow older by being adaptable and by planning ahead for your future.

The decline in the amount of time spent working is a major change of our industrialized and computerized society. Today, the average American spends only about 14 percent of his or her life working compared with about 30-40 percent for early agrarian cultures. This leisure time provides you with the freedom to explore a myriad of recreational, developmental, and professional choices.

Private pensions have been a major factor contributing to the increase in retirements and leisure activities. Nearly 60 percent of American workers are covered by private pension plans. Although social security provides some basic benefits, your financial independence in your senior years will likely come from your pension, savings, investments, and other private financial resources. For an independent and fulfilling life you will need to set financial goals and work to achieve them. You will need to be knowledgeable about your pension benefits, entitlements, and other sources of assistance.

As an elderly person, you will face many of the same legal issues as most other people, plus many more, such as pension rights, social security benefits, Medicare and Medicaid, health care, elderly housing, estate planning, making a will, probate, disability, consumer protection, taxes, and many others. You will be impacted greatly by increasing medical costs, poor economic conditions, crime, consumer fraud, and other societal ills.

The staggering problem of access to health care in America has generated a lot of public attention over the past few years. Over 40 million Americans lack health insurance. One-third of the U.S. population with incomes below the poverty level do not even qualify for Medicaid. While nearly 98 percent of older Americans are enrolled in Medicare, most remain unprotected against the catastrophic costs of long-term care and medication.

According to the U.S. Senate Special Committee on Aging, seniors are often seen as "easy marks" and specifically targeted for abuse by criminals. When victimized they suffer heavier losses and are slower to recover. The Committee identified consumer fraud as a widespread abuse, with home repair, medical insurance, nursing home, housing, investment, automobile, vacation, and funeral frauds being the most common. Today, every state and the District of Columbia has some form of consumer protection law. These laws prohibit several categories of practices aimed at consumers, including false, deceptive, or unfair acts and practices lacking in good faith. The most important way you can protect yourself against consumer fraud is through consumer education and awareness, and also by following some common sense precautions.

For many seniors, particularly in retirement years, dealing with everyday life can be like starting over. You must find the right place to live, make new friends and contacts, develop new skills, and perhaps start a new job. You may have special therapy, transportation, and personal care needs. Emotional and psychological support are also essential. As a senior, you will need to keep a position of value and respect in society to maintain your well-being and a healthy attitude.

Although planning ahead is the best way to an independent and fulfilling senior life, many of us do not take the time to do the things necessary to prepare for the future. Now, if not sooner, is the time to do the thinking and acting for managing difficult choices and crisis situations which are likely to arise in the years ahead. Act now before you are limited by physical disability or mental incapacity to make decisions for yourself.

Ensure that, if ever you cannot make decisions for yourself, others will represent your wishes, preferences and best interests. Designating a person to make decisions for you, through a power of attorney or medical directive, may help to avoid lengthy and costly court proceedings to establish guardianship. Put your wishes and decisions in writing to decrease the chances of future mismanagement and mistreatment. Prepare your will now if you have not done so at this point in your life. A will can provide a good inventory of your property and clear instructions on how you want it distributed. Look at a living trust, wherein you transfer property to yourself or someone else as trustee, if you are interested in a quicker alternative to probate.

Review your medical and life insurance needs routinely. Decide if whole, term or some other variant of life insurance is best for you. Pay careful attention to your investments and estate planning strategies to maximize benefits for you and your loved ones. Maintain good credit references and learn how to verify and correct your credit rating. Be aware of age discrimination and what remedies you may have if you have been discriminated against.

Many resources are available to seniors to foster self-reliance and fulfillment. These include senior centers, special housing, nursing and meals services, family service agencies, agencies on aging, senior associations, community centers, churches, and others. Senior organizations and advocacy groups demonstrate your social and political influence as senior citizens.

The American Association of Retired Persons (AARP), with a membership of nearly 30 million, is a tremendous resource of information and support for seniors. Other senior organizations include the 4 million-member National Council of Senior Citizens (NSCS) founded by the AFL-CIO, and the National Alliance of Senior Citizens (NASC), which has over 2 million members.

*Senior Counsel* has been compiled as an additional resource for people age fifty and older to help you attain independence and fulfillment during your senior years. This book provides some basic answers to many legal, financial, and social issues facing seniors every day. It should serve as a handy, simple, and enlightening reference to help you maximize your enjoyment and achievements in life. In some complex situations you may need to consult a legal, financial, or medical professional. But in all cases, *Senior Counsel* will offer invaluable guidance as you develop your strategies for age fifty and beyond.

# CHAPTER 1

# ATTAINING YOUR SELF-FULFILLMENT

## Focus on Yourself

What do you want most out of life? Financial security? A successful career? A close and loving family? A sense of purpose? Surely each of us wants all of these things and more to attain happiness and self-fulfillment in life. Unfortunately, most people never reach self-fulfillment or don't appreciate it when they do. People generally do not take the time and effort to enjoy the things that are most rewarding for them. Most of you simply follow the traditions presented to you and assume that you have no real control over your fate, destiny, and overall happiness. Nothing could be further from the truth.

You hold the key to your self fulfillment and inner happiness. You must decide whether an unfulfilling life of mediocrity is acceptable to you. Each of us, whether we chose to follow them or not, have inner drives, visions, and consciousness. Self-fulfillment is attained by following your inner self.

In the early to mid 1900's people had clearer definitions of success and happiness and a relatively stable model for achieving them. For men, this model was the tradition-oriented "organization man" with family values and strong loyalty to his job. For women it was almost complete devotion to home and family.

So much has changed since the 1950's. Men and women alike want more and more out of life. You want more out of your job and career than money. You want more out of life than the traditional linear life cycle of going to school, starting a career, raising a family, retiring, and dying. You want more out of relationships than convenience and pleasing others. Most of all, you want a meaningful and quality lifestyle which gives you a sense of purpose and accomplishment.

The sophisticated population of the 1980's and 1990's is exploring alternative models of lifestyles and personal success and are confronted with a wide variety of possibilities. As a result, life in the 1990's is harder to manage and control. Those of you born between the 1940's and 1960's are likely to face the 1990's as a decade of scarce promotions and advancement opportunities, frustrations, stress, burn out, and psychological problems. Both your professional and personal relationships are likely to be more temporary because of ever increasing job mobility and divorce rate. This simply means that alternative means of satisfying your aspirations need to be found as you progress through the stages of life.

With each stage in life will come constantly changing focus and interests. Your mid-life transition will likely start in your forties and continue into your fifties. You start to restabilize your choices and lifestyle. You will also seek to create a better fit between the world and yourself. It is important to realize and resolve the differences between your inner self and the realities of your particular circumstances. You are likely to take a new look at life ambitions and contemplate career changes. In fact, it may be imperative to change so that your goals can be accomplished. You are also likely to become a mentor and share your knowledge and skills with young associates and friends.

Around sixty you can expect to go through a mellowing of feelings and relationships. You develop a greater comfort with yourself and start to define your accomplishments and measurements of success, rather than have others define them for you. You start to live for yourself at this stage and not primarily for others.

Also in your sixties and beyond you can expect to go through a review of your life. You come to accept what has transpired in your life and realize that it does have worth and meaning. Self fulfillment is reached when you come to value yourself and the choices you have made. There is typically an eagerness to share everyday human joys and interactions and your family is a very important focal point.

You also become aware of your ageing, physical limitations and mortality. Although death is always a new presence and a closer reality, you shouldn't let it consume the rest of your life. Remember, you still have nearly a quarter of your life to live and these could be the most fulfilling years of your life.

An important part of self fulfillment is focusing on yourself and your career. The responsibility of career and professional development rests with the individual. Organizations are less effective in providing traditional career guidance and growth. However, a large number of people are just not prepared to manage their careers and therefore do not reach their career expectations.

To be successful you must have a macro, long-range objective focusing on where you ultimately want to be. Although your goals will change over your lifetime, review every potential opportunity, position, and employer in terms of your long-range career objectives. Some times you may have to accept short-term trade-offs for some long-term benefits. Important training opportunities and contacts can be gained from some low-paying and otherwise unexceptional jobs.

Always try to broaden your background and interests, while at the same time specializing in at least one area; preferably two or more. Be careful not to limit yourself to isolated and overly specialized job assignments. Keep your awareness for opportunities that may become available to you while in your current position. Look at college or other professional training for your further development; particularly if your employer will pay for the costs. Most major corporations and professional associations offer educational assistance and continuing education as part of their benefits package.

Honestly and objectively evaluate yourself and your performance. Recognize when you have obtained all you can from a particular situation and when you have also outstayed your opportunities. Don't view a change as an admission of failure, rather as an honest reflection of your limitations and contributions.

With our healthier, longer lives and changing needs and priorities, the way our work and career fit into our lives is also dramatically changing. People are redefining the traditional patterns of work and retirement. Rather, people are re-entering the work force on several occasions during their lifetime. We are also learning the importance of enjoying our leisure time well before retirement. Even our attitude toward retirement is changing, because our perception of retirement and senior life is changing. We are beginning to look forward to retirement with confidence and excitement.

Too few people plan for their retirement until shortly before it

comes. Yet, retirement is such a drastic change in your way of life —
all within a twenty-four hour period. Make sure that you avoid retirement shock by planning ahead and keeping a healthy attitude. Be willing to adapt to change as you did as a kid starting kindergarten, or as
a young adult getting married and starting a family. Our lives are always in a state of flux and change. Effectively managing that change
will make the difference between being happy or miserable. Happiness, success, and self fulfillment do not happen by accident.

There are several attitudes with which you can embark on your senior years. You may take a depressing "it's all over" attitude, and be
like many seniors who live lonely and emotionally disturbing later
years. You may also take an attitude of denial, refusing to accept your
seniority and forever trying to prove your youthfulness. This attitude
can have humiliating and tragic consequences because of your refusal
to deal with the physical reality of aging. The best and healthiest attitude in growing older is to be realistic and face your limitations and
potentials. Assess your assets and your liabilities and take advantage of
your strengths and capabilities. Learn to accept the things in life that you
can't change, and strive to change for the better those things that you can.

Try to maintain close contact with family and friends, and come to
rely on them for help when you need it. Don't feel any guilt for asking
for their help. At the same time be willing to assist others when you
can. Remember that family and friends can't always be there for you
because of any number of reasons. They may be far away, travelling
constantly, overworked, or facing other demands in their lives. This
means that you must be realistic in your expectations of others in planning for your senior years.

You need to decide on your financial priorities for your older adulthood. Make sure that you will receive the maximum benefits from your
pension, investments, Social Security, and other sources. Put your financial goals on paper and review them regularly to make sure that
you are achieving your objectives.

Maintaining good health is always important, but it is especially
so in your senior years. Although most senior citizens are in good
health, many are not and often do not seek treatment for health problems. It is important that you learn to understand the aging process to
distinguish between problems that require medical treatment and oth-

ers which do not need attention. You will need to establish a close and ongoing relationship with a doctor that you feel comfortable with and trust and respect. Discuss your complete medical history with your doctor, including any medications you are taking and complications you may have had in the past. Ask your doctor for recommendations and information about diet, weight, stress, exercise, medications, therapies, and anything else that you don't understand about your health. Don't be embarrassed to discuss your medical and emotional problems with your doctor.

The best prescription for good health and independence in your senior years is following your good judgment and your doctor's advice, and always keeping a positive spirit.

Again, remember to plan ahead and prepare for the future. You should decide now, while you are in sound physical and mental health, how you would like to handle situations relating to your aging, such as disability, life supporting medical treatment, or mental incapacity. Take the steps now to ensure that your wishes are carried out, such as making a will, medical directive, power of attorney, organ donor pledges, or other documents. Explain your decisions to your family and others who may have to carry out your wishes.

Staying independent and living at home is usually the preferred arrangement for most older persons. However, physical, medical, or financial problems can often prevent this from happening. There are a variety of services available for seniors to foster independent living. You may now be able to arrange for meals, assistance in grooming, dressing, shopping, health care, and various other personal care services to be delivered at your home. Many communities offer a number of these services to help you with your daily requirements, and also allow you to socialize with other people. Senior centers, churches, and other group settings provide seniors with opportunities to interact with their peers, as well as offering a variety of health care and social services.

Nevertheless, there is about a 25 percent chance that you will need to reside in a nursing home at some point in your life. Today, about 5 percent of the senior population is living in one of the nearly 20,000 nursing homes in the United States. Costs for a year's stay in a nursing home can average between $25,000 to $50,000, and little of this cost is reimbursed by Medicare or private insurance. The eventuality of a nursing home stay should be planned for to avoid wiping out your family resources. Think about how you will meet the expenses and cope with an institutional environment. What quality of care will be provided? Will it be convenient for your family and friends to visit you?

Keep in mind at all times that the basis to a happy senior life is the process of living to the fullest. Your senior years should be ones of peace and comfort spent in close, endearing relationships with family and friends. They should be a time for engaging in rewarding and satisfying activities and endeavors, and a time for helping others and sharing your knowledge and wisdom. They should also be a time for self-development and personal enrichment.

Millions of senior Americans participate in continuing adult education. This is an excellent avenue for personal development and socialization. A network of several hundred colleges, schools, and other institutions, called Elderhostel, offers low-cost, short-term residential academic programs for older adults. Adult education programs are also sponsored by local public school systems. Investigate these programs to see if they can offer some benefit for you. Take advantage of museums and libraries. These can also be very useful institutions for learning, enrichment, and leisure-time activities.

The key to fulfilling senior years is to always look forward, plan ahead, value relationships, take good care of yourself, and maintain a healthy attitude. Your senior years can be the time for exploring new professional, social, and cultural interests; re-establishing old friendships; enjoying travel and true leisure and attaining real self-fulfillment. Age fifty and beyond can be the time of your life.

### Finding Peace with Stress

A major key to happiness is finding inner peace despite the stress of everyday life. You need stress in your life or life would be dull and unexciting. Although stress add challenges and opportunities, too much stress can seriously effect your physical and mental health. Your challenge in this stress-filled world is to make the stress in your life work for you instead of against you.

Stress comes from physical, mental, and emotional activities that you undertake every day. Stress is so personal that things that may be relaxing to you may be stressful to someone else. For instance, you may be the type of person who likes being busy and active most of the time. A day of "taking it easy" or "doing nothing" at the beach may make you feel unproductive and frustrated. Yet others may find such days quite relaxing.

Find out what you like and relax your way. Oftentimes, too much stress is caused by trying to conform to other people's expectations.

Too much emotional stress can lead to physical illnesses, such as high blood pressure, ulcers, and heart disease. It can also lead to depression, mental illness, and even suicide. Your recognition of the early signs of over-stress and doing something about them can make a big difference in the quality of your life.

The National Institute of Mental Health offers these important points on helping you deal with stress:

**Try physical activity.** When you are nervous, angry, or upset, release the pressure through exercise or physical activity. Running, walking, playing tennis, or working in your garden are just some of the activities you might try. Physical exercise will relieve that "up tight" feeling, relax you, and turn the frowns into smiles. Remember, your body and your mind work together.

**Share your stress.** It helps to talk to someone about your concerns and worries. Perhaps a friend, family member, teacher, or counselor can help you see your problem in a different light. If you feel your problem is serious, you might seek professional help from a psychologist, psychiatrist, social worker, or mental health counselor. Knowing when to ask for help may avoid more serious problems later.

**Know your limits.** If a problem is beyond your control and cannot be changed at the moment, don't fight the situation. Learn to accept what is—for now—until such time when you can change it.

**Take care of yourself.** You are special. Get enough rest and eat well. If you are irritable and tense from lack of sleep or if you are not eating correctly, you will have less ability to deal with stressful situations. If stress repeatedly keeps you from sleeping, you should ask your doctor for help.

**Make time for fun.** Schedule time for both work and recreation. Play can be just as important to your well-being as work; you need a break from your daily routine to just relax and have fun.

**Be a participant.** One way to keep from getting bored, sad, and lonely is to go where it's all happening. Sitting alone can make you feel frustrated. Instead of feeling sorry for yourself, get involved and become a participant. Offer your services in neighborhood or volunteer organizations. Help yourself by helping other people. Get involved in the world and the people around you, and you'll find they will be attracted to you. You will be on your way to making new friends and enjoying new activities.

**Check off your tasks.** Trying to take care of everything at once can seem overwhelming, and, as a result, you may not accomplish anything. Instead, make a list of what tasks you have to do, then do one at a time, checking them off as they are completed. Give priority to the most important ones and do those first.

**Must you always be right?** Do other people upset you—particularly when they don't do things your way? Try cooperation instead of confrontation; it's better than fighting and always being "right." A little give and take on both sides will reduce the strain and make you both feel more comfortable.

**It is OK to cry.** A good cry can be a healthy way to bring relief from your anxiety, and it might even prevent a headache or other physical consequence. Take some deep breaths; they also release tension.

**Create a quiet scene.** You can not always run away, but you can "dream the impossible dream." A quiet country scene painted mentally, or on canvas, can take you out of the turmoil of a stressful situation. Change the scene by reading a good book or playing beautiful music to create a sense of peace and tranquility.

**Avoid self-medication.** Although you can use prescription or over-the-counter medications to relieve stress temporarily, they do not remove the conditions that cause the stress in the first place. Medications, in fact, may be habit-forming and also may reduce your efficiency, thus creating more stress than they take away. They should be taken only on the advice of your doctor.

**The art of relaxation.** The best strategy for avoiding stress is to learn how to relax. Unfortunately, many people try to relax at the same pace that they lead the rest of their lives. For a while, tune out your worries about time, productivity, and "doing right." You will find satisfaction in just being, without striving. Find activities that give you pleasure and that are good for your mental and physical well-being. Forget about always winning. Focus on relaxation, enjoyment, and health. Always be good to yourself.

# CHAPTER 2

# YOUR HEALTH CARE ALTERNATIVES

Good health and access to health care will always be important, especially in your senior years. Yet, increasing hospital costs, doctor's fees, and other medical costs have left tens of millions of Americans without health insurance or the means to pay for adequate health care. In planning for your senior years, make sure that health care financing is a top priority. Review your needs for medical coverage and compare the various options. Understand what types of coverage you can obtain through Medicare, Medicaid and private health insurance.

## Medicare

### What is Medicare?

Medicare is the federal health insurance program for people age 65 or older, certain disabled individuals under age 65 who have been collecting Social Security disability benefits for at least 24 months, and people of any age who have permanent kidney failure. While Medicare does not cover all medical expenses, it provides some basic protection against the cost of health care. Medicare was finally signed into law in 1965 by President Lyndon Johnson, despite strong opposition from many who believed that government regulation would lead to socialized medicine and a decline in the health care delivery system. But the concept for such a health care program goes as far back as the early 1900's.

Do not confuse Medicare with its companion program Medicaid. Medicaid, which is run by state welfare or human service agencies and funded partially by the federal government, is a health insurance program for people with low income and limited assets. A discussion of the Medicaid program appears later in this chapter (see page 46).

The Health Care Financing Administration is the agency which runs the Medicare program and the Social Security Administration is the agency which handles Medicare enrollment and provides general information. You may qualify for Medicare or Medicaid or both.

There are two basic parts to the Medicare Program:

- Hospital Insurance (also called "Part A"). It helps to pay for in-patient hospital care and certain follow-up services. It is financed by part of the payroll (FICA) and self-employment taxes that also pay for Social Security.

- Medical Insurance (also called "Part B"). It helps pay for doctor's services, outpatient hospital care, and certain follow-up services.

These two types of Medicare coverage involve different types of medical costs and different enrollment rules, and they will be discussed separately within this chapter.

## Are You Eligible for Medicare?

### Part A — Hospital Insurance
The majority of people 65 or older are eligible for Medicare hospital insurance based on their own earnings record or that of their spouse. If you meet the following requirements, you will be eligible for Medicare hospital insurance at 65:

- You are getting Social Security or Railroad Retirement benefits (Railroad Retirement benefits are equivalent to the Social Security benefits that a railroad employee or beneficiary would have been entitled to receive if the employee's service had been covered under the Social Security system rather than the Railroad Retirement system); or

- You are not getting Social Security or Railroad Retirement benefits, but you have worked long enough to be eligible for them; or

- You would be entitled to Social Security benefits based on your spouse's earnings record, and your spouse is at least sixty-two (you should be aware that your spouse does not have to apply for benefits in order for you to be eligible based on your spouse's earning record); or

- You have worked long enough for the federal, state, or local government to be insured for Medicare.

Prior to age sixty-five, you are eligible for Medicare hospital insurance if:

- For twenty-four months, you have been getting Social Security disability benefits (in this case you will be automatically enrolled in Medicare).

- You have worked long enough for the federal, state, or local government and you meet the requirements of the Social Security disability program.

For individuals who receive a disability annuity from the Railroad Retirement board, you should contact your Railroad Retirement office for information on hospital insurance eligibility and any applicable waiting period.

Based on your earnings record, your spouse, divorced spouse, widow or widower, or a dependent parent may qualify for hospital insurance when he or she becomes sixty-five. Further, hospital insurance eligibility may apply to disabled widows and widowers under sixty-five, disabled divorced widows or widowers under sixty-five, and disabled children.

Individuals with permanent kidney failure are subject to special rules. The rules state that you are eligible for hospital insurance at any age, if you receive maintenance dialysis or a kidney transplant, and:

- You are insured or are getting monthly benefits under Social Security or the Railroad Retirement system, or

- You have worked long enough in government to be insured for Medicare.

Based on your earnings record, your spouse or child may be eligible for hospital insurance if he or she receives maintenance dialysis or a kidney transplant, regardless of whether anyone else in the family is receiving benefits.

In the event you are ineligible for hospital insurance in the ways outlined, you may be eligible on the basis of government employment in which you paid the Medicare payroll tax. If you are employed by the government and you become disabled before sixty-five, you may be in a position to receive Medicare based on your government work. As a general rule, a twenty-nine-month waiting period will apply before hospital insurance benefits can start. To avoid losing benefit protection under these circumstances, Social Security Administration suggests you contact them right away.

If you are sixty-five and do not meet the qualifications for hospital insurance, you can still purchase coverage, in a manner similar to buying private insurance. The basic premium for this insurance was a little over $190 per month in 1992. If you choose to enroll in hospital coverage, you will also have to enroll in Medicare medical insurance and pay its monthly premium of about $32. You must be a lawfully admitted permanent resident and must live in the U.S. for five years before you can buy Medicare insurance.

### Part B — Medical Insurance

As a general rule, anyone who is sixty-five or older may enroll in Medicare medical insurance by paying a monthly premium. The same general rule applies to anyone who is under sixty-five and eligible for Part A, hospital insurance. You generally do not need any Social Security or government work credits to obtain this part of Medicare. Note that aliens sixty-five or older who are not eligible for Part A, hospital insurance, must be lawfully-admitted permanent residents and must live in the U.S. for five years before they can enroll in Part B, medical insurance.

If you have questions about whether you qualify for Medicare or if you need more information, you may contact the Social Security Administration at 1-800-772-1213 between 7:00 A.M. and 7:00 P.M. every business day. If you receive a Railroad Retirement annuity or Railroad Retirement benefit based on disability, you should contact a Railroad Retirement office.

## Enrolling in Medicare

The enrollment rules for Parts A and B of Medicare are different and you should understand what is required for signing up for Medicare. First, let's review the enrollment procedures for Part A of Medicare.

### Enrollment under Part A

Although an application for hospital insurance under Part A typically must be made, for many people there is automatic enrollment. For example, if you are receiving Social Security or Railroad Retirement benefits when you become sixty-five, you will be automatically enrolled in Part A, hospital insurance. About two to three months before you turn sixty-five, you will get a package in the mail that will contain your Medicare card, along with information about the Medicare program. Also included will be instructions asking you to decide if you want to pay a monthly premium to sign up for Part B, the medical insurance portion of Medicare. If you do not want Part B coverage, you must follow the instructions that come with your Medicare card. If you elect Part B coverage, the premiums for such are automatically deducted from your monthly Social Security check.

If you are planning to retire when you reach sixty-five, you should contact the Social Security Administration about three months before your sixty-fifth birthday. Social Security Administration will sign you up for Medicare at the same time you apply for Social Security benefits. There is no requirement that you must retire in order to get Medicare Part A. However, you will still need to contact Social Security about three months before your sixty-fifth birthday to sign up for Medicare even if you do not retire.

Individuals who are government employees or retirees who are eligible for Medicare because of government work should also contact the Social Security Administration about three months before their sixty-fifth birthday to apply for hospital insurance. A government employee who becomes disabled before 65 may be eligible for Medicare hospital insurance based on his or her government work. As a general rule, there is a twenty-nine-month waiting period before Part A starts. Again, contact your Social Security office to avoid loss of any Medicare protection.

If you are a disabled person under sixty-five, you will be automatically enrolled in hospital insurance and will receive, about three months before you become eligible for Medicare, a Medicare enrollment package containing your Medicare card and information about the program. You become eligible for Part A after you have been entitled to disability benefits for twenty-four months. You will be asked in the package whether you want to pay a monthly premium for Part B, medical insurance.

A disabled widow or widower between fifty and sixty-five who has not applied for disability benefits because he or she is already getting another kind of Social Security benefit may still be able to get Medicare Part A, hospital insurance. You should contact Social Security as soon as possible so that you will not lose any Medicare protection for which you are eligible. Further, if you or a family member have permanent kidney failure, you should contact your Social Security office to inquire about eligibility and enrollment in Medicare.

If you are an individual who used to get disability insurance benefits and Medicare, but lost them solely because you are working, you can purchase Part A, hospital insurance, if you continue to be disabled. And, if you do not meet the regular requirements for entitlement to Medicare, you can purchase coverage by contacting your Social Security office. You should note that you do not have to enroll in Medicare medical insurance unless you choose to do so.

### Enrollment Under Part B

If you are enrolled in Part A, you generally may choose to enroll in Part B for a monthly premium. Everyone who enrolls in Part B must pay a monthly premium, as explained below.

Certain people who receive Part A benefits must enroll in Part B. If you are eligible for Medicare benefits because you fall within the following categories, you must enroll in Part B:

• You have chronic kidney failure.

• You are not insured under the Social Security or Railroad Retirement System, but wish to receive Medicare benefits. (In this case you must pay for both the monthly Part A and Part B premiums.)

Most people who have the option of enrolling in Part B choose to do so because it is a very wise buy. The federal government pays approximately 75 percent of the cost of your Part B premiums. It is also extremely unlikely that you could purchase similar private insurance coverage at the current monthly premium cost.

Do not delay enrolling in Part B. If you do not enroll in Part B within the prescribed time, your coverage may be delayed and you may be charged a penalty for late enrollment.

If you are receiving Social Security or Railroad Retirement benefits, you will receive a Medicare enrollment package two to three months before becoming eligible for Medicare. The package will advise you that you are automatically enrolled in both parts of Medicare. However, you have the option to turn down Part B, medical insurance, since there is a monthly premium. You would still receive Part A, hospital insurance.

For enrollment in other situations you should contact your Social Security office to apply for Part B, medical insurance, if you:

- plan to continue working past sixty-five; or

- had Part B medical insurance coverage in the past, but eliminated it; or

- turned down Part B medical insurance when you became entitled to Part A hospital insurance; or

- are sixty-five but you are not eligible for hospital insurance; or

- are eligible for Medicare based on government work; or

- have permanent kidney failure; or

- are a disabled widow or widower between fifth and sixty-five and you are not receiving disability benefits; or

- live in Puerto rico or outside the U.S.

There are two types of enrollment periods for Part B medical insurance: the initial enrollment period and the general enrollment period. It is important for you to know that each period has a specific time frame for enrolling, if you want medical insurance coverage.

The initial enrollment period is seven months. When you are about to become eligible for medical insurance, you have seven months to sign up. This seven-month period begins three months before you first become eligible and ends three months after that month.

When your coverage begins depends on when you sign up. For example, if you enroll during the first three months, your medical insurance will start with the month you actually become eligible. If you sign up during this period, there will be no delay in your coverage.

If you sign up during the last four months, your coverage will start one to three months after you sign up. So, you can see why it is so important to avoid any delay.

If you do not sign up during the initial seven-month enrollment period, you cannot sign up until the next "general enrollment period." This period runs from January 1 to March 31 of each year.

If you enroll during the general enrollment period, your coverage will not start until the following July. In addition, you may be required to pay a monthly premium that is ten percent higher for each twelve-month period you could have enrolled, but were not enrolled. This 10 percent premium surcharge for late enrollment may not apply if you had employer group health coverage.

### Terms to Know to Understand What Medicare Covers

Listed below are definitions for several terms used frequently when discussing the subject of health insurance and health care delivery systems. You will need to know these terms to understand what specific coverage you are obtaining under Medicare.

**Acute Care:** Care for persons with short-term illness.

**Approved Charges:** The approved or allowable dollar limit Medicare sets on how much it will pay a provider of medical services for any given treatment or procedure. The fees charged by the medical provider may be above the Medicare limit, up to a predetermined government-imposed ceiling.

**Benefit Period:** Under Medicare, a benefit period begins the day you enter a hospital and ends when you have been out of the hospital for 60 days in a row.

**Coinsurance:** A form of cost-sharing where an insured individual is required to pay a percentage of covered expenses to a provider.

**Co-Payment:** Another word for "coinsurance." It may be either a percentage of an approved charge or a flat dollar amount.

**Custodial Care:** Care that can be given safely and reasonably by a person who is not medically skilled, and which is given mainly to help the patient with daily living.

**Deductible:** The amount you must pay before the insurance benefits are payable. This payment is a type of cost-sharing.

**Integration:** The way in which a private health insurance plan fits—or "integrates"—with Medicare medical insurance.

**Long-Term Care:** A broad range of health, social, and supportive services to meet the needs of individuals with some form of disability.

**Medigap:** Private health insurance which is designed to supplement or fill the gaps in Medicare coverage.

**Out-of-Pocket Expenses:** Personal payments made for health care not paid for by public or private insurance. The term includes deductible and coinsurance payments, along with payments for products and services that are not covered under insurance plans.

**Pre-Existing Condition:** A medical condition that exists at the time you begin coverage under a health insurance plan.

**Primary Payer:** The health insurance plan that pays first on your hospital and medical bills, as required under legal rules. If the primary payer does not pay all your expenses, the secondary payer may pay the remaining expenses, subject to any deductibles.

**Reserve days:** Under Medicare, an extra sixty hospital days you can use if you have a long illness and have to stay in the hospital for more than 90 days. You are entitled to only sixty reserve days in your lifetime.

**Secondary Payer:** The health insurance plan that pays after the primary plan has paid hospital and medical expenses.

**Skilled Nursing Facility:**  A medically oriented facility used following recuperation from surgery or in other situations requiring around-the-clock medical care.

## What Does Medicare Part A (Hospital Insurance) Cover?

Medicare Part A covers inpatient hospital care, skilled nursing facility care, home health care, and hospice care. Hospitals, skilled nursing facilities, home health care agencies, and hospices are called "providers." If you are hospitalized, your provider will submit their claims directly to Medicare. It is not your responsibility to submit claims for your provider's services.

Your provider will, however, charge you for any part of the Part A deductible you have not met and any coinsurance you owe. It is your responsibility to pay these charges.

Note that when your provider sends a Part A claim for payment, you will get a "Notice of Utilization." This will explain the decision that Medicare made on the claim.

**Inpatient Hospital Care:**  Medicare Part A will pay for up to ninety days in any Medicare-participating hospital during each benefit period. To be covered, your doctor must prescribe inpatient hospital care for treatment of your injury or illness, and you must require the kind of care that can only be provided by a hospital. For example, in 1992, Part A paid for all covered services for the first sixty days, except for a deductible of $652. For the sixty-first through the ninetieth days in a hospital, the patient paid $163 per day, while Medicare paid for the remainder of all covered services.

If you are out of the hospital for at least sixty days in a row and then return, you will start a new benefit period, and your ninety days of coverage will start all over again.

If you need more than ninety days of inpatient care during any benefit period, you may decide to use some or all of your sixty reserve days. For each reserve day used in 1992, Part A pays for all covered expenses except for $326 per day. Reserve days are not renewable, and once you use a reserve day, you never get it back.

Examples of services and supplies covered by Part A, hospital insurance, include:

- semi-private room and meals

- regular nursing services

- anesthesia services and operating and recovery room costs

- intensive care and coronary care

- drugs, lab tests, and X-rays

- medical supplies and appliances

- rehabilitation services, such as physical therapy

- preparatory services related to kidney transplant surgery

**Skilled Nursing Facility Care:** In the event you need inpatient skilled nursing or rehabilitation services following a hospital stay, and you meet certain other conditions, Part A helps pay for up to one 100 days in a Medicare-participating skilled nursing facility in each benefit period. Part A pays for all covered services for the first 20 days. For the 21st through the 100th days, it pays for all covered services except for a specified amount per day ($81.50 per day in 1992).

Examples of the services and supplies Medicare pays for when you are in a skilled nursing facility are listed below:

- semi-private room and all meals

- regular nursing services

- rehabilitation services, such as physical therapy

- drugs, medical supplies, and medical appliances

You should be aware that Medicare does not pay for custodial care.

**Home Health Care:** In the event you are confined to your home and meet certain other conditions, Part A can pay the full approved cost of home health visits from a Medicare-participating home health agency. No limit is applied to the number of covered visits you can have.

Examples of services Medicare Part A pays for when you need home health care include:

- part-time skilled nursing care

- physical therapy

- speech therapy

Part A also covers part-time services of home health aides, occupational therapy, medical social services, and medical supplies and equipment.

**Hospice Care:** A facility that provides pain relief and other support services for terminally ill people is known as a hospice. Part A of Medicare can assist in paying for hospice care for terminally ill individuals, if the care is provided by a Medicare-certified hospice and certain other conditions are met.

Part A can pay for a maximum of two ninety-day periods and one thirty-day period of hospice care. The benefit periods may be used together, resulting in a total of 210 consecutive days of hospice care. If the benefit periods are exhausted and you remain terminally ill, your hospice benefits will be extended indefinitely.

Listed below are examples of items that Part A covers when hospice care is needed:

- doctors' services and nursing services

- medical appliances and supplies, including outpatient drugs for relief of pain

- physical and speech therapy

- home health aide and homemaker services

- medical social services

- counseling

- respite care (inpatient care on a short-term basis in order to give temporary relief to the person who generally assists with home care of the patient)

## What Does Medicare Part B (Medical Insurance) Cover?

Part B helps pay for doctors' services and other medical services and supplies not covered by Part A, hospital insurance. Thus, Part B is helpful if you are sick and do not need to be hospitalized. Prior to Part B paying for covered services, an annual deductible must be met. For example, the 1992 annual deductible was $100. After the deductible is met, Medicare will generally pay 80 percent of the approved amount for covered charges throughout the remainder of the year. It is your responsibility to pay the remaining 20 percent of the charges (i.e., coinsurance) plus the expenses over and beyond the Medicare-approved amount.

Listed below are examples of doctors' services covered by Medicare:

- medical and surgical services, including anesthesia

- diagnostic tests that are a part of your treatment

- X-rays

- radiology and pathology services by doctors while you are a hospital inpatient or outpatient

- treatment of mental illness (payments for outpatient treatment are limited to 50 percent of approved charge instead of 80 percent)

- services of your doctor's office nurse

- drugs that cannot be self-administered, blood transfusions, and other medical supplies

Examples of other services covered by Part B, medical insurance, include:

- outpatient hospital services you receive for diagnosis and treatment of an illness, including care in an emergency room or outpatient clinic of a hospital

- an unlimited number of home health visits if you do not have hospital insurance and if certain conditions are met

- ambulance transportation

- home dialysis equipment and support services

- outpatient physical therapy and speech pathology services

- radiation treatments

Medicare determines what is a reasonable charge for each service you receive. If the charges for your services are more than the Medicare-approved amount, you generally will owe the Medicare coinsurance (20 percent of the Medicare-approved amount), plus any charges above the Medicare-approved amount.

If your doctor accepts "assignment," you pay only the coinsurance amount. Thus, by choosing a doctor that accepts assignment, you could save many dollars. "Assignment" is a method by which Medicare pays your doctor. If your doctor "accepts assignment," he or she agrees to accept the "Medicare-approved" charge as total payment for the services that he or she has provided. Doctors who accept assignment are said to be "Medicare-participating."

To find out if your doctor accepts assignment, you can:

1. Call the Medicare carrier in your state and ask for a free copy of the *Medicare-Participating Physician/Supplier Directory* for your area. Medicare "carriers," also called "intermediaries," are health insurance organizations that are under contract with Medicare to process Medicare claims.

2. Ask your doctor/supplier if he or she accepts assignment. Often Medicare-participating doctors/suppliers display emblems or certificates which show that they accept assignment on all Medicare claims.

After your doctor/supplier sends in a Part B claim, Medicare will send you a notice called an "Explanation of Medicare Benefits." This form will show you what Medicare paid for and why. For example, if you received services from a doctor, this notice will contain the following information:

- whether your doctor took assignment on your claim;

- the date and type of services that you received;

- the amount billed and the amount approved;

- the amount Medicare paid;

- whether you have met your annual deductible; and

- the amount for which you are responsible.

Be sure that you review this form carefully and save it for your records. If you suspect a mistake, call or write the carrier that handles your claim.

If you believe that payment has been incorrectly denied, you have the right to ask the carrier to review the decision. Often, asking for a review is worth the effort. A majority of reviews are resolved in favor of the beneficiary. If you are unable to resolve your dispute with the carrier, you can take legal action before an administrative law judge or in court.

## What Does Medicare Exclude?

The Medicare program is designed to provide basic health care coverage for the elderly and the disabled, but it does not pay all your medical expenses. Listed below are examples of the services and supplies not covered by Medicare:

- custodial care

- most nursing home care

- care you get outside the U.S. (Canada and Mexico may be exceptions if inpatient care is given in a Medicare-certified hospital)

- routine checkups and the tests directly related to these checkups (please note: some mammograms and Pap smears are covered)

- routine dental care and dentures

- most immunization shots

- prescription drugs

- routine foot care

- medical tests for, and the cost of, eyeglasses or hearing aids

- personal comfort items, such as a telephone or television

### What Happens if You Have Other Health Insurance?

If you have other health insurance when you become eligible for Medicare, you need to decide whether it is worth the monthly premium cost to you to sign up for Part B, medical insurance.

Here are some tips to help your decision-making process:

- Find out how your private health insurance plan "integrates" with Part B.

- Determine how you and your family members will be impacted with or without Part B coverage.

- Keep in mind that most private plans, similar to Medicare, do not cover all health services.

- Remember that most nursing home care is not covered by private health insurance policies or Medicare.

- Protect yourself and be sure not to cancel any health insurance you now have until your Medicare coverage actually begins.

You should be aware of the following special rules, if you have health insurance from an employer group health plan:

- You can wait to enroll in Medicare medical insurance during a seven-month "special enrollment period," if you work past sixty-five— or are sixty-five or older and the spouse of a worker of any age. The enrollment period begins with the month the group health coverage ends or the month employment ends, whichever comes first. If you meet certain requirements, you will not have to pay monthly premiums that are 10 percent higher for late enrollment in Medicare.

- In a group health plan that covers at least one employer with twenty or more employees, the group health plan is required by law to offer workers who are sixty-five or older the same health benefits that are provided to younger employees. Further, the group health plan must also offer the spouses who are sixty-five or older (regardless of the age of the worker) the same health benefits given younger spouses. If you or your spouse continue to belong to your employer's group health plan, Medicare will be the secondary payer and the employer plan will be the primary payer. If you reject your employer's plan, Medicare will be the primary health insurance payer. You should be aware that the employer is not allowed to offer you Medicare supplemental coverage if you reject its health plan.

• If you are under sixty-five, disabled, and have health coverage under your employer's health plan or a family member's employer health plan, Medicare will be the secondary payer. The employer plan must be a "large group health plan", that is, a plan that covers employees of at least one employer who has 100 or more employees. In this situation, you will have a special enrollment period and will not be subject to the 10 percent premium surcharge.

• If you are under sixty-five, entitled to Medicare because of permanent kidney failure and have employer group health coverage, Medicare will be the secondary payer for an initial 12-month period. When that period ends, Medicare will be your primary payer.

## Health Maintenance Organizations and Medicare

As a general rule, Medicare beneficiaries have options with respect to how and where they receive their Medicare-covered services. Many choose a particular doctor or hospital approved under Medicare. Under this arrangement, the bill is sent to Medicare after the service is provided. You (or your Medigap plan) are responsible for any amounts that Medicare does not cover. However, you also have the option of signing up for a Health Maintenance Organization (HMO) or Competitive Medical Plan (CMP).

HMOs or CMPs are health care delivery systems that provide health care in exchange for a monthly, fixed fee. Under these plans, Medicare beneficiaries receive all Medicare-covered hospital and medical insurance benefits through the plan. The cost of this type of plan to you is known in advance and is generally limited to the fixed monthly premiums and minimal copayments.

At no extra cost to you, some HMOs and CMPs provide services beyond what Medicare covers. Examples of such services include prescription drugs and hearing aids. Most HMOs and CMPs have limits on care that you should be aware of before enrolling. Call or visit a Social Security office if you want to find out how to contact an HMO or CMP in your area for more information.

There are certain advantages to joining a Medicare HMO:

• In an HMO, you generally pay a monthly fee, which entitles you to a wide range of medical services. In exchange for the fee, you will not be charged substantial additional costs for your medical care. People who participate in HMOs tend to use their service more frequently and at earlier stages of illness.

• HMO doctors routinely accept Medicare assignment. The HMO may also absorb the Medicare deductibles or coinsurance and provide additional benefits beyond Medicare-approved services.

• HMOs tend to emphasize preventive health care, an attractive benefit for many people.

You should be aware that there are also certain disadvantages of joining a Medicare HMO:

• The main disadvantage is that you are not able to choose your own doctors and hospital. In general, you must obtain all your health care services through the HMO. In many cases, however, this is not a real problem because many HMOs have excellent doctors and maintain first rate health care facilities.

• To be eligible for a Medicare HMO, you must live in the HMO's geographical area for at least nine months of the year. Therefore, if you travel a great deal, an HMO may not be a viable option for you.

- Like other Medigap supplements, HMOs do not cover every possible health problem. For example, long-term care, as well as routine dental care, eyeglasses, and hearing aids are generally not covered.

### Health Care Protection from the Veterans Administration (VA), CHAMPUS or CHAMPVA Program

If you are a veteran who was not dishonorably discharged, you may be eligible for a variety of benefits through the Veterans Administration. These benefits include medical service, such as hospitalization, nursing home care, examinations, outpatient medical and dental treatment, and prosthetic devices.

A summary of the federal benefits available to veterans and their dependents is contained in the publication *Federal Benefits for Veterans and Dependents* (VA IS-1). This publication discusses medical, educational, loan, insurance, compensation, pension, and other programs administered by the Veterans Administration and other agencies. To purchase this publication, send a written request and $2.50 to the Superintendent of Documents, U.S. Government Printing Office, Washington, D.C. 20402.

If you have health care protection with the VA, CHAMPUS, or CHAMPVA, your health benefits may change or end when you become eligible for Medicare. Before you decide whether to enroll in Medicare Part B, medical insurance, you should contact the VA, Department of Defense, or a military health benefits advisor for information.

### Health Care Protection from the Indian Health Service, a Federal Employee Plan, or a State Medical Assistance Program

If you fall within one of these categories, you should contact a health benefits advisor in the appropriate office. He or she should be able to provide information to help you decide whether it will be to your advantage to have Medicare Part B, medical insurance.

## Medigap Insurance

Medigap insurance, sold by private insurance companies, is a form of coverage designed to fill the gaps in Medicare protection. As you know, the expenses not covered by Medicare are your financial responsibility. Examples of such expenses include: Medicare deductibles, premiums, any charge above and beyond Medicare-approved limits, coinsurance and the cost of any service (including most long-term care) or supplies not covered by Medicare. Since these expenses can be substantial, you should consider a Medigap policy for financial protection against noncovered medical care costs. Additional information on purchasing Medigap or other private health insurance can be found in chapter 10 beginning on page 158.

## Types of Private Health Insurance

There are many types of insurance in the marketplace you can purchase that will cover some or all of the medical costs Medicare does not cover. Descriptions of the most common ones follow:

**Medicare Supplement:** These policies pay part or all of Medicare's deductibles and coinsurance amounts. Some Medicare supplement policies pay for health services that are not covered by Medicare.

You should be aware that recent federal legislation simplifies comparison shopping for any policy held to be, or marketed as, a Medicare supplement policy (the legislation does not apply to employer or union policies). The U.S. Congress, in its legislation, directed the National Association of Insurance Commissioners to design standard Medicare supplement plans, along with standardized (and clearer) language, definitions,and terms. These actions were taken because many consumers were confused by complicated provisions and had difficulty choosing from among the hundreds of policies available to them. As a result of the legislation, there are now ten standard plans, the first of which contains only basic benefits and is designated as "Plan A." In each of the other nine plans, designated as Plan B through J, you would get basic benefits plus one or more additional benefits. Each state is required to implement the federal provisions.

For further information on these plans, consult the *1992 Guide to Health Insurance for People With Medicare* (Publication No. HCFA 02110).

In addition to the ten standard plans, another available option is Medicare Select. This is a preferred provider arrangement, initially available in fifteen states, in which lower premiums may be charged in return for your agreeing to use the services of particular health care providers. The states with Medicare Select are: Alabama, Arizona, California, Florida, Indiana, Kentucky, Michigan, Minnesota, Missouri, North Dakota, Ohio, Oregon, Texas, Washington, and Wisconsin.

For further information on Medicare Select, you should contact your state insurance department.

**Major Medical Expense:** These policies help provide coverage for the high cost of serious illness or injury, including some health services not covered by Medicare. The policies often have a large deductible and may not cover Medicare's deductibles and coinsurance amounts. Make sure that you thoroughly understand the coverage you will be obtaining before purchasing major medical insurance.

**Employer Group Insurance:** Many employers provide group health insurance for their employees. Some plans also offer spousal benefits. Upon your retirement, it may be possible to convert your employer group insurance coverage to a suitable individual Medicare-supplement policy when you reach age sixty.

If this is the case with your former employer, carefully compare the benefits and costs of your plan with other supplemental policies. If you switch to another supplemental policy, be sure to continue coverage under your old policy long enough to cover any waiting periods the new policy may have. A waiting period is the time between the date when you become insured and the date when the policy will pay benefits for a pre-existing condition or certain other specified illnesses.

Do not drop your policy with your former employer without adequate advice. If the premium is paid by your former employer, or even if a small amount is paid by you, it is sometimes wise to retain the policy and buy a minimum benefit supplemental policy for complete coverage. Contact your employer's personnel office for additional information.

Some associations and organizations offer similar group health insurance to its members.

## Tips for Buying Private Health Insurance

The following suggestions will help you in making the best private health insurance decision for yourself:

❏ Comparison shop with respect to coverage and cost. Make a chart that will allow you to see how the different plans compare with respect to such items as deductibles, coinsurance, and prescription drugs.

❏ Buy only the amount of insurance you reasonably need.

❏ Look at whether the policy pays a set dollar amount or a percentage of the cost of care. Keep in mind that inflation causes policies with fixed dollar amounts to lose relative value over time.

❏ Look at how long the coverage will last.

❏ Check for waiting periods, pre-existing conditions, exclusions, and noncovered medical services, such as treatment of mental illness, alcoholism, or drug addition.

❏ Find out how much nursing home care and home health care cost in your area, in order to determine if policy coverage will be adequate.

❏ Check on your right to renew the policy. Automatic renewal policies offer the best protection.

❏ Beware of illegal insurance sales practices! You should not believe anyone who tells you that he or she is from the government and tries to sell you insurance. Medicare supplement policies are not sold or serviced by the Medicare program or any other state or federal government agency. Further, it is illegal for any insurance company or agent to knowingly sell you a policy that duplicates Medicare coverage or your private health plan. Insurance companies or agents that violate this law are subject to federal penalties. Call your state insurance department or the U.S. Department of Health and Human Services at 1-800-638-6833 if you think you have been a victim of an illegal insurance sales practice.

❏ Do not let a salesperson pressure you. Take the time needed to make an informed decision.

❏ When you receive your policy, do not delay reading it. Make sure that it provides the coverage you ordered.

### Qualified Medicare Beneficiary Program

If you receive Medicare benefits and have little income or resources, you should be aware of the Qualified Medicare Beneficiary (QMB) program. This program for low income Medicare beneficiaries can save you money on out-of-pocket medical costs—even if you do not receive Supplemental Security Income (also called "SSI").

If your annual income is below the national poverty level and you do not have access to many financial resources, you may qualify for government assistance under the QMB program. The national poverty income levels for 1992 was $6,810 per year for an individual and $9,190 for a couple in all states except Alaska and Hawaii. The income limits for Alaska were $8,500 for one person and $11,570 for a couple. The income limits for Hawaii were $7,830 and $10,570 for one person and a couple, respectively. In all cases, financial resources in the form of cash and other liquid assets (such as bank accounts, stocks, and bonds) usually cannot exceed $4000 for one person or $6000 for a couple.

In the event you qualify for the QMB program, your state will pay your Medicare premiums, deductibles, and coinsurance. Since your state is the only entity that can decide if you qualify for help under the QMB program, you should contact your state or local medical assistance (Medicaid) agency, social services office, or welfare office if you think you may qualify.

It is important to note that in order to qualify, you do not have to be on welfare and you must not be eligible for Medicaid. The state Medicaid agency or welfare office is contacted because it is the entity providing you with the financial assistance. The term used to describe this arrangement is "Medicaid buy-in." The "Medicaid buy-in" benefit is one of the few remaining vestiges of the Medicare Catastrophic Coverage Act of 1988, which was almost completely repealed in 1989. Strong protests concerning high costs and lack of coverage for nursing home care, among other things, caused the legislation to meet its early demise.

## Medicaid

The Medicaid program was enacted in 1965 as Medicare's companion program. It is a joint federal-state medical assistance program that is operated by the states with partial federal funding. The Medicaid program supplements Medicare by providing comprehensive health care benefits for individuals ages sixty-five and older and disabled individuals who have very low incomes and assets. Individuals eligible for Medicaid include:

- Persons receiving Aid to Families with Dependent Children (AFDC) benefits.

- Persons receiving SSI benefits.

- Persons with low income (defined by each state) who meet their individual state's eligibility requirements.

- Low income pregnant women and children under the age of six.

The Medicaid program was originally thought of as a vehicle for providing health care for the poor, without regard to age. Today Medicaid is a major payer of long-term care, especially inpatient skilled nursing home care. Often, individuals with medical expenses have been forced to "spend down" their income and assets to the pre-set level that triggers or initiates Medicaid eligibility. On this point, you should note that there are "spousal impoverishment" rules. The rules are designed to assist beneficiaries in avoiding the use of their entire life savings before qualifying for Medicaid nursing home coverage.

By law, every state Medicaid program is required to pay for medical expenses generally included under Medicare Part A (Hospital Insurance) and Part B (Medical Insurance), including:

- Inpatient hospital services

- Outpatient hospital services

- Skilled nursing facility care

- Physicians fees

- Laboratory tests

- Home health care services

Some states may choose to provide additional Medicaid coverage for benefits such as dental care and prescription drugs.

In the event you are eligible for Medicaid, the need for Medigap insurance should be reevaluated. It is likely that the benefits you purchase under Medigap insurance would duplicate your benefits under Medicaid. Further, your Medigap premiums could be financially prohibitive.

## Nursing Homes

The term "nursing home" means different things to different people. For some, any permanent place of residence for older people, other than their own home, is considered to be a nursing home. For others, it is a place where older people can receive continuing medical care, and, for still others, a warehouse for unwanted older persons.

We will use the term "nursing home" to mean a housing arrangement that provides a complete spectrum of health, social, and supportive services to older persons in need of assistance on a long-term or rehabilitative care basis. Although nursing homes primarily serve an older population, they also provide care to any person, regardless of age, who is in need of long-term or rehabilitative services unavailable through home care or hospitals.

Nursing homes are generally divided into three major categories: (1) skilled care nursing homes; (2) intermediate care nursing homes; and (3) custodial- or residential-care nursing homes. The different types of nursing homes, most of which are privately owned and operated, reflect the functions provided by the facilities and the needs of the residents. Both the federal and state governments have strict rules (though less strict for custodial care nursing homes) which regulate how the homes are staffed and managed. Federal standards must be met for Medicare and Medicaid reimbursement and each home must be licensed by the state in which it operates. A brief description of each type follows.

**Skilled Care Nursing Homes:** These facilities are for patients who require intensive, around-the-clock supervision and complex medical care by a registered nurse, under the direction of a physician.

**Intermediate Care Nursing Homes:** These nursing homes are for patients who benefit from around-the-clock assistance because of disabilities, but who can still perform many daily life activities alone, such as dressing and eating. This type of facility provides supportive care with low level of medical care.

**Custodial- or Residential-Care Nursing Homes:** These facilities, also referred to as board-and-care or personal-care homes, are for patients who require supervision with respect to daily life activities. As a general rule, the patients do not require medical care.

When a long-term illness strikes, most seniors find that the long-term care that they need, such as nursing home care, are not adequately covered by Medicare, other public programs or their private insurance. Because nursing home care is often needed over an extended period of time, nursing home costs are one of the greatest threats to the financial security of senior citizens and their families. Remember that Medicare only covers 100 days in a skilled nursing facility immediately following a hospital stay. Many private long-term care insurance policies have limitations and exclusions which severely restricts coverage for nursing home care. This means that Medicaid has become the primary source of funding for nursing home care for most seniors.

The eligibility requirements for Medicaid varies from state to state, but typically requires that your income and assets be lower than the levels established by the state in which you live. You should contact the appropriate agency on aging, public welfare or social services which handles Medicaid applications in your state for specific eligibility requirements.

Many states use the eligibility rules for Supplemental Security Income (SSI) under Social Security in determining qualifications for Medicaid. These eligibility rules for SSI are discussed further in Chapter 3. The rules for eligibility typically require that your income be below established poverty guidelines and that your cash and liquid assets not exceed prescribed amounts (i.e. $2000 for individual and $3000 for couples in 1992). The SSI rules also permit you to keep other assets and still be eligible for Medicaid; such as, your family home, household goods up to a total of $2000, up to $4500 in automobiles and other vehicles, certain life insurance and funds for burial expenses.

The eligibility rules place some restrictions on the transfer of assets to become eligible for Medicaid. Assets transferred to or held in trust for a Medicaid applicant will be counted as available resources in determining eligibility. After July 1, 1988, an institutionalized applicant for Medicaid can be denied eligibility if he or she transferred assets at less than fair market value within thirty months of applying for Medicaid. This period of ineligibility generally lasts until the time required to "spend-down" the uncompensated value of the transferred assets on medical care, but cannot exceed thirty months. Transfer of a home is excluded from these rules if the transfer is to a spouse, dependent or disabled child, or to a sibling or non-dependent son or daughter under certain conditions.

If your income or assets exceed the eligibility guidelines for Medicaid, you will be notified when you apply that you are over-income. A "spend-down" amount will be specified which you must spend toward allowable expenses before you are eligible for Medicaid benefits.

Since the financing of nursing home care is extremely expensive, be sure to read any admission documents and contracts very carefully. The advice of an attorney knowledgeable in this area is suggested, given the complexity of the rules and other issues relating to nursing home care. You should seek the attorney's advice before you or someone in your care enters the home. Without a comprehensive review, you or a relative may be held personally liable for expenses.

Under federal law, nursing home residents have rights that must be met by every nursing home participating in Medicare or Medicaid. Such rights include receiving information about the following:

- their residential rights

- the services offered by the nursing home and the fees for those services

• plans for their medical care and treatment

Additionally, patients have the right to make choices for themselves about physicians, activities in which they engage, and to voice grievances; to have privacy in social, religious, medical and communication arenas; and to be free from abuse and restraint. Patients must be treated with dignity and respect.

## Hidden Traps in Nursing Home Agreements

When reviewing a nursing home agreement, you should be on the look out for the following:

- Admission fees: check current status of state and federal law regarding the permissibility of such fees.

- Differential rates and rooms for private-pay residents

- Medicare coverage: check who covers costs in absence of Medicare eligibility.

- Payment-in-advance clauses

- Personal care expenses

- Application fees

For more information on this subject, request the American Association of Retired Persons' publication, *Nursing Home Life: A Guide for Residents and Families*. AARP's address appears in the Appendix.

There are many alternatives for individuals who do not require nursing home care. Those alternatives range from living in one's own home to living in a form of shared housing. Such options, along with other support systems and services, such as elder care and senior centers, are widely available in many states. You should contact your state or local agency on aging for additional information.

# CHAPTER 3

# YOUR SOCIAL SECURITY BENEFITS

### Social Security is for Everyone

Almost every person in the United States is either paying Social Security taxes or getting Social Security benefits—or is related to someone who is. While many of us associate Social Security primarily with retirement, it also provides, among other things, vital income to families of workers who are disabled or who die before retirement age. About 40 million Americans receive some form of a Social Security benefit. That figure equals about one out of every six Americans.

The Social Security system, created under the Social Security Act of 1935, was designed to "provide for the general welfare." It covers a broad range of programs, including: retirement insurance; disability insurance; survivor's insurance; hospital and medical insurance for the aged and disabled; black lung benefits; supplemental security income (SSI); unemployment insurance; and varied public assistance and "welfare" services. This chapter will focus mostly on the "typical" Social Security benefits, i.e., retirement, disability, survivor's, Medicare, and SSI benefits.

A longstanding debate continues regarding the financial solvency of the Social Security system. However, in a 1992 publication, the Social Security Administration answers the question, "Will Social Security be there when I need it?" with a straightforward, "Yes it will," and goes on to give an explanation. It says that Social Security's financial troubles in the 1970s and early 1980s, resulting from high inflation and other economic problems, no longer exist. Rather, due to adjustments in Social Security taxes and an improved economy, the system is in "excellent shape—and will be for many years to come."

Contributions to Social Security, stemming from taxes paid by employers, employees, and the self-employed, are collected by the Internal Revenue Service and paid into the United States Treasury as internal revenue collections. The amounts collected are appropriated to specific trust funds. The portions of funds not needed for current withdrawals, that is, the extra monies—referred to as "reserves"—are invested in Treasury bonds. Current figures show that the system is solvent and building a large reserve, which is expected to reach $8 trillion by the year 2027. However, the large influx of baby boomers into their retirement years during the early twenty-first century still raises questions about the solvency of Social Security.

## Who Pays Social Security Taxes?

Employers, employees, and the self-employed pay Social Security taxes. These taxes are used to pay for all Social Security benefits. Additionally, a portion of these taxes are used to pay for Medicare coverage. SSI is financed through general tax revenues, not Social Security taxes. Here's how it works:

If you work for someone else, you and your employer pay taxes for both Social Security and Medicare. In 1993, you and your employer will each pay 7.65 percent of your gross salary, up to a limit established by an act of Congress or by a formula tied to cost-of-living increases in Social Security benefits. In 1993, the limit is $57,600. The limits in 1992 and 1991 were $55,500 and $53,400, respectively. For planning purposes, keep in mind that the tax and earnings bases are generally announced in October or November of the year prior to the year in which the increase is to take effect.

The 7.65 percent represents a combination of two rates: the Social Security rate (6.20 percent) and the Medicare (hospital insurance) rate (1.45 percent). If you make more than $57,600 in 1993, you will continue to pay the Medicare portion of the Social Security tax up to a limit of $135,000. The limits for 1992 and 1991 were $130,200 and $125,000, respectively.

If you work for yourself, you pay 15.3 percent of your taxable income into Social Security, up to the limit of $57,600 for 1993 (the same earnings base used for employees and employers). As a general rule, the same limits on taxable income that apply to wage earners also apply to the self-employed, with some exceptions. When filing your tax return, there are special deductions you can take that are intended to offset your tax rate. You should consult a competent tax advisor on this subject, if you have questions after reading IRS Form 1040 or reviewing Social Security's fact sheet, *If You're Self-Employed* (Publication No. 05-10022).

Self-employed individuals continue to pay the Medicare portion of the Social Security tax (2.9 percent) up to a limit of $135,000 for 1993...the same as for wage earners. As a general rule, self-employment income would be your net earnings from a trade or business carried on as a sole proprietor or as a member of a partnership.

Since 1957, members of the U.S. armed forces have been covered by Social Security. Social Security taxes are paid on their cash compensation and additional earnings credits are received, up to a maximum, recognizing the value of the food, housing and clothing they receive. Where military service is shorter than two years, the additional credits may not always be given.

## What Does Social Security Cover?

The major programs covered by the U.S. Social Security system are: retirement; disability; survivors; Medicare; and SSI. Let's take a look at the specific benefits offered under Social Security, starting with the retirement benefits.

## Retirement Benefits

### Full Retirement

You will be eligible for your full Social Security benefit at the age of sixty-five, if you were born before 1938. However, if you were born in 1938 or later, you will be subject to the 1983 amendments to the Social Security Act. As a result of these amendments, beginning in the year 2000, the age at which full benefits are payable will increase in gradual steps from age sixty-five to age sixty-seven.

The following table from the Social Security Administration shows how the full retirement age will increase:

### Age to Receive Full Social Security Benefits

| Year of Birth | Full Retirement Age |
| --- | --- |
| 1937 or earlier | 65 |
| 1938 | 65 + 2 months |
| 1939 | 65 + 4 months |
| 1940 | 65 + 6 months |
| 1941 | 65 + 8 months |
| 1942 | 65 + 10 months |
| 1943 - 1954 | 66 |
| 1955 | 66 + 2 months |
| 1956 | 66 + 4 months |
| 1957 | 66 + 6 months |
| 1958 | 66 + 8 months |
| 1959 | 66 + 10 months |

**Reduced Benefit for Early Retirement**

Regardless of what your "full" retirement age is, you may start receiving benefits as early as age sixty-two. But, if you start your benefits early, they will be reduced a small percentage based on the number of months you will receive checks before you reach full retirement age. For example, if your full retirement age is sixty-five, the reduction for starting your Social Security benefit at age sixty-five is 20 percent; at age sixty-three, it is 13 1/3 percent; and at age sixty-four, it is 6 2/3 percent.

If you were born after 1937, thereby making your full retirement age older than sixty-five, you still will be able to take your retirement benefits at age sixty-two, but the reduction in your benefit amount will be greater than it is for people retiring now. For example, someone retiring at age sixty-two now will receive thirty-six months' benefits before reaching the full retirement age of sixty-five, resulting in a 20 percent reduction. An individual whose full retirement age is sixty-seven will receive benefits for sixty months' between age sixty-two and full retirement age. This result is a 30 percent reduction.

The general rule is that early retirement will give you about the same total Social Security benefits over your lifetime, but in smaller amounts to account for the longer period you will receive them.

Poor health causes some people to retire early. If poor health keeps you from continuing your work, consider applying for Social Security disability. The disability benefit amount is the same as a full unreduced retirement benefit. You should contact Social Security for more information on this subject.

### Delayed or Late Retirement

If you decide to continue working full-time beyond your full retirement age and, accordingly, do not sign up for Social Security until later, you can increase your Social Security benefit in two ways:

Your extra income generally will increase your "average" earnings, which is the basis for determining the amount of your retirement benefit. It follows that the higher your average earnings, the higher your Social Security benefit will be.

Your Social Security benefit will be increased by a certain percentage if you delay retirement. This special credit varies depending on your date of birth. The increases will be added automatically from the time full retirement age is reached until you start taking your benefits, or you reach age 70. The chart below shows the increase that applies to you:

**Chart of Increases for Delayed or Late Retirement**

| Year of Birth | Yearly Percentage Increase |
| --- | --- |
| 1916 or earlier | 1% |
| 1917-1924 | 3% |
| 1925-1926 | 3.5% |
| 1927-1928 | 4% |
| 1929-1930 | 4.5% |
| 1931-1932 | 5% |
| 1933-1934 | 5.5% |
| 1935-1936 | 6% |
| 1937-1938 | 6.5% |
| 1939-1940 | 7% |
| 1941-1942 | 7.5% |
| 1943 or later | 8% |

As an example, if you were born in 1943 or later, Social Security will add an extra 8 percent to your benefit for each year you delay signing up for Social Security beyond your full retirement age. The 8 percent per year impacts people turning age sixty-five in the year 2008 or later.

## Disability Benefits under Social Security

Although the dictionary defines "disability" as "a physical or mental condition that prevents a person from leading a normal life," the Social Security definition of disability is more specific and is generally related to your ability to work. In order to qualify for a Social Security disability, you must have a physical or mental impairment that is expected to keep you from doing any "substantial" work for at least one year (as a general rule, monthly earnings of $500 or more are considered substantial). Alternatively, you must have a condition that is expected to result in death. Social Security is not intended for temporary conditions or "partial" disabilities. In order to qualify for disability benefits, you must have earned a minimum number of quarters of Social Security coverage (as defined later in this chapter), subject to certain rules about earning some of these quarters in recent years.

Social Security benefits can be received at any age. If you are getting disability benefits at age sixty-five, they will become retirement benefits, although the amount remains the same. If you retire or become disabled certain members of your family may also qualify for benefits based on your Social Security record. These family members include:

- Your unmarried son or daughter, including a stepchild, adopted child, or, in some cases, a grandchild. The child must be under eighteen or under nineteen if in high school full time.

- Your unmarried son or daughter, eighteen or older, if he or she has a disability that started before twenty-two. If a disabled child under eighteen is receiving benefits as a dependent of a retired, deceased, or disabled worker, Social Security should be contacted to have his or her checks continued at eighteen on the basis of disability.

- Your spouse who is sixty-two or older.

- Your spouse at any age if he or she is caring for a child of yours who is under sixteen or disabled and also receiving checks.

- In the event of your death, certain family members may qualify for disability benefits, such as:

- Your disabled widow or widower fifty or older. The disability must have started before your death or within seven years after your death.

- If your widow or widower caring for your children receives Social Security benefits, she or he is eligible if she or he becomes disabled before those payments end or within seven years after they end.

- Your disabled ex-wife or husband who is fifty, or older if the marriage lasted ten years or longer.

Since disability is one of the most complicated of all Social Security programs, you should call or visit your Social Security office to get more information.

Individuals with HIV infection or AIDS may also qualify for disability benefits under two sets of circumstances: (1) when, because of the disease, they must severely limit the amount of work they do and (2) when they are no longer able to work. For more information on this subject, you should request the booklet, *A Guide to Social Security and SSI Disability Benefits For People With HIV Infection* (Publication No. 05-10020) or contact your Social Security office.

### Supplemental Security Income Benefits

Supplemental Security Income, generally called "SSI," is a program administered by Social Security, but for which benefits are financed by the general revenue funds of the U.S. Treasury. Benefits do not come from Social Security taxes or Social Security trust funds.

SSI makes monthly payments to people who are sixty-five or older, blind, or have a disability, and who have low incomes and few assets. Children and adults are eligible for SSI benefits because of blindness or disability. On occasion, a person whose sight is not poor enough to be considered blind may be able to get benefits as a disabled person.

Additionally, to get SSI you generally must reside in the United States and be a U.S. citizen or be an alien living in the U.S. legally.

Eligibility for SSI also depends on what you own and how much income you have. The word "income" in this context means money you have coming in as wages, Social Security checks, and pensions. Further, it means "non cash" items you receive such as the value of food, clothing, and shelter.

If you are married, Social Security will also look at the income of your spouse and the things he or she owns. If you are under eighteen, it may look at the income of your parents and the things they own. Similarly, if you are a sponsored alien, Social Security may look at the income of your sponsor and what he or she owns.

The amount of income you can have and still receive SSI benefits depends on whether you work and the state in which you live. While there is a basic national payment, some states add money to the national payment, resulting in higher SSI rates and higher income limits than others. You can contact Social Security to find out the income limits in your state.

In determining you eligibility for SSI, Social Security does not include the following:

- The first $20 of most income received in a month;

- The first $65 a month you earn from working and half the amount over $65;

- Food stamps;

- Most food, clothing, or shelter you get from private, nonprofit organizations; or

- Most home energy assistance.

For students, some of your wages or scholarships may not count. Generally, you are eligible for SSI if your monthly income was less than $422 for an individual or $633 for a couple in 1992.

For individuals who are disabled and work, Social Security does not count any wages you use to pay for items or services needed to work because of your disability. As an example, if you need a wheelchair, the wages you use to pay for the wheelchair are not included in income. Additionally, Social Security does not count any wages a blind person uses to pay expenses that are caused by working. If, for instance, a blind person uses wages to pay for transportation to and from work, the transportation cost is not counted as income.

Assets (the things you own) that are considered by Social Security in determining your eligibility for SSI include items such as real estate, personal belongings, bank accounts, cash, and stocks and bonds. However, Social Security does not count everything you own. For example, Social Security does not include:

- The home you live in and the land it is on.

- Your personal and household goods up to a limit of $2000 in total value.

- Your car generally does not count.

- Burial plots for you and immediate family members.

- Up to $1,500 in burial funds for you and your spouse.

- The cash value of life insurance policies with face values of $1500 or less.

- If you are blind or have a disability, some items may not count if you plan to use them to work or earn extra income.

An individual may be able to get SSI if the assets counted by Social Security are no more than:

- $2000 for one person, or

- $3000 for a couple

These limits do not change from state to state as they do in the income category.

Adults and children with disabilities can get SSI if their income and assets are below specified limits discussed in earlier sections. In general, most of the rules used to decide if a person has a Social Security disability will apply to SSI. Given that Social Security recently developed new standards for evaluating disability in children applying for

SSI benefits, it encourages new or previously denied cases to apply or reapply for SSI disability benefits. The SSI program, similar to Social Security, has special plans designed to help people who want to try going back to work without the risk of abruptly losing their benefits.

The majority of individuals who receive SSI can also get food stamps and "Medicaid" assistance. Medicaid helps pay doctor and hospital bills. You should contact Social Security for information on nutrition programs and a local social services office for more information about Medicaid. Also, see chapter 2 for a discussion on the Medicaid program.

### Medicare Benefits

Medicare is the U.S.'s health insurance program for people sixty-five or older, certain disabled individuals under sixty-five and people of any age who have permanent kidney failure, and it provides basic protection against the cost of health care. Since the subject of Medicare is covered in chapter 2, only a brief overview will be provided here.

There are two parts to Medicare:

- Hospital Insurance (also called "Part A"). It helps pay for inpatient hospital care, and certain followup services.

- Medical Insurance (also called "Part B"). It helps pay for doctor's service, outpatient hospital care, and certain related medical services.

As a general rule, Part A of Medicare is financed by payroll and self-employment taxes. Part B is financed by monthly premiums from those who enroll and partially by the general revenues of the federal government. Part A benefits are provided on the basis of past work, while Part B benefits are provided only if you pay the monthly premiums. Virtually everyone who is eligible for Part A through a work record, a spouse's record, or payment of the Medicare tax as a government employee, can sign up for Part B. Part B is an optional program which requires the payment of monthly premiums. Part A is free when you are eligible for it, since it was paid for by your taxes while you worked.

## Survivors' Benefits under Social Security

Survivors' benefits are those benefits that certain members of your family may be eligible for upon your death based on your Social Security record. Family members who can receive Social Security benefits include:

- A widow or widower who is sixty or older;

- A widow or widower who is fifty or older and disabled;

- A widow or widower at any age if she or he is caring for a child under sixteen or a disabled child;

- Children if they are unmarried and:

  — Under eighteen; or

  — Under nineteen and in an elementary or secondary school as a full-time student; or

  — eighteen or older and severely disabled, with the disability having started before age twenty-two;

- Your parents, if they were dependent on you for at least half of their support.

A special one-time lump sum death benefit of $255 is payable to your surviving spouse who was living with you at the time of your death. If there is no spouse living with you, the lump sum payment can be made only to certain members of your family.

The lump-sum benefit is made in addition to, and does not affect, monthly benefits to which the widow or widower may be entitled. If there are no eligible survivors, the benefit is not paid.

Application for the lump-sum benefit must be filed within two years of the insured's death. The exception to this rule is that no application is required of a beneficiary who was entitled to a wife's or husband's benefits on your earnings record for the month prior to your death.

Your ex-spouse may be eligible for benefits on your earnings record when you die, even if you have remarried. In order to qualify for benefits, your former spouse must:

- be at least sixty years of age (or fifty, if disabled) and have been married to you for at least ten years;

- be any age if caring for a child who is eligible for benefits on your record;

- not be eligible for an equal or higher benefit on his or her own record;

- not be currently married, unless the remarriage occurred after sixty—or fifty for disabled widows. If your ex-spouse remarries at sixty or older, after having been married to you for at least ten years, he or she at age sixty-five will be eligible for a widow's benefit on your record, or a dependents benefit on the record of his or her new spouse, whichever is higher.

If your ex-spouse receives benefits on your Social Security account, it will not affect the amount of any benefits payable to other survivors based on your record. Likewise, benefits payable to a divorced spouse are not reduced because some other person is being paid benefits on the same account.

### Benefits for Your Family

Once you start collecting Social Security retirement or disability benefits, other members of your family may also be eligible for payments, including your spouse, children, grandchildren, and divorced spouse. As a general rule, a spouse and other dependents will be eligible for a monthly benefit that is up to 50 percent of your retirement or disability benefit, subject to a maximum family benefit.

Upon your retirement, your dependents can collect the following amounts:

**Your spouse:** at age sixty-five or older — 50 percent; under age sixty-five and caring for a child under sixteen or disabled — 50 percent; at age sixty-two — the rate is reduced by a small percentage for each month before age sixty-five. The lowest reduced benefit currently is 37.5 percent at age sixty-two.

**Children:** if under age eighteen, 50 percent; if older and disabled (and the disability began before age 22), 50 percent.

**Divorced spouse:** at age sixty-five, 50 percent; at age sixty-two, reduced benefit, if the marriage lasted ten years or more. Note that an ex-spouse will not qualify for benefits on your record if his or her own Social Security record or someone else's provides an equal or higher benefit.

**Grandchildren:** If under eighteen, living in your home and you provide at least half of his or her support, 50 percent.

The Social Security law places a limit on the amount of money that can be paid to your family based on your Social Security record. The limit is generally equal to about 150 to 180 percent of your retirement benefit. The range may be lower for disability benefits. Where the sum of the benefits payable on your account is greater than the maximum family benefit, the benefits to your family will be reduced proportionately to bring the total within the limit. However, other benefits will not be affected. The benefit payable to a divorced spouse is not included in your maximum family benefit calculation, except for a surviving divorced spouse who qualifies only on the basis of caring for your child.

## When Will You Qualify for Social Security Benefits?

Social Security work credits are earned as you work and pay taxes. They are generally the prerequisites to getting benefits out of the system. An exception to this general rule is that some people can get benefits as a dependent or survivor on another person's Social Security record.

Most people earn four credits per year, which is the maximum that can be earned in one year. In 1992, workers earned one credit for each $570 in earnings. Every year, the amount of money needed to earn one credit is adjusted.

The number of credits needed to qualify for Social Security depends on your age and the type of benefit for which you might be eligible. The majority of people need forty credits (ten years of work) to qualify for benefits. Fewer credits are needed by young people to be eligible for disability benefits or for their dependents to be eligible for survivors' benefits if they should die.

It is likely that you will earn more credits than you need during your working lifetime to be eligible for Social Security. While the extra credits themselves will not increase your Social Security benefit, the income you earn while working will increase your benefit.

In order to qualify for disability benefits for you and your family under Social Security, you must have worked long enough and recently enough under Social Security. The work credit requirements needed for disability benefits depend on your age at the time you become disabled:

- Under age twenty-four. You need six credits in the three-year period ending when your disability starts.

- Ages twenty-four to thirty-one. You need credit for having worked half the time between twenty and the time you become disabled. For example, if you were disabled at age twenty-seven, you would need credit for three years of work out of the six years since your twenty-first birthday.

- Age thirty-one or older. You must have earned the same number of credits needed for retirement. Additionally, you must have earned at least twenty of the credits in the ten years immediately before the disability starts. The following chart shows the work credits needed for disability qualification:

| If Born After 1929, And Become Disabled At Age: | Credits You Need |
|---|---|
| 31-42 | 20 |
| 44 | 22 |
| 46 | 24 |
| 48 | 26 |
| 50 | 28 |
| 52 | 30 |
| 53 | 31 |
| 54 | 32 |
| 55 | 33 |
| 56 | 34 |
| 57 | 35 |
| 58 | 36 |
| 59 | 37 |
| 60 | 38 |
| 61 | 39 |
| 62 or older | 40 |

| If Born Before 1930, And Become Disabled Before Age 62 In Year: | Credits You Need |
|:---:|:---:|
| 1986 | 35 |
| 1987 | 36 |
| 1988 | 37 |
| 1989 | 38 |
| 1990 | 39 |
| 1991 or later | 40 |

Special rules apply for blindness. For example, the required work credits, earned at any time after 1936, need not be recent credit. Further, you may be eligible for a disability "freeze" if you continue to work. In this case, your future benefits, figured on your average earnings during your working life, will not be reduced because of relatively low earnings in those years when you are blind.

As a general rule, citizens and those with lawful alien status will earn credits toward qualification for benefits for all services performed in the U.S., regardless of the citizenship or residence of either the employee or employer. Qualification will be based on work credits as discussed earlier in this chapter.

If you work outside the U.S., special rules apply. For more information, contact your Social Security office regarding any totalization agreement, which is a bilateral arrangement between the U.S. and a foreign country that prevents double Social Security taxation of U.S. citizens employed aboard and that assures continuity of coverage for U.S. citizens who divide their working careers between work covered by the U.S. Social Security system and by a foreign Social Security or pension system. U.S. citizens can travel or live in most foreign countries without affecting their eligibility for Social Security benefits. You should note that there are a few countries, such as Albania and Cuba, where Social Security checks cannot be sent.

Note that if you did not work long enough to qualify for Social Security, or if you receive only a minimal benefit, you may be eligible for Supplemental Security Income (SSI) discussed earlier in this chapter.

## How and When Do You Apply for Social Security?

You must apply to receive Social Security benefits because the government will not automatically do it for you. An application for benefits can be made at any Social Security office. Social Security has about 1300 offices in cities and towns across the United States. You can visit the office nearest you or you can call: 1-800-772-1213 from 7:00 A.M. to 7:00 P.M. every business day or your local Social Security office (check telephone listings under "U.S. Government"). The easiest way to file a claim is to call the toll free number, 1-800-772-1213, ahead of time for an appointment.

You should apply for disability, survivor's and SSI benefits as soon as you are eligible. Social Security Administration suggests that you sign up for retirement benefits three months before you want your benefits to start.

Some of the records you may be asked to provide, depending on your claim, include:

- Your Social Security card or a record of your number;

- Your birth certificate;

- Children's birth certificates or adoption papers and Social Security numbers if they are applying;

- Your most recent W-2 form, or your tax return if you are self-employed.

- Worker's death certificate.

- Proof that the deceased supported you, if you are a dependent.

Even if you do not have all the documents you need, do not delay signing up for Social Security benefits. The Social Security Administration will help you get the needed information or advise you of other acceptable proof.

Your Social Security or SSI payments can either be deposited directly into your bank account or sent to you in the mail. In addition to being safer and more convenient than checks, direct deposit is more efficient and saves money for the federal government. In order to choose direct deposit, have your checkbook or any papers that show your bank account number with you when you sign up for Social Security.

## How Much Will Your Benefit Be?

Your Social Security benefit is based on factors such as your date of birth, the type of benefit for which you are applying and your earnings averaged over most of your working life. The easiest way to find out the benefits you will receive is by contacting the Social Security Administration. The Social Security Administration will provide you with a detailed, written personal estimate of your retirement, disability, and survivors benefits upon your request. Ask for Form SSA-7004 (Request for Earnings and Benefit Estimate Statement).

In about six weeks or less, you will receive a statement that will indicate:

- the number of credits that you have earned;

- the number of credits that you still need to earn to receive retirement, disability, and survivor's benefits;

- a list of your earnings subject to Social Security tax, as well as your Social Security tax payments by year;

- estimates of your monthly retirement benefits at ages sixty-two, sixty-five, and seventy; and

- estimates of disability and survivor's benefits for you and your dependents.

Do not be surprised if the statement that you receive does not include information for the last two years. It sometimes takes the Social Security Administration that long to update your records.

You can check the accuracy of the statement that you receive with your old W-2 forms (Wage and Tax Statements). This is the form that your employer is required to give to you each year so that you can complete your annual income tax return. The form states the amount that you have earned for the year and the amount of payroll taxes that your employer withheld from your paycheck. Your employer is required to match this payroll tax amount. Thus, the Social Security taxes that are posted under your name each year should equal two times the amount of payroll taxes that were withheld from your paycheck and also self-employment taxes.

Although it is your employer's responsibility to submit Social Security taxes on your behalf, you should periodically check your earnings record to make sure there are no mistakes. Sometimes, an employer may forget to submit the payroll taxes. Or, if you have changed your name, your earnings may be mistakenly posted to someone else's record.

In any case, it is a good habit to check your record every two or three years. It is a simple and painless procedure that could prevent you from losing many thousands of dollars in benefits.

## Defending Your Rights to Social Security Benefits

When the Social Security Administration makes a decision that affects your eligibility for Social Security or SSI benefits, it will send you a letter that explains the decision. If you disagree with the decision, you have the right to appeal it, and ask the Social Security Administration to review your case. This request must be submitted within sixty days after the date of the initial determination by either completing a "Request for Reconsideration Form" or by writing a letter to any Social Security Office.

The appeals process within the Social Security system involves three steps. If you are unsuccessful after these steps, your fourth step would be to bring a civil case in the federal courts. The complete appeal process is given below:

- Reconsideration by the Social Security Administration

- Hearing before an administrative law judge or hearing examiner

- Review by an appeals council established within the Social Security Administration

- Requesting a federal court hearing

You have sixty days from the time you receive the decision to file an appeal to the next level. Social Security assumes that you received the decision five days after the date on it, unless you can show that you received it later. You have the right to be represented by a qualified person (including an attorney) of your choice when dealing with the Social Security Administration.

For additional information, call or visit any Social Security Office to ask for a copy of the following fact sheets: *The Appeals Process* (Publication No. 05-10041) and *Social Security and Your Right to Representation* (Publication No. 05-10075).

## Will Your Social Security Benefit Be Taxed?

Some people who get Social Security will have to pay taxes on their benefits. Those impacted are people in higher income tax brackets. However, no more than one-half of the Social Security benefit will be taxed. For a federal tax return filed as an "individual," you may have to pay taxes on your Social Security benefits if your adjusted gross income exceeds a threshold income level of $25,000. For a federal tax return filed jointly, you may have to pay taxes on your Social Security benefits if your combined income exceeds a threshold of $32,000. The term "combined income" is defined as your and your spouse's adjusted gross income (from your Form 1040) plus nontaxable interest and one-half of your Social Security benefits.

## Working While Receiving Social Security

The Social Security Act limits the amount of money you can earn and continue to receive all of your Social Security retirement benefits. This restriction, often referred to as a retirement earnings test or earnings limit, impacts people under the age of seventy who collect Social Security retirement, as well as the benefits of dependents and survivors. After 1982, persons age seventy and older are allowed unlimited earnings without any loss of benefits under the annual earnings test. Individuals who work and collect disability or SSI benefits have different earnings requirements.

For example, in 1992, you could earn up to $7,440 and still collect all of your Social Security retirement benefits, if you are under age sixty-five. For every $2 earned over the limit, $1 would be withheld from your benefit. For those ages sixty-five through sixty-nine, you could earn up to $10,200 and still collect all of your Social Security retirement benefits. For every $3 earned over the limit, $1 would be withheld from your Social Security benefit.

Earnings included for this purpose are income from a job or the net profit from self-employment. Bonuses, commissions, and vacation pay are counted. However, the following items are not counted as earned income: pensions, annuities, investment income, interest, and Social Security, veteran's, and other government benefits.

## Other Information Concerning Social Security

Once you start collecting benefits, you should let Social Security know when events occur that could affect your benefits. Examples include:

- Moving
- Getting married or divorced
- Changing your name
- An income or earnings change
- Birth or adoption of a child
- Imprisonment of a beneficiary
- Leaving the United States
- Death of a beneficiary

If you are unable to manage your financial affairs, Social Security, following a careful investigation, will appoint a relative, friend, or another interested party to handle your Social Security matters. This individual is referred to as your "representative payee." Your Social Security benefits will be made payable in the representative payee's name on your behalf.

## Your Social Security Number

Your Social Security card contains a number used for recordkeeping purposes, such as recording earnings and monitoring benefits. It is also used by banks, insurance companies, other businesses, and government agencies as a form of identification. In the event you lose your card or need to change the name on your account or need to apply for a Social Security number, contact Social Security for an application form. The application contains information on the documentation you will need to submit.

Since federal tax returns must show a Social Security number for dependents age one and older, parents should generally apply for a Social Security number for children when they provide information for the child's birth certificate. Many states make the Social Security number a part of the birth registration procedure. If you have grandchildren who become your dependents, you may find they already have a number. If not, call or visit your Social Security office to get an application.

# CHAPTER 4

# UNDERSTANDING YOUR PENSION PLAN

## The Importance of Your Pension

With almost 60 percent of the workers in the United States covered by private pensions, you can easily see that your pension is an important financial resource for your senior years. In fact, your pension, personal annuities and savings, and Social Security benefits are likely to be the only sources of income after you retire. Therefore, it is important that you understand if and when you are covered by a pension plan and to what benefits you may be entitled.

You need to know whether your employer has a pension plan. Employers are not required to have pension plans for their employees, although most large and medium-sized companies do. You also need to know if you are specifically covered by your employer's pension plan, because it is not required that all employees be included.

A pension is basically a program under which your employer or union contributes money to a fund during your years of work to provide income to you after you retire. Your pension differs from an Individual Retirement Account (IRA) or private annuity in that a pension is generally employer-financed, while you typically fund and maintain your IRA and other private annuities.

## Your Pension Rights under Federal Laws

Although your employer does not have to set up a pension plan, if one is set up, it must meet certain federal requirements. Most of the required standards for pension plans are provided by the federal

Employee Retirement Income Security Act (ERISA) of 1974. Exempt from ERISA are governmental plans (including Railroad Retirement Act plans and plans of certain international organizations), certain church plans, plans maintained solely to comply with workers' compensation, unemployment compensation, or disability insurance laws, plans maintained outside the United States primarily for nonresident aliens, and excess benefit plans (plans maintained solely to provide benefits or contributions in excess of those allowable for tax-qualified plans) which are unfunded. Additional rules apply to pension plans under the Labor Management Relations Act, covering union members, Age Discrimination in Employment Act of 1967, prohibiting age discrimination, the Civil Rights Act of 1964, and the federal tax laws. Your rights as a pension plan participant are generally defined in Title I of ERISA.

Your employer's pension plan may not cover all employees. The pension laws and regulations allow employers to include or exclude certain categories of employees from a pension plan, provided that the plan does not discriminate in favor of shareholders, officers, and other highly-paid employees.

ERISA does not apply to small employers having less than twenty-five employees. If you are covered by a pension plan which is not regulated by ERISA, you must rely on your plan documents for your rights to pension benefits.

## Requirements for Participating in a Pension Plan

Under the ERISA laws, employees who are at least twenty-one years old and have worked for their employer for at least one year typically must be allowed to participate in the employer's pension plan. There are several exceptions for schools, plans providing full vesting after three years and other special situations. The one-year requirement for participation in a pension plan can generally be met by twelve months of continuous full or part-time employment or employment for 1000 hours in a twelve-month period.

Certain pension plans which provide for a fixed amount to be paid to employees (for example, $1,000 per month for each year of service) may require five years of service prior to retirement before you can collect a pension. These are called "defined benefits" plans and are the most common pension plans.

Another type of pension plan is the "defined contribution" plan wherein your employer contributes a fixed amount into the pension plan for each year of your service. Your retirement benefits under a "defined contribution" will depend on the amount of your employer's contributions and how well the plan performs over your work life.

Pension plans may not exclude an employee solely on the basis of part-time or seasonal employment if the employee has a "year of service" as defined by ERISA. Generally, a year of service is 1,000 hours of service during a twelve-month period. Plans of the maritime industry may designate 125 days as constituting a year of service. In the case of a seasonal industry where the customary period of employment is less than 1,000 hours during the year, a year of service is to be defined by regulation.

There are other circumstances where an employee who may have less than 1,000 hours of service must be deemed to have completed a "year of service." Some plans, instead of counting all hours of service from records, use an equivalency permitted by regulations to determine hours of service. In such cases, employees who meet specified requirements must be treated as having the equivalent to 1,000 hours of service even though they may not actually have 1,000 hours of service. Plans which use another alternative method of crediting service (called "elapsed time") base eligibility to participate on whether one year has elapsed while the employee is employed with the employer, irrespective of the number of hours of service completed.

Participation cannot be denied an employee because he or she begins employment late in life if the plan provides defined contributions such as profit sharing, stock bonus, or money purchase plans. Plans providing defined benefits (not contributions) are permitted to exclude from pension plan participation an employee who begins employment within five years of the plan's normal retirement age. However, for plan years starting on or after January 1, 1988, employers no longer will be able to exclude from plan participation employees who start work within five years of a plan's normal retirement age. For collectively bargained plans, this rule is effective on the earlier of (1) the later of January 1, 1988, or the date on which the last of the contracts expires, or (2) January 1, 1990. A "floating" normal retirement age, which could be no later than the fifth anniversary of the employee's participation in the plan, could be established.

After you have met the requirements for participation in a pension plan you begin to accumulate benefits toward retirement. The amount of your retirement benefits are normally determined by the number of years you have worked with your employer.

## Becoming Vested under a Pension Plan

Although you accrue retirement benefits while participating in a pension plan, you do not have a right to these benefits unless they are vested. Accruing benefits over long periods means little if you can lose these benefits. Accordingly, through its vesting provisions, ERISA assures employees who work for a specified minimum period under a pension plan of at least some pension at retirement. ERISA's vesting provisions generally did not become effective until the first day of 1976. If your service ended before that date, your rights would be governed by the rules of your plan.

When you become vested in your pension plan, you have a legal right to receive a pension at retirement age under your plan. Vesting is different from participating because vesting guarantees your right to a pension. Participating means only that you have qualified to be a part of the plan. For example, you might begin participating in a pension plan after one year of service, but the plan might provide that you work for five years before you become vested. This would mean that if you left the employer at any time before five years of service, you would not be vested and therefore would receive no pension benefits.

The ERISA laws establish minimum vesting requirements for pension plans. Before 1976 pension plans could require you to work your whole life for one employer before any pension benefits were vested. From 1976 to 1989 the typical vesting requirement was 10 years of service. Since 1989 pension plans are required to provide minimum vesting under either a five-year, 100 percent vesting rule, or a seven-year, graded vesting rule. Remember different vesting rules apply to people who stopped working under a pension plan before 1989. The five-year, 100 percent rule requires that employees be fully vested after five years of service. The seven-year rule requires that employees be vested according to the following schedule: 20 percent after three years, 40 percent after four years, 60 percent after five years, 80 percent after six years and 100 percent after seven years. Some union-negotiated pension plans paid for by more than one company can follow a ten-year, 100 percent vesting rule where employees are fully vested after ten years of service. Pension plans can provide for more rapid vesting schedules than those required by ERISA.

### Counting Your Years of Service

Your rights with respect to participation, vesting, and benefit accrual are generally determined by reference to years of service and years of participation completed by you and any breaks in service incurred. Whether an employee has completed a year of service is generally measured in terms of the number of hours of service credited to the employee during a 12-consecutive-month period designated by the plan.

It is important to examine your plan documents carefully so you will know exactly what "service" is counted in determining a "year of service" and "years of participation" under your plan and what periods are not counted for participation, vesting, and benefit accrual. You need to know this so you will not inadvertently incur a break in service or fail to participate, accrue benefits, or have periods counted for vesting.

ERISA and its regulations set minimum standards for defining "years of service" and "hour of service" under pension plans. These are minimum standards only, so plans may define these terms more liberally to benefit you. ERISA defines "year of service" for purposes of participation and vesting as a twelve-month period during which an employee has 1,000 hours of service. An employee who works an average of twenty hours a week will have over 1,000 hours of service in a year. Remember, in the maritime industry 125 days may be designated as constituting a year of service and, in the case of seasonal industries, ERISA specifies that "year of service" be defined by regulation.

ERISA also protects you from loss of pension benefits because of short breaks in service. As a general rule for vesting purposes you must be credited with a year of service for each year that you work 1,000 hours or more. Every hour for which you are paid counts toward the 1,000-hour requirement, including vacation days, sick days, personal days, and holidays.

Pension plans are also allowed to calculate years of service by counting your continuous years of employment from your date of hire. If you are laid off or disabled under this plan, you must be given vesting credit for one year after your date of layoff or disability.

In determining your rights to pension benefits, your employer usually must give you credit for all the years you worked for your employer after age eighteen. You must also be given credit for the time you were in the military service if you returned to the same job after leaving the military.

ERISA also provides that the employer credit you for years worked before a break in service if you were away from that employer for less than five consecutive years. This five-year break in service rule does not cause you to lose credit for the years you left because of pregnancy or to take care of a new born child, or for years in which you worked more than 500 hours for the employer.

If your pension plan requires ten years for vesting, you generally must be credited with prior years worked if your break in service was less than the time you worked for the employer before the break.

Even with the break-in-service rules discussed earlier, your employer may require that you work at least one year after the break to receive credit for previous years.

### Protection from Pension Plan Amendments, Terminations, and Mergers

If you have vested rights under a pension plan, you will not lose these rights if you left your employer for any reason. You keep your vested benefits even if you left to work for a competitor or other employer. Your employer is also prohibited from amending its pension plan to take away your accrued or vested benefit.

Your employer can make changes to its pension plan if they do not affect your accrued or vested benefits. Also any changes to the plan would generally only apply to the years after the change and not to the years you have already worked.

Some of your pension benefits are protected even if your employer terminated the pension plan, or goes out of business because of financial problems. Nearly all employees covered by defined benefits plans are protected by insurance under the Pension Benefit Guaranty Corporation ("PBGC"). The PBGC insurance only protects vested benefits, so you are not protected if you have not vested under your pension plan. Additionally, PBGC insurance protects only your basic retirement benefits up to a maximum amount, but not many of the special benefits you may have under your pension plan.

For further information on plan termination insurance, you should write to the PBGC. The address is 2020 K Street, N.W., Washington, D.C. 20006, Attention: Coverage and Inquiries Branch.

The Internal Revenue Code also provides some protection in the event of a termination or partial termination of a tax-qualified retirement plan. The Internal Revenue Code provides for full and immediate vesting of all accrued benefits, to the extent then funded, upon the complete or partial termination of a tax-qualified plan. However, benefits vested solely because of the termination or partial termination of a plan, rather than because of completion of the required number of years of service, are not guaranteed by the PBGC. Therefore, whether benefits vested in the event of a termination or partial termination will actually be paid would depend on whether the plan is sufficiently funded to pay those benefits.

If you are covered by a "defined contribution" pension plan, it is not insured by PBGC. If your plan terminates, you will be paid whatever funds are in your account.

If your pension plan was started within the five years before the plan is terminated, then your benefits may not be insured. Also, if your pension plan was improved within five years before it is terminated, these improvements might not be insured. Lump sum death benefits and disability benefits are usually not insured. Additionally, the PBGC insurance generally provides maximum age sixty-five benefits of only about $2,000 per month.

If your pension plan is terminated for any reason other than financial problems, you will get all of the benefits you have earned under the plan. If your total benefits are $3,500 or less, you are likely to be paid in a lump sum after the plan is terminated. Otherwise the pension plan funds are generally used to purchase insurance annuities which will pay your pension benefits when you retire.

In the case of a merger or consolidation of plans or a transfer of assets or liabilities from one plan to any other plan, each participant must be entitled to receive a benefit after the merger which is at least equal to the value of the benefit he or she would have been entitled to receive before the merger. The before-and-after merger benefits are determined as if the plan had been terminated.

ERISA also protects participants of certain pension plans from financing which is inadequate to pay the promised benefits. In order to make sure that sufficient money is available to pay promised pension benefits to employees when they retire, ERISA sets down rules for funding pension plans. Funding is monitored by actuaries and adjusted every three years to assure the soundness of plans.

ERISA protects employee pension plans from financial losses caused by mismanagement and misuse of assets through its fiduciary provisions. A fiduciary who breaches any responsibility or duty under ERISA may be personally liable to make good any losses to the plan resulting from such a breach and to restore to the plan any profits made through improper use of plan assets. A fiduciary is also subject to such other equitable or remedial relief as a court may deem appropriate, including removal.

### Payment of Your Pension

The normal retirement age under most pension plans is age sixty-five, and you are likely to receive maximum benefits when you retire at that age. If you retire before age sixty-five, your pension benefits will probably be reduced under most plans. If you continue to work under your pension plan after age sixty-five, federal law requires that you be paid a pension by April 1st of the year after you turn seventy and one-half.

Your pension benefits are normally paid to you after your retirement as a monthly amount for the rest of your life. Some pension plans may allow you to elect other payment methods, such as a lump sum or payment over a certain period of time.

Your pension benefits normally stop upon your death, except that your spouse is entitled to receive a part of your benefits. Your spouse will typically receive for life one-half of your vested pension benefits, unless you and your spouse jointly have elected another alternative.

A spouse is entitled to continue to receive benefits even after remarriage. You and your spouse can waive these surviving spouse benefits in writing. If you are unmarried at the time of your death, no pension benefits are required to be paid unless your pension plan specifically provides for such.

If you are divorced, your ex-spouse may still be entitled to a part of your pension benefits. Your pension benefits are considered as marital property in most states. They can be divided at divorce by court order and your pension plan can be required to pay a portion to your ex-spouse.

You retain your vested rights to a pension even if you are covered by another pension plan, profit-sharing plan, Individual Retirement Account or Social Security. However, some pension plans reduce your pension benefits based on the amount you will receive as Social Security. For service after 1989, the reduction for Social Security can not exceed 50 percent of your pension benefits.

Your pension benefits are not reduced because of unemployment payments that you are receiving. However, if you are collecting workers' compensation, your pension payments can be reduced.

## Obtaining Information on Your Pension Plan

ERISA requires plan administrators—the people who run pension plans—to give you in writing the most important facts you need to know about your plan. They must also provide you plan documents at reasonable cost if you make a written request.

ERISA requires that plan information be disclosed to participants and, in some cases, their beneficiaries, as well as to the government. Most plans are required to file financial reports with the Internal Revenue Service and summary plan descriptions with the U.S. Department of Labor. Some types of plans have been exempted from certain of the reporting and disclosure requirements through regulation. Other plans have been provided with alternative methods of complying with the reporting and disclosure requirements. The exemptions are alternative methods of compliance have been granted in order to avoid imposing unreasonable administrative burdens on plan administrators without adversely affecting the rights of participants.

The summary plan description must be furnished to participants and beneficiaries. It must give information on what the plan provides and how it operates. It also must be written in a manner to be understood by the average plan participant and, in an accurate and comprehensive manner, advise participants of their rights and entitlements.

The administrator must furnish automatically to participants and beneficiaries receiving benefits:

- the summary plan description, within 90 days after a person becomes a participant or beneficiary or within 120 days after the plan becomes subject to the reporting and disclosure provisions of the law

- summaries of any changes in the information required to be contained in the summary plan description, within 210 days after the end of the plan year in which the change is adopted

- an updated summary plan description every five years if there have been any plan amendments; and, if no amendments have been adopted, a new summary plan description every ten years

- a summary of the annual report, within nine months after the end of the plan year, or two months after the filing of the annual report if an extension has been granted for the filing of this report.

The administrator must furnish automatically to each pension plan participant:

- a statement of the nature, form, and amount of deferred vested benefits after your employment has ended

- information on pension plan survivor coverage.

If requested in writing, the administrator must furnish to any pension plan participant or beneficiary, a statement of total benefits accrued, accrued benefits which are vested, if any, or the earliest date on which the accrued benefits will become vested. This statement need not be furnished more than once in a twelve-month period. Plans to which more than one unaffiliated employer contributes must furnish the statement only to the extent provided by regulations.

The administrator must furnish to any participant or beneficiary within thirty days of written request and for which a reasonable charge may be made:

- additional copies of the latest updated summary plan description

- the latest annual report (Form 5500, 5500-C, 5500-R).

- the documents under which the plan is established or operated, such as the plan rules or the trust agreement

- terminal reports, if any.

Plans must also respond to written benefit claims. If a claim for benefits is denied in whole or in part, the administrator must write to the participant or beneficiary to explain why the benefits were denied and advise how the denial may be appealed.

The Internal Revenue Service will furnish to the Social Security Administration information on deferred vested benefits of plan participants who have terminated employment during a plan year before retirement. The Social Security Administration will provide that information to employees involved and their beneficiaries upon request and automatically when they apply for Social Security benefits.

Employees who are "interested parties," as defined by Internal Revenue Service regulations, must be notified of a request to the Internal Revenue Service for a determination on the tax status of a plan. Tax qualification gives tax benefits to a plan, the employer, and the employees participating in the plan. "Interested parties" have the right to see the application for approval and the supporting documents.

Summary plan descriptions and annual financial reports are on file and available for examination at the Department of Labor in Washington, D.C. Copies may be obtained for a small cost by writing to the Department of Labor, Public Disclosure Room, Room N-5707, 200 Constitution Avenue, N.W., Washington, D.C. 20210. The telephone number is (202)523-8771.

The Treasury Department must make available for public inspection applications for qualification of pension, profit sharing, and stock bonus plans, applications for tax exemption by organizations claiming to be tax exempt under section 501(a) of the Internal Revenue Code, documents supporting these applications, and letters or other documents issued by the Internal Revenue Service in response to the applications. Plans covering twenty-five or fewer participants are exempt from the public inspection provision. Information from which the compensation or deferred compensation of any participant could be determined is not subject to inspection.

Disclosable documents may be examined in Room 1567 of the National Office of the Internal Revenue Service, Washington, D.C., by submitting a request in writing to the Director, Disclosure and Security Division, Internal Revenue Service, P.O. Box 388, Ben Franklin Station, Washington, D.C. 20045. The documents filed in a particular district office of the Internal Revenue Service may be examined in that district office by sending a written request to the public disclosure officer of the district office. Photocopies of documents, for which a duplication charge is made, may also be obtained through written requests.

Be sure to retain copies of your pension plan summary, benefit statements, detailed pension plan document, and any other agreements relating to your employment. Understand what benefits you have earned and can count on for your retirement years. See your plan administrator, personnel officer, or a pension benefits lawyer if you need assistance.

### Filing a Claim for Your Pension

Employee benefit plans must have a reasonable and written procedure for processing written claims for benefits and for appeals if the original claim is denied. Therefore, if you believe you are entitled to a benefit from a pension or welfare benefit plan, you should write to the administrator of your plan to file a claim.

If a claim for benefits is denied, the participant must be notified in writing (generally within ninety days after the claim is filed) of the reason(s) for the denial and the specific plan provisions on which the denial is based. Any notice of denial must also tell you what additional information may be required in order to perfect your claim and find out how to appeal the denial.

You have at least ninety days in which to appeal a denial. A decision on your appeal generally must be made within sixty days unless the plan provides for a special hearing or the decision must be made by a group which meets only on a periodic basis. The decision on review must be furnished to the claimant and include the reasons for the decision, together with references to plan documents.

If your claim is denied and you believe you are entitled to benefits, you may wish to write to the plan administrator to request a copy of the complete plan rules. A reasonable charge (up to twenty-five cents a page) may be made for copies of the plan rules. You could then compare the plan rules with the plan provisions cited by the plan in the denial to determine whether the rules have been properly applied.

You should consult your summary plan description if you have any questions about how your plan processes claims.

## Taking Legal Action against Your Pension Plan

Participants and beneficiaries of a pension plan may bring a civil action:

- to compel a plan administrator to supply plan documents requested in writing by the participant or beneficiary within thirty days of the written request. A plan administrator who, in the court's judgment, fails to supply the information within the required time (unless the failure to supply the information results from circumstances reasonably beyond his or her control) may be personally liable to the individual who made the request for a fine of up to $100 per day.

- to enforce rights under the plan and to recover benefits due.

- to clarify his or her right to future benefits.

- for appropriate relief from breach of fiduciary duty.

- to enjoin any act or practice which violates any provision of Title I of ERISA (that is, the reporting and disclosure, participation, vesting, benefit accrual, break in service, joint and survivor, funding, and fiduciary provisions) or the terms of the plan, or to obtain other equitable relief.

- to enforce the right to receive a statement of vested benefits upon termination of employment.

- to obtain review of a final action of the Secretary of Labor, to restrain the Secretary from taking action contrary to ERISA, or to compel the Secretary to take action.

- to obtain review of any action of the PBGC (or a receiver or trustee appointed by the PBGC) which adversely affects the participant or beneficiary.

U.S. district court have exclusive jurisdiction over civil and criminal actions brought under Title I of ERISA, except that cases pertaining to benefit recovery or clarification of future benefit rights brought by participants and beneficiaries may also be brought in state courts. U.S. district courts have jurisdiction to grant relief without respect to the amount in controversy or the citizenship of the parties. In any action under title I of ERISA by a participant or beneficiary the court in its discretion may allow reasonable attorney fees and costs of action to either party.

An employee who has qualified as an "interested party" under regulations of the Secretary of the Treasury (as well as an employer and a plan administrator) may appeal to the U.S. Tax Court a determination by the Secretary of the Treasury concerning the initial or continuing qualification of a retirement plan or the Secretary's failure to make a determination.

You and your beneficiaries cannot be discharged, fined, suspended, expelled, disciplined, or discriminated against for exercising any right or prospective rights under a plan or ERISA or for giving information or testimony in any inquiry or proceeding relating to ERISA. Moreover, the use of violence, coercion, intimidation, and the like to interfere with rights or prospective rights under a plan or ERISA is punishable by a fine up to $10,000 and/or up to one year in prison.

It is unlawful to discharge, fine, suspend, or discriminate against any participant or beneficiary for the purpose of interfering with the attainment of any right to which he or she may become entitled under the plan or the law. This provision prohibits the practice of promising pensions and then dropping a worker to avoid paying a pension.

### Other Retirement Plans

In addition to your regular employer-sponsored pension plan, there are a variety of other retirement arrangements you might want to consider. Arrangements such as an Individual Retirement Accounts (IRA) or 401(k) plan may be invaluable as an additional source of retirement income.

Under the tax laws beginning in 1987, certain people can open or continue to contribute to IRAs. The amount contributed may be claimed as a deduction on your federal income tax return. Earnings on your IRA contributions are not taxable until you begin withdrawing benefits at age fifty-nine and one-half or later. Therefore, you may contribute to your own retirement plan and have earnings on those contributions accumulate on a tax-free basis. When you begin to withdraw the accumulated funds, the benefits will be taxable but you may be in a lower tax bracket than when you were employed.

Deductible IRA contributions are permitted unless (1) an individual or married couple has an adjusted gross income (AGI) above a specified phase-out level; or (2) the individual (or, if married, neither the individual nor the spouse) is an active participant in an employer-maintained retirement plan for any part of the plan year ending with or within the individual's taxable year.

If either spouse was covered under a plan, then the AGI test would apply. Couples with AGI under $40,000 can deduct $2,000 (plus $250 for a non-working spouse or a spouse who elects to be treated as having no compensation). The amount they could deduct would generally be reduced proportionately for income above $40,000 and totally phased out at $50,000. A single person with AGI under $25,000 could deduct $2,000, and this generally would be reduced proportionately and phased out at $35,000.

Individuals may make non-deductible IRA contributions to the extent they are not eligible to make deductible contributions and earnings on such contributions are not subject to tax until they are withdrawn.

If you receive a lump sum payment from a tax-qualified pension plan due to retirement, disability, termination of your employment, or termination of your pension plan, you may be able to defer taxes by depositing the funds in an IRA. This is called tax-free rollover. Later, you could transfer this sum tax-free to a new employer's pension plan if the plan permits it.

The rules governing IRAs are administered by IRS. For further information, contact the nearest IRS office listed in your local telephone directory.

PBGC also gives advice and assistance on evaluating the economic desirability of establishing IRAs and rollovers. For a copy of their booklet on IRAs, write to PBGC, Coverage and Inquiries Branch, 2020 K Street, N.W., Washington, D.C. 20006.

The tax laws also allow employers to establish a salary reduction plan, known as a 401(k) plan. This operates similarly to an IRA, in that you set aside part of your salary—the amount is set by the company and the tax laws, but it can exceed the maximum required for IRAs. The amount set aside, and the earnings, are not taxable income until distributed. However, unlike IRA's, sometimes the employer may match your contribution. The money in your 401(k) plan is somewhat accessible in hardship situations. Also you can usually borrow from your 401(k) plan.

# CHAPTER 5

# ACHIEVING EFFECTIVE FINANCIAL AND ESTATE PLANNING

## Managing Your Money

Unless you are independently wealthy, you will invariably have some concerns during your lifetime over money and finances. In fact, even the wealthy must deal with the issue of money management or their fortunes could be easily lost. It is especially important for senior citizens and those preparing for their senior years to do effective financial planning.

So many of your dreams will depend on financial security—a home, college for the kids, vacation, a happy retirement. It is up to you to make these dreams come true by setting and attaining financial goals. Review your financial status on a regular basis by determining your net worth and analyzing how your assets are allocated. Prepare a budget to keep track of your cash in-flows and out-flows. Keep your financial records (such as receipts, check books, bank statements, and other important documents) organized and in a safe place. Set realistic, yet aggressive, goals for savings and investments to provide resources for emergencies and retirement. Do some estate planning to minimize taxes and administrative expenses, and to maximize value for your family, heirs, and other beneficiaries. Take steps as early as possible to lay down a financial foundation on which you can build a secure future.

Determining your net worth periodically lets you know where you are financially. Your net worth is calculated by totalling all of your assets and subtracting all of your debts and other liabilities. Start with the preparation of a net worth statement by listing all of your assets and their value. This should include cash, checking and savings accounts, certificates of deposits, stocks, bonds, IRA accounts, life insurance cash values, real estate, automobiles, and personal property. Next, list all of your liabilities, including mortgages, personal loans, credit cards, taxes, and any other debts. The sum of your assets minus your liabilities will tell you how much you are worth.

Preparing a budget helps you keep track of where your money is going. It also helps in predicting how you will spend money in the future. Budgeting is an important process in setting financial goals and making sure that you are taking the right steps toward meeting them. Start by listing all your sources of monthly income such as salary and wages, pension, annuities, Social Security, interest, dividends, rental income, gifts, and any other money that you receive. Then itemize all of your monthly expenses and expenditures including mortgage, rent, taxes, utilities, insurance, repairs, loans and credit card payments, food, clothing, transportation, recreation, and the like. Ideally, your income should be more than your expenses and expenditures, especially during your pre-retirement years, to allow for savings. A successful strategy for maximizing your financial security in your senior years should comprise (1) controlling your personal debt and expenditures, (2) saving regularly, (3) taking full advantage of tax-deferred and tax-free income plans, and (4) maintaining a diversified and risk-balanced investment portfolio.

Look at ways to control your personal debt by minimizing use of credit cards and consumer credit. Try to pay cash for most of your purchases, if possible. Remember that interest on consumer loans is no longer tax deductible. Avoid a lot of impulse buying because it can wreck your financial planning. Do you spend too much on gifts? Entertainment and dining out? Vacations? Clothing? Although you should enjoy life, finding ways to curb your spending can help you in saving and investing and meeting your financial goals.

Learn to use the equity in your home to help manage your credit and advance your financial plans. Unlike consumer interest, home mortgage and home equity interest is tax deductible. Consider getting a home equity loan to pay off consumer loans and consolidate debt. It will likely save you taxes and interest in the long run.

You should also use your employer-sponsored 401(k) savings to maximize your financial benefit. Try to contribute as much money as possible to your 401(k) plan. The earnings that you save are usually tax-deferred, and many employers match your 401(k) contribution. You can typically borrow money from your 401(k) at below market interest rates and the interest is also tax-deferred income to you. You can advantageously use your 401(k) loans to pay off credit cards and other consumer debts.

Your investment strategy should be one of prudent risk-taking. With most investments, the greater risks usually provide the potential for a greater return to you. However, your level of risk taking typically changes over the various life cycles. At a younger age you can afford to take greater risk as you strive to build up your investment assets. When you approach retirement, your risk factor should decline as you focus on minimizing losses and preserving asset value. To help reduce overall risk of loss, your investment portfolio should always be diversified into a variety of investment vehicles.

A good financial planner can be helpful in analyzing your finances and recommending how to improve your financial situation. They can assist you in preparing a financial plan based on your personal history and financial goals. Before you select a financial planner be sure to investigate his or her background and experience. For further information on financial planners contact the following organizations:

**National Association of Personal Financial Advisors**
1130 Lake Cook Road, Suite 105
Buffalo Grove, Illinois  60089
1-800-366-2732

**Institute of Certified Financial Planners**
7600 E. Eastman Avenue, Suite 301
Denver, Colorado  80231
(303) 751-7600

**International Association for Financial Planning**
2 Concourse Parkway, Suite 800
Atlanta, Georgia  30328
(404) 395-1605

Securities and Exchange Commission
Office of Filings, Information, and Consumer Services
450 5th Street, N.W.
Washington, D.C. 20549
(202) 272-5624

## Your Investment Options

There are a myriad of savings and investment vehicles available for both short-term and long-term financial goals. These include everything from the simple savings account with banks, credit unions, and savings and loans associations to U.S. Government securities, corporate and municipal bonds, mutual funds, annuities, stocks, real estate, and commodities. An effective investment strategy is to balance risks, yield, taxes, inflation, and liquidity with the best mix of investment channels.

The U.S. Government offers securities which are very safe with guaranteed rates of return. Treasury bills are issued for periods of thirteen, twenty-six, or fifty-two weeks and are redeemable for the face amount. You pay a discounted amount, and the yield over the time period of the bills is the difference between the face value and the discounted price. You can purchase treasury bills directly from your local federal reserve bank without paying any fees or through an intermediary bank or broker.

The U.S. Treasury also offers EE and Series HH savings bonds. EE bonds mature in twelve years and guarantee a minimum 6 percent rate. If held for five years or longer you will typically earn a competitive market-based rate on EE bonds. You purchase EE bonds at a discounted price and receive the face value of the bond on maturity. The interest you earn on EE bonds is exempt from state and local income taxes, and you pay no federal taxes on the interest income until you cash in the bonds. Series HH bonds are also exempt from state and local taxes and earn 6 percent annual interest which is paid semi-annually. The EE and HH savings bonds are very safe investments and can usually be purchased through banks and other financial institutions, or your employer by payroll deduction.

Municipal bonds are another relatively safe investment vehicle. Although their yields are usually lower than most riskier investments, the interest earned is typically exempt from federal, state, and local taxes. Municipal bonds can be a useful investment medium if you are in a high tax bracket.

Corporate bonds are an additional investment medium which can offer attractive yields at relatively low to medium risks, depending on the financial health of the issuing company and its bond rating. Bonds with the highest grade are rated as "AAA," and these typically offer a lower yield than the lower grade bonds. Corporate bonds are usually issued from one to thirty years and are redeemable for the face value at maturity. You purchase the bonds at a discounted price which fluctuates according to market conditions.

You are probably already familiar with the savings plans offered by your bank, such as the traditional passbook savings account. Banks also offer certificates of deposit with varying maturity periods and interest rates. There are usually penalties for early withdrawal of funds from certificates of deposit. Money market accounts are also available at most banks and generally earn a higher yield than your passbook savings account. The money market accounts may provide check-writing and other privileges, and may be subject to minimum balance requirements and administrative fees. Your accounts with federally insured banks and credit unions are insured up to $100,000 per depositor.

Annuities from insurance companies or other financial establishments are investment vehicles which guarantee a fixed income for life or a specified number of years. If you want a guaranteed income without having to worry about managing assets to attain it, then you should consider purchasing an annuity. The interest is usually tax-deferred until you make withdrawals. Annuities are only as good as the company issuing them, so be sure to investigate the financial health of the company before purchasing an annuity.

Riskier investments include equity or ownership vehicles such as stocks, mutual funds, commodities, and real estate. When you purchase stock, you are buying part ownership in a company. The value of your stock will go up and down depending on the financial performance of the company and other economic conditions. The stock may also pay dividends determined by company profits. Regular ownership in a company is evidenced by common stock which has no guaranteed rate of return; in fact, the return can be negative. Preferred stock usually offer a specified dividend rate and is paid off before common stock if the company dissolves.

Mutual funds are a mechanism for you to pool your assets with other investors for investing in a variety of vehicles. Some mutual funds can be speculative and extremely risky and others can be conservative depending on how the fund makes investments. It is very important that you evaluate a fund's historical performance and financial stability before investing in mutual funds.

Real estate and commodities are purely speculative investments and involve a lot of risk. With these investments you are gambling on the future value of assets such as real property, precious metals, foreign currencies and feed stocks. Always obtain professional advice before investing in high risk ventures.

## The Financial Perspective of Estate Planning

"The pen is mightier than the sword," particularly when it comes to estate planning. If you take the time to put pen to paper and plan your estate, you can save a significant portion of your wealth for your family and other heirs.

Without proper planning, your estate will be exposed to taxes, probate and legal fees, and may be significantly depleted leaving little or nothing for your family or heirs. In the absence of a clear plan, there may be disputes about distribution of your assets, resulting in a waste of time and additional legal and administrative fees. With planning, you can determine the value of your estate and make decisions while you are alive that will preserve it for your heirs later. Through the use of various tools of estate planning, like charitable trusts, living trusts and life insurance you may be able to avoid some tremendous costs to your estate.

An estate plan is normally used to preserve your estate today and minimize the cost associated with dividing and transferring the value to your heirs later. The plan should also consider ways to accomplish other goals you have for assets that you have accumulated during a lifetime. If your estate plan costs you more than it saves, it is an ineffective plan.

Your estate plan should take into account the following costs:

- Appraisals

- Tax filing costs

- Probate fees

- Legal fees

- Auction fees

- Estate taxes

- Administrative fees

To the extent that you can minimize or eliminate these costs, you will preserve more of your estate's value for your heirs.

There are two provisions in the tax law that determine the amount that may be passed to heirs without incurring estate taxes. The first is that when an estate is left to a surviving spouse, regardless of size, there is no estate tax due. The amount that may be passed to a spouse at death is unlimited. This is the unlimited marital deduction.

The second provision involves the Unified Credit which pertains to amounts passed to other heirs. Currently, the tax law allows for a credit of $192,800 against estate taxes due. This credit is equivalent to the tax due on $600,000 of assets. Therefore if you die with an estate of $600,000 or less there would be no estate taxes due, in most cases. A married couple may leave $1,200,000 to heirs since they are entitled to two unified credits.

Note that in many cases one of the unified credits is lost at the death of the first spouse unless the couple take steps necessary to preserve that credit. Remember, as long as money passes to one spouse there are no estate taxes because of the unlimited marital deduction. But, upon the death of the second, taxes will be due on any amount over $600,000. One basic element of estate planning for married couples should be preserving both unified credits. Working with a good estate planner can help you maximize benefits under the tax laws.

The key to estate planning is establishing goals. Prior to deciding on use of estate planning devices such as a will or various trusts, you should decide what you would like to accomplish with your estate. Is preservation for your heirs important? Would you like to maximize the value to you now or your heirs later? Are you willing to sacrifice a portion of what you have today to leave more for others later? Would you consider gifting assets to charity? Don't get lost in the details on the type of trusts or wills needed because these are merely tools to be used to accomplish the objectives. Rather than thinking about the how and what kind of will or trust, think of the why. Let the professionals worry about how to put your wishes into proper form. Tell your estate planner or attorney what you want accomplished so they can help you accomplish your goals.

There is cost involved in setting up an estate plan. However, by investing money and time today, you may be saving your heirs not only thousands of dollars but also legal and emotional distress later.

### Checklist for Setting Up An Estate Plan

❑ Determine the current value of your estate. Include all assets plus the death benefit from insurance on your life if you are also the owner of the policy. Include cash value of policies that you own even if you are not the insured.

❑ Set goals; what would you like to accomplish with your assets? Do you want to preserve the full value for relatives, charity, or others? Any specific bequests (the family heirloom to your daughter)? Any special needs that should be addressed, like providing for the care of a minor or handicapped heir?

❑ Evaluate your present situation. What costs would be incurred if your estate were settled today, and how would assets be distributed to heirs? Do you have a current will? Does it reflect your true wishes? Make an itemized list of costs for settling your estate. Include funeral expenses, estate, income taxes, probate, legal fees, and payment of creditors. Will there be a cash shortage in settling the estate? If so, it may be necessary to sell assets to cover the shortage. Oftentimes a forced sale of assets could result in diminished market value. This is your "before" picture. A financial analysis done by a financial planner should accomplish the above. The analysis should also point out the dollars that may be saved by making changes in your present situation.

❑ Compare your "before" picture with your goals. Are changes desirable? Together with your estate planning professional determine what changes need to be made to accomplish your goals.

❑ Determine the cost that would be incurred to make changes to your "before" picture.

❑ Evaluate "after" picture. How will circumstances differ when changes are in place? What problems will an estate plan solve? Will you eliminate cash shortages? Will there be a change in the value of estate to your heirs? Will asset distribution be correct? Is there a benefit to you today?

❑ Compare costs versus benefits and make a decision on your course of action. Develop an action plan to complete all necessary steps. Include a time frame to get things done.

❑ Implement the plan. The best laid plans do not accomplish a thing. If you do not follow through and actually implement the plan, you have wasted time and money.

❑ Review annually. Since everything changes, laws, value of your estate, your personal preferences, etc., you should establish a time for review of your plan at least once a year.

Since estate planning involves financial and legal issues, it is best done through the coordinated efforts of financial and legal professionals that specialize in the area of estate planning. If your estate is complex you should enlist the help of professionals who can effectively coordinate and use all the available tools to accomplish your goals. Do not make the mistake of using an attorney to do the financial analysis or allow the financial professional to do your legal work. Use only financial planners or attorneys that have special expertise in estate planning.

## Estate Planning Devices

A will and trust arrangement can be used as effective estate planning devices. A will is a set of final instructions showing how you would like your property distributed. See chapter 12 for a more detailed discussion on wills. Although none of us like to think of our own demise and the need for a will, it is a necessary document if you have assets and would like to have these distributed according to your wishes. In the absence of a will, court proceedings may be necessary to determine how your estate should be distributed. Thus, a will should be a part of any estate plan.

A revocable living trust is a legal arrangement to hold property during one's life for the benefit of others at one's death. It may be used jointly with your will. The revocable living trust may be changed at anytime by the grantor (the person who sets up the trust). Assets continue under the control of the grantor. This type of trust is normally set up to avoid the time and costs of probate. See chapter 12 for more discussion on living trusts.

An irrevocable trust is another arrangement for holding property and can be useful in estate planning. The irrevocable trust, once established, generally can not be changed and the grantor gives up control over assets transferred to the trust.

Another estate planning device is the charitable remainder trust which allows gifting of assets to a charity without giving up income from the assets during your lifetime. Assets are placed in trust for the benefit of a charity at the death of the grantor. During the grantor's lifetime the trust will pay an income stream to the grantor. The grantor will normally receive an income tax deduction when assets are placed into the trust. The amount of the income tax deduction is calculated using IRS guidelines. This type of trust is used to provide income today. It is particularly useful when a sale of highly appreciated assets are involved.

Life insurance can be used as an effective estate planning device to transfer the value of assets to heirs. Since life insurance usually avoids probate and administrative expenses, it is an excellent way to transfer assets. See chapter 7 for a more detailed discussion on life insurance.

Gifting and joint ownership arrangements may also be used as part of an overall estate plan. Each one has its advantages and disadvantages. Prior to using a gifting or joint ownership arrangement make sure you fully understand that this also means giving up control over your assets. You can make gifts to an unlimited number of people or organizations without paying federal gift taxes, provided that these gifts do not exceed $10,000 ($20,000 for married couples) per person each year. No taxes are paid on gifts of any amount between spouses.

Because tax and estate laws are constantly changing, always seek the advice of a knowledgeable attorney or estate planner before making gift and estate planning decisions.

CHAPTER **6**

# MANAGING YOUR CREDIT

## Why Good Credit is Important

As you grow older your need to maintain a good credit rating becomes of paramount importance. You typically will not have the money yourself to purchase many of the big ticket items in your life, such as a car, house, or college education. Even your ability to obtain medication and medical treatment may very well depend on your credit rating. Thus, having access to credit is very important if you are to acquire and enjoy most major assets during your lifetime. Furthermore, changes in your life, such as divorce, loss of income, relocation, retirement, education for your children, and loss of a spouse, may all trigger a need for you to obtain credit or review your current credit history. Maintaining a good credit history and establishing sources of credit should always be a part of your financial planning.

Although lenders consider a variety of factor in deciding whether to give you credit, most of them rely heavily on your credit history. So, building a good credit history is essential if you want to be able to borrow money. If you have no reported credit history, it may take time for you to establish credit. Although this problem affects young people more than it does senior citizens, there is a large number of seniors (particularly widows and divorcees) who have not established their own credit.

If you do not have a credit history, you should begin to build one. If you have a steady income and have lived in the same area for at least a year, try applying for credit with a local business, such as a department store. Or you might borrow a small amount from your credit union or the bank where you have checking and savings accounts. A local bank or department store may approve your credit application even if you do not meet the standards of larger creditors. Before you apply for credit, ask whether the creditor reports credit history information to credit bureaus serving your area. Most creditors do, but some do not. If possible, you should try to get credit that will be reported. This builds your credit history.

If you do not have a credit file, you can visit or write your local credit bureau and request that a file be started on you. Most credit reporting agencies will require that you provide them with your identification, your address (last five years), social security number, place of employment, and verification of income. If you do not have employment income, take copies of Social Security, disability, pensions, annuities, alimony, and retirement checks. Remember that, under the law, employment income must be treated the same way as retirement or disability income in determining if credit is to be granted. If you have prior creditors, contact them to obtain copies of your last credit transactions. Also, if you have a bank account, attempt to get a letter of reference from your banker and submit these to the credit reporting agency.

Open checking and savings accounts at several financial institutions if you do not have any. These may be useful as credit references and as easier sources of credit because of your ongoing relationship. Most creditors will not extend you credit unless you have at least three good credit references. Apply for a major credit card. If you do not qualify, check to see if you can offer collateral or have someone cosign.

The Federal Trade Commission enforces a number of federal credit laws and provides free brochures and publications on many credit-related issues. The Federal Reserve System and the Federal Deposit Insurance Corporation also provide free consumer pamphlets and handbooks on a variety of credit topics. Much of the following information was provided by these sources.

### How Credit Bureaus Work

Credit reporting agencies, often called credit bureaus, are companies that gather information on credit users and sell that information in the form of credit reports to credit grantors, such as banks, finance companies, and retailers. Credit bureaus keep records of consumers' debts and how regularly these debts are repaid. They gather information from creditors who send computer tapes or other payment data to credit bureaus, usually on a monthly basis, showing what each account-holder owes or has paid. The data show if payments are up-to-date or overdue, and if any action has been taken to collect overdue bills. The credit bureau adds this data to existing information in consumer files, creating a month-by-month history of activity on consumer accounts.

If you have been denied credit because of information that was supplied by a credit bureau, the Fair Credit Reporting Act requires the creditor to give you the name and address of the credit bureau that supplied the information. If you contact that bureau to learn what is in your file within thirty days of receiving a denial notice, the information is free. If not, the credit bureau may charge you a small fee (i.e., $10-$30).

You always are entitled to learn what is in your credit file, but credit bureaus vary in how they disclose this information. Most will send you a printed copy of your credit report. Some, however, will ask you to visit the bureau to review your record or will give you information over the telephone once you have provided proper identification.

Once you have received your credit report, make sure that you understand the report. Often, credit reports are computer coded for recordkeeping purposes, and, thus difficult to understand. If you do not understand your report, the credit bureau is required by law to give you an explanation of what your report says. If you still do not understand, you can set up an appointment with a credit counselor to discuss your report.

## How to Conduct Your Own Credit Check-Up

Even if you have not been denied credit, you may wish to find out what information is in your credit file. Some financial advisors suggest that consumers review their credit reports every three or four years to check for inaccuracies or omissions. This could be especially important if you are considering making a major purchase, such as buying a home. Checking in advance on the accuracy of information in your credit file could speed the credit-granting process.

To find which credit bureaus have your file, check the Yellow Pages under credit bureaus or credit reporting agencies for the phone numbers and addresses of the bureaus near you. The names and addresses of the four major credit reporting agencies are given at the end of this chapter. When you contact them, give all identifying information, such as your full name, Social Security number, current address, former address, and spouse's name (if applicable). Ordinarily, a credit bureau will charge $10 to $30 to give you your credit file information. To get a complete credit picture, ask all local credit bureaus if they maintain a file on you.

If you are married, you and your spouse probably have individual credit files. These files may contain identical or different information, depending on whether you and your spouse have shared or separate accounts. You and your spouse may find it helpful to review and compare your credit histories together.

Credit information on accounts opened before June 1, 1977, that are shared by a husband and wife often are reported only in the husband's name. However, creditors must report the credit history individually, in the name of each spouse, if you ask them to do so. Newer accounts should be reported on an individual basis automatically. If you find this is not the case, write to the creditor and request that the account be reported in both names. This will help both of you build a credit history.

## What a Credit Report Covers

Contrary to myth, a credit bureau neither tracks all aspects or your personal life nor evaluates credit applications. Credit bureaus are simply organizations that collect and transmit four principal types of information.

**Identification and employment data:** Your name, birth date, address, Social Security number, employer, and spouse's name are routinely noted. The bureau also may provide other information, such as your employment history, home ownership, income, and previous address, if a creditor requests it.

**Payment history:** Your account record with various creditors is listed, showing how much credit has been extended and how you have re-paid it. Related events, such as referral of an overdue account to a collection agency, may be noted as well.

**Inquiries:** Credit bureaus are required to maintain a record of all creditors who have requested your credit history within the past six months. They normally include such creditor inquiries in your credit file for at least this long.

**Public record information:** Events that are a matter of public record and are related to your credit-worthiness, such as bankruptcies, foreclosures, or tax liens, may also appear in your report.

### How to Correct Errors in Your Credit Report

Your credit file may contain errors that can affect your chances of obtaining credit in the future. Under the Fair Credit Reporting Act, you are entitled to have incomplete or inaccurate information corrected without charge.

If you dispute information in your report, the credit bureau must reinvestigate it within a "reasonable period of time," unless it believes the dispute is "frivolous or irrelevant." To check on the accuracy of a disputed item, the credit bureau will ask the creditor in question what its records show. If the disputed item is on the public record, the credit bureau will check there instead. If a disputed item cannot be verified, the credit bureau must delete it. If an item contains erroneous information, the credit bureau must correct the error. If the item is incomplete, the bureau must complete it. For example, if your file showed accounts that belong to another person, the credit bureau would have to delete them. If it showed that you were late in making payments but failed to show that you are not longer delinquent, the credit bureau would have to add information to show that your payments are now current. Also, at your request, the credit bureau must send a notice of the correction to any creditor who has checked your file in the past six months.

If the reinvestigation does not resolve your dispute, the Fair Credit Reporting Act permits you to file a statement of up to 100 words with the credit bureau explaining your side of the story. Employees of the credit bureau often are available to help you word your statement. The credit bureau must include this explanation in your report each time it sends it out.

Your credit file may not contain information on all of the accounts you have with creditors. Although most national department store and all-purpose bank credit card accounts will be included in your file, not all creditors supply information to credit bureaus. For example, some travel-and-entertainment and gasoline card companies, local retailers, and credit unions do not report to credit bureaus.

No one can legally do a credit check on you without your authorization. Moreover, you want to avoid going from one creditor to another within a short period of time applying for credit. Each time that you complete a credit application, a credit report is usually run on you and reported to the credit bureau. Furthermore, sometimes credit checks are run on you without your knowledge, usually by places that offer instant credit, like used car lots and discount stores. If no credit account is opened as a result, then perspective creditors may view all the inquiries as rejections of your application for credit and feel uneasy in extending you credit. If you discover that there are unauthorized or numerous inquiries on your report, you should write a letter to the credit bureau and request that these inquiries be removed.

If you have been told that you were denied credit because of an "insufficient credit file" or "no credit file" and you have accounts with creditors that do not appear in your credit file, you can ask the credit bureau to add this information to future reports. Although they are not required to do so, for a fee many credit bureaus will add other accounts, if verifiable, to your credit file.

### How Time Affects Your Credit Report

Under the Fair Credit Reporting Act, credit bureaus can report most negative information for no more than seven years. The seven-year period runs from the date of the last regularly scheduled payment that was made before the account became delinquent unless the creditor later took action on the account, such as charging it off or obtaining a judgment for the amount due. If a creditor took such an action, the seven years would run from the date of that event. For example, if a retailer turned over your past-due account to a collection agency in 1977, a credit bureau may report this event until 1984. You should be aware that if you made a payment after 1977 on this account, your action would not extend the permissible reporting period beyond 1984.

There are exceptions to the seven-year rule. Bankruptcies may be reported for ten years. Also, any negative credit-history information may be reported indefinitely in three circumstances:

- If you apply for $50,000 or more in credit;

- If you apply for a life insurance policy with a face amount of $50,000, or more;

- If you apply for a job paying $20,000 or more (and the employer requests a credit report in connection with the application).

You can contact the credit bureau if you believe negative information is being reported beyond the permitted period and ask that it be removed.

## What You Can Do if You Have a Poor Credit History

Before creditors will give you credit, they look at how you have paid your bills in the past. Negative information in your credit file may lead creditors to deny you credit. Information that is considered negative includes late payments, repossessions, accounts turned over to a collection agency, charge-offs (accounts viewed as a "loss" by a creditor), judgments, liens, and bankruptcy.

A poor credit history that is accurate cannot be changed. There is nothing that you (or anyone else) can do to require a credit bureau to remove accurate information from your credit report until the reporting period has expired. However, this does not necessarily mean that you will be unable to obtain credit during the period. Because creditors set their own credit-granting standards, not all of them look at your credit history in the same way. Some creditors may look only at more recent years to evaluate you for credit, and they may grant you credit if your bill-paying history has improved. Before applying for credit, it may be useful to contact creditors informally to discuss their credit standards.

If you cannot obtain credit based on your own credit history, you may be able to do so if someone who has a good credit history cosigns a loan for you—this means the cosigner agrees to pay if you do not. Or you may be able to obtain a small loan or a credit card with a low dollar limit by using your savings account as collateral. If you pay promptly and your creditor reports to a credit bureau, this new information will improve your credit history picture.

## How to Deal with Mounting Bills

A sudden illness or the loss of your job may make it impossible for you to pay your bills on time. Whatever your situation, if you find that you cannot make your payments, contact your creditors at once. Try to work out a modified payment plan with your creditors that reduces your payments to a more manageable level. If you have paid promptly in the past, they may be willing to work with you. Do not wait until your account is turned over to a debt collector. At that point, the creditor has given up on you. Most creditors do not want to spend time and money to collect delinquent accounts—all they want is their money! Therefore, in most cases, your creditors will be willing to work with you through your crisis. For example, you may want to offer your creditor interest payments on your debt and delay payments on your principal until your condition changes; also, check to see if your debt is covered by a payment protection plan or other insurance that would pay your debt. In some cases you may be able to get your creditor to accept a partial payment as satisfaction in full for your debt. In any event, you want to keep an open dialogue with your creditor keeping him abreast of your situation.

If you do work out a debt-repayment plan, ask your creditors to report your new, smaller payments to the credit bureau as timely. Otherwise, the credit bureau may report these payments as delinquent because you are paying less than the amount agreed to in your original credit agreement.

Automobile loans may present special problems. Most automobile financing agreements permit your creditor to repossess your car any time that you are in default on your payments. No advance notice is required. If your car is repossessed, you may have to pay the full balance due on the loan, as well as towing and storage costs, to get it back. If you cannot do this, the creditor may sell the car. Do not wait until you are in default. Try to solve the problem with your creditor when you realize you will not be able to meet your payments. It may be better to sell the car yourself and pay off your debt. This would avoid the added costs of repossession and a negative entry on your credit report.

## Where to Find Low-Cost Help

If you cannot resolve your credit problems yourself or need additional assistance, you may want to contact the Consumer Credit Counseling Service (CCCS). This is a non-profit organization with more than 200 offices located in forty-four states that counsels indebted consumers. CCCS counselors will try to arrange a repayment plan that is acceptable to you and your creditors. They also will help you set up a realistic budget and plan expenditures. These counseling offices, which are funded by contributions from credit-granting institutions, are offered at little or no cost to consumers. You can find the CCCS office nearest you by checking the white pages of your telephone directory or by sending a self-addressed stamped envelope to:

**National Foundation for Consumer Credit**
8611 Second Avenue, Suite 100
Silver Spring, Maryland 20910
(301) 589-5600

In addition, nonprofit counseling programs are sometime operated by universities, military bases, credit unions, and housing authorities. They are likely to charge little or nothing for their assistance. Or, you can check with your local bank or consumer protection office to see if it has a listing of reputable, low-cost financial counseling services.

## The Cost of Credit

If you are thinking of borrowing or opening a credit account, your first step should be to figure out how much it will cost you and whether you can afford it. Then you should shop around for the best terms.

Two laws help you compare costs:

• Truth in Lending requires creditors to give you certain basic information about the cost of buying on credit or taking out a loan. These "disclosures" can help you shop around for the best deal.

- Consumer Leasing disclosures can help you compare the cost and terms of one lease with another and with the cost and terms of buying for cash or on credit.

Credit costs vary. By remembering two terms, you can compare credit prices from different sources. Under Truth in Lending, the creditor must tell you (in writing and before you sign any agreement) the finance charge and the annual percentage rate.

The finance charge is the total dollar amount you pay to use credit. It includes interest costs, and other costs, such as service charges and some credit-related insurance premiums.

## How Age Affects Your Credit

In the past, many older persons have complained about being denied credit just because they were over a certain age. Or when they retired, they often found their credit suddenly cut off or reduced. So the law is very specific about how a person's age may be used in credit decisions.

A creditor may ask your age, but if you are old enough to sign a binding contract (usually eighteen or twenty-one years old depending on state law), a creditor may not:

- turn you down or offer you less credit just because of your age;

- ignore your retirement income in rating your application;

- close your credit account or require you to reapply for it just because you reach a certain age or retire; or

- deny you credit or close your account because credit life insurance or other credit-related insurance is not available to persons your age.

Creditors may "score" your age in a credit-scoring system, but, if you are sixty-two or older, you must be given at least as many points for age as any person under sixty-two.

Because individuals' financial situations can change at different ages, the law lets creditors consider certain information related to age—such as how long until you retire or how long your income will continue. An older applicant might not qualify for a large loan with a 5 percent down payment on a risky venture, but might qualify for a smaller loan—with a bigger down payment—secured by good collateral. Remember that while declining income may be a handicap if you are older, you can usually offer a solid credit history to your advantage. The creditor has to look at all the facts and apply the usual standards of creditworthiness to your particular situation.

## ADDRESSES OF FOUR MAJOR CREDIT REPORTING AGENCIES

| CRA NAME | ADDRESS/PHONE | CREDIT REPORTING TERRITORY |
|---|---|---|
| TRW Credit Information | P.O. Box 74929<br>Dallas, Texas 75374<br>(714) 991-5100 | Pacific Coast<br>Rocky Mountain<br>South Western<br>New England<br>Mid Atlantic<br>New England |
| Trans-Union Credit Information | P.O. Box 7000<br>North Olmstead, Ohio 44070 (312) 408-1050 | Pacific Coast<br>Rocky Mountain<br>Mid West<br>Southern |
| Associated Credit Service | P.O. Box 674422<br>Houston, Texas 77267<br>(713) 878-1900 | Mid West<br>South Western<br>Mid Atlantic |
| OBI-EQUIFAX | P.O. Box 740241<br>Atlanta, GA 30374<br>1-800-685-1111 | Pacific Coast<br>Rocky Mountain<br>Southern<br>New England |

# CHAPTER 7

# Maintaining Good Life Insurance

## Do You Need Life Insurance?

Is life insurance really necessary? Should you buy whole life or term? How much life insurance do you need? What company should you consider? These are just a few of the questions that surface as you think of life insurance. From a financial perspective insurance serves a necessary function. Few of us would go without auto or home insurance. Likewise, if an unexpected death would cause financial problems for you, your dependents, your business, or others, then life insurance might be prudent to cover the potential loss. Also, if your debts exceed your available assets you should consider life insurance to cover the shortage to avoid creating a financial burden for your family. Insurance is a necessity to protect you against a possible unacceptable financial loss.

Life insurance is basically a contract between you and an insurance company. This contract is typically referred to as an insurance policy. The insurance company usually agrees to pay a "benefit" at the death of the "insured" to a designated "beneficiary" in exchange for a monthly "premium." The policy owner may name the insured and beneficiary. The policy has a time component, death benefit, a premium, and may include other terms governing the relationship between you and the insurance company. The policy may include savings, dividends, and special provisions for loans, along with riders that cover special circumstances.

With any insurance, the risk of a devastating financial loss is passed off to an insurance company that has the resources to cover the loss. When considering life insurance you should be certain the company you choose has the financial reserves necessary to cover expected losses. Be sure the insurance company is likely to be around with the dollars necessary if you need them. Don't buy insurance from a company that does not have a good reputation and a high rating by BEST, Standard & Poor's, or Moody's agencies.

Every policy has premiums—the amount you submit to the insurance company in exchange for the coverage you receive. But premiums vary with the type and amount of insurance and other factors. Some policies have cash value after a period of time; meaning that they are a form of investment or savings which allows you to get a return over time for some of your premium payments.

Like most financial products, life insurance policies cover a wide range. Among the life insurance policies offered are term, whole life, single premium life, joint life, second to die, universal and variable life, to name a few. What should you know about life insurance in order to make an intelligent choice? Do you need to understand every facet of every available policy? With a basic understanding of the way life insurance works and your own long term financial needs, you will be in a good position to make a intelligent selection.

## Types of Life Insurance: Their Advantages and Disadvantages

Basically, there are only two types of life insurance, term and cash value (commonly referred to as whole life). Insurance companies vary these term and cash value policies and mix the two in single policies to satisfy market demands. As you consider the products on the life insurance market be aware that life insurance products are tailored to meet specific needs and objectives. If you do not have the time to thoroughly review the market, get a competent, trusted agent who will be concerned about your insurance needs and your financial situation. Try to find an agent who has knowledge of a wide range of products so that he or she will make the best recommendations for your particular circumstances.

There is a wide range of products available when choosing life insurance. Insurance companies are combining investment options and flexibility to create life insurance and investment products for specific groups. With this variety, you should be able to find life insurance that fits your needs and makes sense for your financial situation.

The main reason for having life insurance is usually for the death benefit. Before making a decision on life insurance you should determine what size death benefit is needed to cover all the financial requirements that would result from a premature death.

For your dependents the value of life insurance is obvious—you can create an "instant estate" providing for a surviving spouse and children to the extent that you can afford and desire to do so. When considering life insurance take some time to do the arithmetic. What sort of financial stability would you want to provide for your family or other beneficiary? What type of financial stability do you and your spouse want to provide each other in the event of a death. Consider things like existing debts, final expenses, and inflation. Do you want to provide for college for children? What about other unexpected expenses?

After selecting the right death benefit, look at the other benefits that may be available from your policy. As with any contract make sure you are getting what you want and make sure you understand your obligation for premium payments; how much and when due. Can you skip payments and retain coverage? How many years do premiums continue? Get an understanding of other benefits that you may acquire and what these will cost you.

From a financial perspective, when you buy a life insurance policy you commit yourself to a small regular financial loss in the form of insurance premiums in exchange for coverage in the event of an unexpected death, which could be accompanied by a much larger financial loss. The policy may offer various incentives to soften or lower the financial cost to you. One key incentive may be a savings or dividend component. For these reasons you should stop thinking about premiums only as a cost of insurance. Your premiums can also be an investment and savings mechanism.

One of the advantages of life insurance in general is that the death benefit passes to the beneficiary free of income taxes. The increase in cash value of a whole life policy also accumulates on a tax deferred basis. However, your death benefit may be subject to death or estate taxes in certain cases.

Let's review some of the common types of insurance you might consider and the advantages and disadvantages of each. These include term insurance and cash value insurance, such as whole life, single-premium whole life, universal life, variable life, first-to-die, and second-to-die.

**Term Insurance:** A term insurance policy provides life insurance for a specified period of time, such as one year, five years, twenty years, or up to a certain age. In some cases there may be provisions for renewal, but premiums will likely increase upon renewal because you are older. Term policies are "bare bones" policies with few extras. If you will need life insurance for a limited period of time and have limited discretionary income, term life insurance may be your best buy. It may be the only way you can afford the coverage you need at this point. If you can afford more and have a long term need for life insurance, perhaps something other than term may be better for you.

Generally, if you will need life insurance for more than ten years, it may be to your advantage to consider cash value policies that offer a savings or investment element. Most term policies expire without ever paying any death benefits. If your insurance needs will extend well into the future, you should be aware of the escalating cost of your term policy. You may reach the point in your older years when the cost of term insurance is out of your reach. Term insurance may be less expensive in the short term, but not in the long term. If you plan to leave a sizable estate to heirs through life insurance, then term policies typically will not be the best choice.

One of the disadvantages of term policies is the termination date. After a specific period of time the term policy will end with no cash value. There are policies available that are guaranteed renewable or that may offer the right to convert the term policy to a cash value policy. But, in most cases term policies will expire with no provisions for renewal or conversion. If your circumstances change or you become uninsurable because of health during the period that you are covered by a term policy, you may be unable to find life insurance when you need it most.

The advantages of term life insurance is its simplicity and low cost, in early years. The disadvantages are its termination date, increasing premiums, and lack of cash value and limited tax advantages.

**Cash Value Insurance:** Cash value life insurance will in general include all the available life insurance, except term insurance. Cash value insurance combines an element of insurance with an investment or savings account. Over time the cash value of the policy should reach or exceed the initial death benefit. There may be good financial reasons for you to choose cash value insurance, particularly if you have a long-term need for life insurance. As with most long term investments there may be a longer period of time before you see a good payoff from a cash value life insurance policy. If you bail out early, you may lose money. However, if your cash value insurance is properly selected to suit your financial circumstances, the return can be very attractive in the long run.

Cash value life insurance has basically two components—the cost component and the savings/investment component. The cost component is the portion of your premium that actually pays for your death benefit coverage. Since cash value policies increase in value as you pay premiums, not all of the premium is used to cover the death benefit. The charge for the death benefit is less than the amount of your premium which results in a balance (cash accumulation) in your account which accumulates over time. As your cash accumulates it earns a return which also accumulates in your account.

The cash value in your policy is generally available through loans or surrender of the policy even before the death benefit is payable. Remember that a key advantage gained for earnings on your cash account is its tax-deferred status. If the value in your cash account does not exceed the amount paid in premiums you may avoid taxes on the earnings because these are viewed as a return of premiums. Cash value insurance policies will typically provide several methods for withdrawing your dollars. The cash value in your insurance policy is usually available quickly and gives you a very liquid asset.

There are typically three ways to get money from your cash value policy. You may borrow against the cash value of the policy, usually at some interest rate which is below the market rate. If you die before the loan is repaid, the amount owed plus any interest will be subtracted from the death benefits which will be paid to your beneficiary. You may also surrender the policy and the insurance company will pay you the cash value. With surrenders there may be a surrender charge, particularly in the early years of a policy. Make sure that you understand any surrender charges, how you may avoid them and when surrender charges will not apply. Lastly, you can typically use the cash value of your policy to buy an annuity that provides a guaranteed monthly income for life.

**Whole Life:** Whole life is one of the most common cash value policies. Whole life policies have a guaranteed death benefit, guaranteed interest rate, and guaranteed premium over the life of the policy. Generally whole life policies pay a lower rate of interest than other cash value policies. Whole life policies are usually designed to have the cash value equal to the death benefit when the insured reaches age 100.

If you have a short term insurance need or if your insurance needs are likely to change, a whole life policy may not be best for you.

The advantages of whole life are its fixed death benefit, fixed premium, lifetime coverage, tax advantages, and cash value. Its disadvantages are its relative inflexibility, low rate of return, and higher initial cost.

**Single Premium Life Insurance:** Single premium life policies are funded with a lump sum investment. This type of policy will credit interest or dividends to the cash account and deduct insurance costs periodically. Single premium policies may offer a very attractive return to the long term investor. In addition to the interest or dividends that you receive on your investment, these earnings will grow tax-deferred as long as the funds stay within the policy.

You may access your cash from a single premium policy via surrenders or loans. With this type of policy, the IRS has closed some of the tax advantages for contracts purchased after June 21, 1988. Distributions in the form of loans or surrenders will be considered a return of earnings first and investment last. In some cases there may be a 10 percent tax penalty for distributions made prior to age fifty-nine and one half.

Advantages of single premium life insurance are its guaranteed return, tax-deferred earnings, and lifetime coverage. The major disadvantage is the large upfront premium.

**Universal Life:** Universal life policies offer you the advantage of changing many of the key elements of your policy; death benefit, premium amount (within limits), length of coverage, timing of premium payments. Typically you may pay premiums at any time and in any amount. You can also change the amount of your insurance relatively easily. Generally these type of policies offer a competitive interest rate on your accumulated funds. Rates are usually guaranteed for one year, and then a new rate is determined subject to a specified minimum rate. You have the option of adding money to your account at any time, thus contributing to a long term, tax-deferred investment vehicle. If your insurance needs change you may increase or decrease the amount of your coverage without surrendering your policy. However, if you are increasing the death benefit, there may be a requirement to prove insurability again.

You may typically access your cash from these policies via loans or surrenders. The insurance company will probably have charges for surrenders during the early policy years. You must be careful not to exceed IRS guidelines regarding the amount you may invest into these policies to avoid tax liability and penalties. Your insurance agent can help you stay within the IRS limits and avoid tax problems.

The advantages of universal life insurance are its flexible death benefit, flexible premium, lifetime coverage, guaranteed return and tax-deferred earnings. The disadvantages are its relative complexity, the need for regular review, and investment charges and expenses. Consider universal life if you have a frequently changing need for long-term insurance and savings.

**Variable Life:** Variable life insurance provides death benefits and cash values that fluctuate, depending on the performance of the investment options that you choose. With variable universal life you will have the opportunity to make decisions regarding the investment of the dollars within your account. Your investment choices usually include stocks, bonds, and money market funds. Although you can realize a higher return with variable life insurance, you also assume the risk of poor investment performance.

The cash value in a variable universal life policy may be accessed through policy surrenders and loans. The policy is subject to IRS rules and regulations on funding and withdrawals. Again, a good agent can help keep you within the guidelines. Agents selling variable life insurance must be registered with the Security and Exchange Commission and licensed by the National Association of Securities Dealers. Your agent should give you a prospectus on any variable life insurance policy which includes an extensive disclosure about the policy.

A variation on variable life policy is variable universal life. The variable universal life may fix the amount of the death benefit and have the value of the accumulation account change with market conditions.

One of the advantages of variable life is that it allows you to choose from a wider range of investment vehicles and integrate your insurance into your overall investment strategy. Other advantages are its lifetime coverage, tax-deferred earnings, and access to cash value. The disadvantages are its relative complexity and investment risks with no guaranteed return.

**First To Die Policies:** First to die policies cover two persons and pay a death benefit on the first death of either of the insured. With the two family income and the financial risk to families at the loss of either wage-earner, first to die policies offer a method of covering two lives at a lower cost. First to die policies are relatively new and are a direct response to the changes resulting from dual-income families.

**Second To Die Policies:** Second to die policies cover two people and pay death benefit on the second death. These policies are generally used in estate planning to replace dollars lost to estate taxes or to provide funds necessary to pay estate taxes due. The policies may also be useful in funding a trust. Because they are based on joint life expectancy, the premiums are usually less than those for two separate single life policies.

### Tax Treatment of Life Insurance

One of the real advantages to investing in life insurance is the favorable tax treatment of distributions from insurance policies. If you are careful about the way you take distributions you may be able to receive your life insurance earnings effectively tax-free. Return of premiums generally are not taxed. Loans against cash values may also avoid taxes. With planning you can effectively withdraw most of the value of your policy through loans and surrenders and avoid any income taxes.

An additional advantage for estate planning may be the death benefit. The death benefit will be paid to your beneficiary and generally will not be subject to income taxes. Although there are a number of methods to obtain the cash value from your life insurance, you should pay careful attention to how you fund the policy and how you take the cash. You should consult your insurance agent or tax advisor to review your specific case and how to comply with IRS regulations. Otherwise, you may be taxed on distributions from your policy first as a return of earnings and may face other tax penalties.

Up until changes made with the Tax Reform Act of 1986, distributions from insurance policies received extremely favorable tax treatment. The Tax Reform Act restricted distributions on policies issued after December 31, 1984, and provided less favorable tax treatment on the distributions from policies issued after that date. Policies issued between December 31, 1984, and June 21, 1988, may also be subject to the more restrictive regulations, depending on the amount put into the policy and whether you have made material changes to the policy.

If you have a policy issued before December 31, 1984, you are in the best position to use it to generate "tax free" income. You may be able to take surrenders up to the full amount you have paid into the policy as a return of principal while avoiding taxes all together. For amounts in excess of your payments (earnings) you may take loans, thus, effectively allowing you to use your earnings tax-free. Again, if the loans are not repaid they will be deducted from your death benefit.

The Tax Reform Act of 1986 placed restrictions on the accumulation of cash value within a life insurance policy and on the amount that you may add to your policy. There are also restrictions on the number of years the policy must be in force prior to taking distributions. If your policy violated these guidelines it will be classified as a modified endowment contract, and you will lose most of the tax advantages on loans and surrenders. Under a modified endowment contract the distributions will always be viewed as earning first and principal or return of premiums last. If you are under fifty-nine and one half you may also have a tax penalty on distribution. Preventing your insurance policy from being classified as a modified endowment contract is crucial in avoiding the more restrictive tax treatment. Although your policy may not be classified as such initially, this may occur later if you violate the guidelines on cash accumulation and funding. A competent insurance agent, tax advisor, or financial planner can help you meet these guidelines.

### Using Life Insurance to Meet Financial Goals

Life insurance policies can be used effectively to accumulate cash for long term goals. For example, your insurance need may be coupled with a long term savings need, such as funding retirement or providing an education fund for children. A cash value policy offers the best opportunities through life insurance to reach some of your long range financial goals.

Remember the variety of options that may be available to you by having a large cash value accumulate within your life insurance policy: (1) You can purchase an annuity, (2) You can borrow against the total cash value, (3) You may surrender the policy for the full cash value, (4) You can use the policy as a gift or transfer wealth to your heirs.

Life insurance can also be used as a means for paying for estate taxes, medical expenses, funeral expenses and other needs.

The first step in utilizing life insurance effectively is to determine your financial needs and the amount of insurance necessary to cover them. Some financial advisors recommend that you should have life insurance equal to five times your total annual earnings. Thus, if your annual income is $50,000, life insurance in the amount of $250,000 is suggested.

However, this general rule may not apply to everyone, because of special circumstances and financial needs. For example, you may want to provide financial stability for your family for five years, pay off your mortgage, and educate your children. If annual income is $50,000, mortgage on your home is $160,000, and cost of education for your children is $60,000, your life insurance needs can be calculated as follows:

| | |
|---|---:|
| Five year income | $250,000 |
| Mortgage | 160,000 |
| Education | 60,000 |
| Total need: | $470,000 |

Less:

| | |
|---|---:|
| Current coverage and investment | $10,000 |
| Savings for education | 10,000 |
| Employer paid insurance | 100,000 |
| Total | $120,000 |
| Life Insurance need: | $350,000 |

Take time to figure your financial needs, including income needs, mortgage, final expenses, education costs, and other debts. Make sure you allow for inflation and subtract present assets that might be used. You can make wise life insurance decisions if you go through a comprehensive review of your responsibilities, financial requirements, and resources. Examine your life insurance needs periodically to take into account changes in family circumstances, living arrangements, and other variables.

Be sure to explain your life insurance coverage to your family and beneficiaries. Give them your agent's name and address and a photocopy of your policy. Your beneficiaries should also know where you keep your life insurance policies, because upon your death they will need to send them to your insurance companies along with a copy of your death certificate to get paid.

## Checklist for Buying Life Insurance

❏ Compute the amount of insurance you need. What amount of financial loss would you like to cover in the event of a premature death? What amount of financial resources have you accumulated to cover the loss?

❏ Determine the type of policy desired. Do you want cash value or term? How many years will you need coverage? Do you have a long term savings need? Is tax deferral on savings important?

❏ Select a competent and trustworthy insurance agent. Purchase your life insurance from a reputable insurance company.

❏ Compare various insurance companies, policy options, and costs.

❏ Read your life insurance policy and make sure that you understand your coverage, exclusions, and other provisions.

❏ Let your family and beneficiaries know about your life insurance policies and where you keep them.

❏ Review you life insurance needs and your insurance policies at least annually. Is the beneficiary correct? Should the amount of insurance be increased or decreased? Should you invest additional cash in a policy or take some of the cash value? Does your insurance fit your estate planning needs?

# CHAPTER 8

# BEING A WISE CONSUMER

## Let the Consumer Be Aware

A missing ingredient in many business transactions is trust and good faith. Wouldn't it be nice if everything your purchased, every contract you entered into, every economic commitment you made, was between you and a person you trusted. There would be less need for receipts, records, and lawyers. Since this will never happen, there is only one thing you can do to keep from being taken advantage of—be an informed consumer.

The market place offers an endless line of products and services. You need to be a smart consumer and do some rational thinking both before and after you make a purchase. Before you make any significant purchase, think about what you really need and what features are important to you. Do comparison shopping among different brands and different stores. For major purchases look for expert product comparison reports. See if your local library has magazines or other publications that compare products and services. Check with your local consumer protection agencies or Better Business Bureau to find out the reputation and complaint record of prospective suppliers of goods and services.

Be sure to read and fully understand the terms of any contract before you sign it. Read the warranties to understand what steps you must take, and what the manufacturer must do, if you have a problem. Know the return and exchange policy.

After your purchase keep all sales receipts, contracts, warranties, and instructions. Read and follow the instructions on how to use the product, and use the product only for the purposes stated in the manufacturer's instructions. If you have problems, report them to the seller or manufacturer. Do not try to fix the product yourself, because this might cancel any warranties on the product.

As a consumer you have the right to receive good quality products and services for your money. Often times you do not. However, if trouble develops with a product or service, there are some things you can do to resolve the problems. Begin by contacting the business from which you bought the product or service. Remain calm and explain the nature of your problem and what action you would like taken. Decide if you want the product repaired or replaced or your money back.

If you are unsuccessful in resolving your complaint with a sales-person or manager at the local level, call or write a letter to the company headquarters. Keep a file of your efforts to resolve your complaints, including the dates and names of the people that you talk with. Also keep in your complaint file copies of your receipts, warranties, and complaint letters. Always retain original copies for your file and never send out documents you cannot replace.

It is important that you complain when you are dissatisfied with a purchase. It is estimated that there are about 80 million customers dissatisfied with purchases each year in this country. Yet, only about 5 percent of the dissatisfied customers ever complain to the seller about their disappointment. Remember, a manufacturer is unlikely to improve goods and services unless you complain when you are dissatisfied.

It is recommended that you make your complaint letter formal by sending the letter to the seller or manufacturer by certified or registered mail. Again, the letter should be specific in describing your problem and the action you would like taken.

### The Cooling Off Rule

A major consumer right with "door-to-door" sales is known as the "cooling off rule." This is a rule of the Federal Trade Commission (FTC) which gives a consumer, who makes a purchase of $25.00 or more through a "door-to-door" sales person, three business days to change his or her mind and cancel the purchase. A "door-to-door" sale is typically any sale made at the buyer's home or anywhere away from the seller's place of business.

The FTC's three-day cooling off rule does not apply to sales that are:

• under $25;

• made entirely by phone or mail;

• initiated by the purchaser for repair of personal property;

• for real estate, insurance, or securities;

• for emergency home repair if the right to cancel is waived; or

• made at the seller's normal place of business.

The FTC requires "door-to-door" sellers to inform you of your cancellation rights. Any contract that you sign for a "door-to-door" sale must provide information about your right to cancel. You should be given a cancellation form which shows the date, name, and address of the seller and the date by which you may cancel. You can cancel your "door-to-door" purchase by mailing a cancellation notice to the seller's address at any time before midnight of the third business day after the date of the contract. Sundays and holidays are not counted in measuring the three-day cancellation period.

Within ten days after you have canceled your "door-to-door" purchase, the seller must refund any money you paid or any property that you used as a trade-in. The federal law provides for penalties against the seller if he fails to do what the law requires. If you have sent a cancellation notice within three days and the seller still refuses to return your money, contact your local consumer protection agency, your state attorney general's office or the Federal Trade Commission. The addresses for these agencies are given in the Appendix.

Senior citizens are generally at a disadvantage when dealing with unknown sellers and are more likely to be taken advantage of. However, there are some things you can do to protect yourself from unscrupulous salespeople:

• Get as much information on the salesperson knocking on your door as possible. Ask for identification; ask what company the salesperson represents. Watch out for scams and con artists.

- Don't pay for items you want right away. Note the price and hold out a few days; shop around for a better deal. Most likely the product or service you want to purchase is being sold by someone else. Compare prices before you buy.

- Don't sign anything unless the following questions are answered to your satisfaction: Exactly what will you receive? Exactly how much are you going to have to pay (including tax, interest, and other charges)? How do you go about getting the product serviced? Will you have to take it or ship it somewhere? Is there a warranty and exactly what is covered by the warranty? How long does the warranty last? Does the company allow refunds and exchanges? Are you going to get the name, address, and phone number of seller or company official? Does the sales contract conform with the words of the seller? Are the terms, warranty, price, and interest rate clearly stated in the contract?

- Make sure everything promised to you is put into writing.

- Insist upon a copy of the contract and any other documents you sign.

## Buying Through the Mail

Millions of consumers order products through the mail each year. If you shop by mail, you have the entire world as a shopping center. Home shopping can offer convenience, wider selection of merchandise, better prices and accessibility to products that are difficult to find. Shopping from catalogs and magazines gives you plenty of time to make a decision on your purchase, without the influence of high pressure sales tactics.

However, the convenience of mail order shopping can become a great disappointment if there are lengthy delays in getting your merchandise, or if it is not what you wanted, or if you never receive it at all. You can protect yourself when shopping by mail by understanding your rights as a mail order shopper and being a cautious consumer.

Always try to deal with reliable and reputable companies. Check with the Better Business Bureau or your consumer protection agency to find information about the company (see the Appendix for addresses). Pay careful attention to the advertisement and other information provided about the product. Do not rely solely on the picture of the item because it could be misleading. Write to the company for additional information if you need more details.

Never pay for a mail order by cash. Rather, use a credit card or pay by check or money order so that you will have a record of payment. Also, keep a copy of your order and any information you have on the product.

The Federal Trade Commission and the U.S. Postal Service enforce laws and regulations which are designed to protect mail order shoppers. The FTC Mail Order Rules provides you with these legal rights when buying by mail:

- Seller must see that you receive the goods no later than the date he promised you would receive them.

- Seller must ship the goods within thirty days of the date he receives your properly completed order, unless the advertisement states the contrary.

- If the seller is unable to meet the shipping deadline, he must notify you when the order will be shipped. If the new shipping date is more than thirty days past the original shipping date, you may, in writing, either accept the new shipping date or cancel the order in writing. However, if you do not cancel this means that you accept the delay.

- If you cancel the order, you are entitled to a full refund within seven business days after the seller receives your cancellation.

- If you paid the bill by charge account and a refund is required, seller must take no more than one billing cycle to adjust your account. Federal credit laws provide that if adjustments in this area take longer, you can stop payment on the charge by notifying the credit card company in writing.

The Mail Order Rule does not cover orders for photo development, seeds, growing plants, book and record club merchandise, magazines (after the first issue), and payment by C.O.D. Neither does it cover orders you charge directly to your credit card using an "800" number. Orders which are charged to your credit card only after the merchandise is sent also are not governed by the Mail Order Rule.

You should not accept merchandise shipped to you which is damaged. If the merchandise is visibly damaged when delivered to you, do not open it. Rather, write "Not Accepted" or "Refused" on it and return it to the seller. New postage is usually not required, unless you have signed for a C.O.D., registered, certified, or insured package.

Merchandise sent to you in the mail that you did not order is yours to keep. This includes any extra merchandise sent with items you did order. You do not have to send it back, and you can not be made to pay for it. Under the law, this is considered a gift. Enjoy it.

If a private delivery service, such as United Parcel Service, brings you merchandise that you did not order, you must do two things before you can legally keep the merchandise:

(1) you must alert the sender (preferably in writing) that you received goods that you did not order;

(2) you must allow the sender a reasonable amount of time to pick the merchandise up at the sender's expense. You should tell the sender what you intend to do with the merchandise if he fails to pick it up.

## Consumer Frauds Against Senior Citizens

Although consumer fraud is a major problem for all consumers, it has a harsher impact on senior citizens. The U.S. Senate Special Committee on Aging has continually investigated the problem of consumer fraud against the elderly. The Committee found the following to be the ten most harmful frauds:

### Medical Frauds

Seniors account for a disproportionate share of total U.S. health care costs. In 1978, persons sixty-five and older represented 11 percent of the U.S. population but, according to the Department of Health and Human Services, accounted for 29 percent of total personal health care expenses. The elderly account for one-fourth of all hospital stays, are twice as likely to visit their physician, and are considerably more likely to use outpatient clinic services. Overall, per capita health expenses are two and one-half times greater for persons over sixty-five than for persons under sixty-five.

In addition, and of particular importance to those seeking opportunities for fraud, seniors are much more likely to have developed chronic ailments. Eighty percent of all seniors are said to have at least one chronic condition. Multiple chronic conditions are common. The most frequently reported chronic conditions according to the National Center for Health Services Research, are arthritis, hypertension, hearing impairment, heart conditions, visual impairments, and diabetes.

Not surprisingly, seniors are particularly concerned about their health. This concern creates a large vulnerability to quacks, miracle cures, hospital frauds, aging cures, medical aids, and other medical frauds of all kinds. Because seniors often forego proper medical care in response to the promises of these charlatans, and the genuine danger from contaminated compounds, respondents ranked medical frauds as the single most harmful fraud against the elderly. Over 17 percent of those responding to the committee's survey identified these frauds as a major concern.

Among the most frequent medical frauds are unproven remedies that promise relief not supported by scientific evidence. Common examples are the various hair restorative compounds, "cures" for baldness, "miracle diet programs," aging inhibitors, "wrinkle reducers," sex aids, cure-alls, and pain relievers. Whatever the price, whatever the product, most of these cons sell hope—hope for the relief of pain, restoration of youth, and delay of death.

### Home Repair and Improvement Frauds

Seventy-one percent of the elderly own their own homes. The majority of these homes were built before 1940. Only 11 percent of the houses where the household was headed by a senior were build since 1970. This combination of the number of elderly who own homes and the age of these dwellings is particularly attractive to phony repairmen. In fact, respondents to the committee's survey indicated home repair and improvement frauds were the most frequent frauds committed against the elderly.

Generally, phony home repairmen make a direct approach. They may appear at the victim's house posing as a city official or claim to have been referred by a neighbor down the street. Whatever the excuse, they quickly note some fundamental flaw in the house that must be repaired immediately. They specialize in roofing and siding, insulation, furnace repair, chimney replacements, wet basements, and driveway topping. Typically, they promise quick, efficient service at bargain rates, take a large downpayment, and never return.

### Bunco Schemes

Bunco is a generic term of swindling schemes or confidence games. There are currently over 800 known bunco schemes. The three most common bunco schemes are:

(1) The pigeon drop: In the most common variation of this scheme, an older person is approached by strangers who claim to have found a large bag containing cash. Through a series of deceptions, the victim is convinced to put up "good faith" money to share in the find. The victim is asked to put the good faith money in a purse or parcel for safekeeping. In the final deception, the victim is distracted and the parcel containing his or her money is switched for another.

(2) The bank examiner: In this scheme, the con artist portrays himself as a good samaritan. He generally poses as a bank official and requests the assistance of the victim in checking on an employee suspected of defrauding the bank. Alternatively, the con may indicate there is reason to believe the victim's records are inaccurate and should be checked. Once the con has the victim's confidence, he persuades the victim to withdraw large sums from his or her bank account.

(3) The phony official: In these cons, the swindler poses as a representative of an official agency, such as Medicare, Social Security, the local zoning board, or some other agency. Once they have made contact, they persuade the victim he or she needs insurance to cover medical costs not covered by Medicare, must repair his home, or replace appliances.

### Insurance Frauds

The National Center for Health Services Research estimated in 1981 that 83.9 percent of the civilian, noninstitutionalized population had full-time, year-round insurance coverage. Those sixty-five and over—

in part because of Medicare—showed year-round coverage rates of 97.8 percent. By contrast, young adults showed year-round coverage rates of 70 percent.

These figures reflect seniors' concerns for the probability and effect of illness which makes them particularly susceptible to insurance frauds. The most flagrant of these abuses involve so-called Medigap insurance and cancer insurances.

Medigap policies are said to be designed to cover the gaps in medicare's coverage. Around 20 million of these policies have been sold to seniors at a cost of about $4 billion.

Cancer insurance is among the hottest insurance sales items. There are currently over 20 million insurance policies in effect. So many questions have been raised with respect to these policies that they may be banned in some states.

The following techniques are often used by unscrupulous insurance agents:

**Stacking:** This term refers to the practice of persuading the victim to buy more policies than are needed.

**Rolling-over:** This technique refers to the practice of attempting to persuade the victim to replace his existing policy with a "better" or "more comprehensive" one.

**Misrepresentation:** This is a deliberate deception as to the policy's coverage.

**Cleansheeting:** Here, the agent simply forges the victim's signature on a new policy.

**Switching:** In this fraud, the salesman switches policies so that the coverage obtained and the premium is different than the victim believed.

### Social Frauds

Social frauds draw on a victim's charity, compassion, loneliness, and vanity. Charity frauds take advantage of the best instincts of people. The most frequent charity frauds involve bogus charities or religious groups, misrepresentation of association with a charity or religious group, and misrepresentation of the benefits or uses of contributions. Companionship clubs or "lonely hearts" clubs prey on the loneliness of its victims. Fear of growing old, becoming isolated and alone, are exploited with phony computer dating services, dancing lessons, or "dues" for social clubs.

### Housing and Land Frauds

Land sales frauds cost U.S. citizens millions of dollars a year. Advertisements are designed to persuade the unwary to buy property they have never seen. All too frequently, the idyllic property in the brochure turns out be swampland, or desert property far from the nearest town.

Similar misrepresentations are made with regard to vacation homes, time-sharing properties, and retirement homes. Often the buyer finds the romantic hide-away he purchased is without utility connections, or that the time-sharing resort sold more time than was available.

### Business Opportunity and Investment Frauds

Twenty-five percent of the elderly have income levels at or near the poverty line. For these people, retirees and others living on fixed incomes, business and investment frauds present a powerful attraction. For a relatively modest investment or through some irresistible business opportunity, the victim is offered the promise of great rewards. In one case, a Cleveland promoter sold jewelry franchises to 540 investors who responded to newspaper ads. The con collected $3.5 million with this scheme. All that the victims received for their investment was $100 worth of costume jewelry.

The other major variation—and one particularly targeted at the elderly—involves work-at-home schemes of all kinds. Some of the more common work-at-home schemes include worm farms, envelope addressing, envelope stuffing, and sew-at-home schemes. One sew-at-home scheme drew 200,000 applicants who were allowed, for a small registration fee, to take a sewing test to see if they qualified for employment. Not surprisingly, no one qualified and  no refunds were given.

### Nursing Home Frauds

About 1.2 million seniors live in the Nation's 25,000 nursing homes. They constitute about 90 percent of all nursing home residents. Further, the probability of being institutionalized increases with age, from one out of hundred in the age group of sixty-five to seventy-four to one out of five of those over eighty-five years old. Abuses in nursing homes have been well publicized during the last decade, largely due to the efforts of the Committee. Most of the concern that has been generated has focused on the quality of care issues and indications of Medicare and Medicaid fraud. Because the government, as the purchaser of services, is so evidently defrauded by these activities, we have often lost sight of the fact that the seniors are often also defrauded. They may be conned into paying an "admission fee" to purchase a place in a medicaid facility, overcharged for specific services, defrauded out of personal maintenance funds, and forced to pay for specific services and supplies that should be included in the home's per diem rate.

One of the more recent variations on this theme in the development of "lifecare" facilities. In these instances, seniors are persuaded to sign over all of their assets with the promise that they will be taken care of until they die. Often, the facility changes ownership or goes out of business, leaving the seniors stranded and exposed.

### Automobile Frauds

Most consumers have had some experience with unreliable automobile salesmen and repairmen. Though these experiences can be aggravating, for the most part they stop short of outright fraud. Automobile frauds consist of fraudulently increasing the profit margin, misrepresenting the car performance or history, or switching vehicles, substituting a similar car with few options or performance problems for the one purchased.

### Funeral Frauds

Funeral frauds feed on the vulnerability of families at the time of a family member's death. They encourage a natural desire to take the best possible care of the departed. Common abuses include:

**Implying there is a legal requirement that the deceased be embalmed before burial:** In most states, there is no such requirement unless the deceased is to be transported by common carrier.

**Unauthorized removal of remains:** Some funeral directors have arrangements with hospitals and nursing homes calling for the delivery of anyone who dies in the facility. In one recent case, when a relative objected, she was allowed to recover the body, but only after paying for "services rendered."

**Refusal to release:** Basically, this con involves holding the deceased hostage until family members make the required payments. In Florida last year, a woman made arrangements over the telephone for her father's funeral. The funeral director agreed to handle the funeral for $495. When the daughter arrived at the funeral home, however, she found the price had doubled. When she objected, she was not permitted to remove the body until she obtained a court order.

**Cash advances:** Many of the services associated with funerals, such as flowers, and obituary notices, are provided by third parties. These services are customarily covered by a cash advance. The abuse enters when the funeral director inflates or misrepresents the actual cost of these services.

While there are federal and state criminal and civil laws to protect against these frauds, people are still falling prey to the frauds every day. Some swindlers are caught and go to jail or pay fines and restitution, but there are always others to take their place. The greatest weapon to protect yourself against them is consumer education. To be forewarned is to be forearmed. That gives potential victims more protection than any book full of laws.

## Smart Consumer Checklists

The U.S. Office of Consumer Affairs, Washington, D.C. 20233 compiles a *Consumer's Resource Handbook* which provides useful information on how to be a smart consumer. Information from this *Handbook* was used to prepare these helpful consumer checklists.

The following suggestions can help you when selecting a credit card company or using your credit cards.

### Credit Card Checklist

❑ Keep in a safe place a list of your credit card numbers, expiration dates, and the phone number of each card issuer.

❑ Credit card issuers offer a wide variety of terms (annual percentage rate, method of calculating the balance subject to the finance charge, minimum monthly payments, and actual membership fees). When selecting a card, compare the terms offered by several card issuers to find the card that best suits your needs.

❑ When you use your credit card, watch your card after giving it to a clerk. Promptly take back the card after the clerk is finished with it and make sure it's yours.

❑ Tear up the carbons when you take your credit card receipt.

❑ Never sign a blank receipt; draw a line through any blank spaces above the total when you sign receipts.

❑ Save your purchase receipts until the credit card bill arrives. Then, open the bill promptly and compare it with your receipts to check for possible unauthorized charges and billing errors.

❑ Write the card issuer promptly to report any questionable charges. Telephoning the card issuer to discuss the billing problems does not preserve your rights. Do not include written inquiries with your payment. Instead, check the billing statement for the correct address for billing questions. The inquiry must be in writing and must be sent within sixty days to guarantee your rights under the Fair Credit Billing Act.

❑ Never give your credit card number over the telephone unless you made the call or have an account with the company calling you. Never put your card number on a post card or on the outside of an envelope.

❑ Sign new cards as soon as they arrive. Cut up and throw away expired cards.

If any of your credit cards are missing or stolen, report the loss as soon as possible to the card issuer. Check your credit card statement for a telephone number for reporting stolen credit cards. Follow up your phone calls with a letter to each card issuer. The letter should contain your card number, the date the card was missing, and the date you called in the loss.

❑ If you report the loss before a credit card is used, the issuer cannot hold you responsible for any future unauthorized charges. If a thief uses your card before you report it missing, the most you will owe for unauthorized charges is $50 on each card. A special note of warning: if an automatic teller machine (ATM) card is lost or stolen, the consumer could lose as much as $500 if the card issuer is not notified within two business days after learning of the loss or theft.

❑ When writing checks for retail purchases and to protect yourself against fraud, you may refuse to allow a merchant to write your credit card number of your check. However, if you refuse, the merchant might legally refuse to sell you the product. There is probably no harm in allowing a merchant to verify that you hold a major credit card and to note the issuer and the expiration date on the check.

❑ If a merchant indicates he or she is using credit cards as back-ups for bounced checks, or refuses your sale because you refuses to provide personal information (including your phone number) on the bank card sales slip, report the store to the credit card company. The merchant might be violating his or her agreement with the credit card companies. In your letter to the credit card company, provide the name and location of the merchant.

### Checklist for Selecting a Financial Institution

Finding the right bank, savings and loan, or credit union means figuring out your own needs first. Answering the following questions should help you identify your "banking personality" and make choosing a financial institution a bit easier.

❏ What is your goal in establishing a banking relationship? Answers might include "to save money," "to have a checking account," "to get a loan," or all of the above.

❏ How much money can you keep on deposit each month and how many checks will you write? Knowing this will help you judge how complex or simple an account you need.

❏ Will you be buying a home or car or making another large purchase in the near future? If so, you will want to find out about the types of loans offered by the institutions you are considering.

❏ If you hope to save for a big expense or toward your child's (or your own) future education, you will also want to find out how many different savings programs are offered.

❏ What time of day do you prefer to do your banking? Do you like the convenience of automated teller machines (ATMs) or do you prefer to deal with live tellers? Answering these two questions will help you determine if you'd be happier at a financial institution with regular, evening, or weekend hours or one with a wide network of ATMs.

❏ What does the financial institution charge for services like cashier's checks, safe deposit boxes, and stop payment orders? Is there a charge for using an automated teller machine? Is there a monthly service charge, or must you maintain a minimum balance in your account to avoid a charge?

❏ Narrow your options to specific financial institutions. Phone or visit several near your home or office, because they are likely to be the most convenient. Take your answers to the above questions with you and find out which accounts and services are most likely to match your needs. Then compare fees and service charges, as well as deposit and loan interest rate.

❏ Price might not be the most important factor in your "banking personality," so you also should take a minute to think about how comfortable you feel at each institution. For example, are your questions answered quickly and accurately? Do customer service personnel offer helpful suggestions?

❑ Remember, you can and should choose more than one financial institution to provide you with different banking services.

❑ Before making your final choice, make sure the institutions you're considering are federally insured. This means your deposits will be protected up to $100,000. All federally insured financial institutions are required to display a federal deposit insurance sign at each teller's window or teller station.

### Home Improvements Checklist

Hiring a contractor to renovate your home, add a room, or make some other improvement can be a confusing maze of contracts, licenses, permits, and payment schedules. The suggestions listed below can help guide you through that maze.

❑ Compare costs by getting more than one estimate or bid. Each estimate should be based on the same building specifications, materials and time frame.

❑ Before choosing a contractor, check with state, county, or local consumer protection agencies to see if any complaints have been filed against the contractor. Ask about information on unresolved cases and how long a contracting company has been in business under its current name.

❑ Ask a potential contractor for a list of previous customers whom you could call to find out about work quality and if they would hire that contractor for future work.

❑ Check with your local building inspections department to see if licensing and/or bonding are required of contractors in your area. If so, ask to see the contractor's license and bonding papers.

❑ Before signing a written contract, be sure it includes the contractor's full name, address, phone number, and professional license number (where required), a thorough description of the work to be done, grade and quality of materials to be used, agreed upon starting and completion dates, total cost, payment schedule, warranty, how debris will be removed, and any other agreement information. Never sign a partially blank contract. Fill in or draw a line through any blank spaces.

❑ Most contractors have liability and compensation insurance to protect the customer from a lawsuit in the event of an accident. Ask to see a copy of the insurance certificate.

❑ If the work requires a building permit, let the contractor apply for it in his name. That way, if the work does not pass inspection, you are not financially responsible for any corrections that must be made.

❑ When you sign a nonemergency home improvement contract in your home and in the presence of a contractor (or contractor's representative), you usually have three business days in which to cancel the contract. You must be told about your cancellation rights and be provided with cancellation forms. If you decide to cancel, it is recommended that you send a notice of cancellation by telegram or certified mail, return receipt requested.

❑ For a remodeling job involving many subcontractors and a substantial amount of money, it is wise to protect yourself from liens against your home in case the contractor does not pay subcontractors or suppliers. If state law permits, add a release-of-lien clause to the contract or place your payments in an escrow account until the work is completed.

❑ If you cannot pay for a project without a loan, add a clause to your contract stating it is valid only if financing is obtained.

❑ When signing a contract, limit your first payment to not more than 30 percent of the contract price. The remaining payments should depend on the progress of the work. Ten percent of the contract amount should be held back until the job is complete, and all problems, if any, are corrected. Some states have home improvement laws that specify the amount of deposit and payment schedule. Check with your state and local consumer protection offices to see if there is such a law in your community.

❏ Thoroughly inspect the contractor's work before making final payment or signing a completion certificate.

### Used Cars/Car Repair Checklist

The following guidelines will help you buy a used car or get your car repaired.

### Used Cars

❏ Decide what kind of car you need and how much you can afford to spend. Talk to owners of similar cars.

❏ Decide whether you want to buy from a dealer or private owner. A car bought from a private owner usually has no warranty.

❏ In a private sale, check to be sure the seller is the registered owner of the car. Make sure you get the car's title and registration, bill of sale, and copies of all other financial transaction papers necessary to register the car in your name.

❏ If you're buying from a dealer, read the contract carefully before you sign, take the time to ask questions about unclear items, and keep a copy of the contract.

❏ Look for and read the buyer's guide which must be displayed in the window of all used cars sold by dealers. The buyer's guide explains who must pay for repairs after purchase. It will tell you if there is a warranty on the car, what the warranty covers and whether a service contract is available.

❏ Comparison shop for price, condition, warranty, and mileage for the model(s) you are interested in buying. Compare available interest rates and other terms of financial agreement.

❏ To estimate the total cost of the car, add the cost of interest for financing, the cost of a service contract (if any), and service or repair expenses you are likely to pay.

❏ Before buying the car, have a mechanic inspect it.

❏ Check the reliability of the dealer with your state or local consumer protection agency. Check the local Better Business Bureau to see if there are complaints against the dealer.

## Car Repair

❑ Check the terms of your car's warranty. The warranty might require the dealer to perform routing maintenance and any needed repairs.

❑ Before having your car repaired, check the repair shop's complaint record with your state or local consumer protection office or local Better Business Bureau.

❑ Some repair shops have mechanics certified by the National Institute for Automotive Service Excellence (ASE) to perform one or more types of services. Be aware, however, that repair shops can display the ASE sign even if they have been tested for only one specialty.

❑ Do not tell the mechanic what you think needs to be fixed or replaced, unless it is obvious. Instead, describe the problem and its symptoms. Let the mechanic determine what needs fixing.

❑ For major repairs, think about getting a second opinion, even if the car must be towed to another shop.

❑ Before you leave the car, make sure you have a written estimate and that the work order reflects what you want done. Ask the mechanic to contact you before making repairs not covered in the work order.

❑ If additional work is done without your permission, you do not have to pay for the unapproved work and you have the right to have your bill adjusted.

❑ Ask to inspect and/or keep all replaced parts.

❑ Keep copies of all work orders and receipts and get all warranties in writing.

❑ Many states have "lemon" laws for new cars with recurring problems. Contact your local or state consumer office for more details.

### Home Shopping Checklist

Today, there are many ways to buy products or services. Some consumers buy items through mail order, telephone, or even television shopping programs. Keep the following tips in mind:

❑ Be suspicious of exaggerated product claims or very low prices and read product descriptions carefully. Sometimes, pictures of products are misleading.

❑ If you have any doubts about the company, check with the U.S. Postal Service, your state or local consumer protection agency, or Better Business Bureau before ordering.

❑ Ask about the firm's return policy. If it is not stated, ask before you order. Is a warranty or guarantee available?

❑ If you buy by telephone, make clear exactly what you are ordering and how much it costs before you give your credit card number; watch out for incidental charges.

❑ Keep a complete record of your order, including the company's name, address, and telephone number, price of the items ordered, any handling or other charges, date of your order, and your method of payment. Keep copies of canceled checks and/or statements. If you are ordering by telephone, get the names of any company representatives with whom you speak.

❑ If you order by mail, your order should be shipped within thirty days after the company receives your completed order, unless another period is agreed upon when placing the order or is stated in an advertisement. If your order is delayed, a notice of delay should be sent to you within the promised shipping period, along with an option to cancel the order.

❑ If you want to buy a product based on a telephone call from an unfamiliar company, ask for the name, address, and phone number where you can reach the caller after considering the offer. It is best to request and read written information before deciding to buy.

❏ Never give your credit card, bank account, or social security number over the telephone as proof of your identity, unless you placed the call or have an account with the company you are calling.

❏ Postal regulations allow you to write a check payable to the sender, rather than the delivery company, for cash on delivery (C.O.D.) orders. If, after examining the merchandise, you feel there has been misrepresentation or fraud, you can stop payment on the check and file a complaint with the U.S. Postal Inspector's Office.

❏ You can have a charge removed from your credit chard bill if you did not receive the goods or services or if your order was obtained through misrepresentation or fraud. You must notify the credit card company in writing, at the billing inquiries/disputes address, within sixty days after the charge first appeared on your bill.

**Checklist for Warranties and Guarantees**

An important feature to consider before buying a product or service is the warranty that comes with it. When reviewing warranties, use the guidelines below:

❏ Do not wait until the product fails or needs repair to find out what is covered in the warranty.

❏ If the product costs $15 or more, the law says that the seller must let you examine any warranty before you buy, if you ask to see it. So use your rights to compare the terms and conditions of warranties (or guarantees) on products or services before you buy. Look for the warranty that best meets your needs.

❏ When purchasing a product or service, ask these questions:
— How long is the warranty, and when does it start and end?
— What is covered? Which parts? What kinds of problems?
— Will the warranty pay for 100 percent of repair costs, or will it pay for parts, but not the labor to do the repairs? Will it pay for testing the product before it is repaired? Will it pay for shipping and/or a loaner?
— Who offers the warranty, manufacturer or retailer? How reliable are they?

❏ Keep sales receipts and warranties in a safe place.

❏ Some states have additional warranty rights for consumers. Check with your state or local consumer protection office to find the laws in your state.

## Sources of Help For Consumers

There are many resources available to you to assist you with consumer problems and inquiries. These include your Better Business Bureaus, state and local consumer agencies, local newspapers, radio and television stations, state attorney general's office and state department on aging. Also available are federal agencies, trade associations, and consumer groups. Look in your telephone directory or visit your local library for the complete names, addresses, and telephone numbers for these organizations.

You can write for a free copy of the *Consumer's Resource Handbook* by writing to the Consumer Information Center, Pueblo, Colorado 81009. This booklet provides a listing of federal, state, and local government agencies, and private businesses and organizations that can help you as a consumer. Some of these listings are included in the Appendix to this book.

For mail order and door-to-door sales inquiries contact:

Federal Trade Commission
Correspondence Branch
Washington, D.C. 20580

For mail order sales inquiries contact:

U.S. Postal Service
Chief Postal Inspector
Room 3517
Washington, D.C. 20260
(202) 245-5445

For complaints and information about mail order sales, write:

Director, Mail Order Action Line Service
Direct Marketing Association
6 East 43rd Street
New York, N.Y. 10017
(212) 689-4977

For complaints and information about door-to-door sales, write:

Code Administrator
Direct Selling Association
1730 M Street, N.W.
Suite 60
Washington, D.C. 20036

Other associations you can contact about specific products or services are listed in directories of trade associations at your local library.

You can also contact consumer groups such as:

American Association of Retired Persons
1909 K Street, N.W.
Washington, D.C. 20049

Consumer Federation of America
Suite 604
1424 P Street, N.W.
Washington, D.C. 20036

Other consumer groups are listed in guides at your local library. Directories of businesses and their addresses can be found there as well. Many directories give the address of top officers, public relations departments, and customer service sections.

# CHAPTER 9

# PROTECTING YOURSELF FROM CRIME

## Are You Safe from Crime?

Crime continues to be a major concern for senior citizens as well as for the rest of the population. Seniors are more likely to be victims of crime because they are perceived to be easy marks by criminals. Whether you are at home, on the streets, or in your car, you can expect to encounter crime. Each year there are more than six million burglaries; one every five seconds with reported losses of nearly $2 billion a year. A car is stolen every thirty seconds amounting to more than one and a half million cars a year at a value of nearly $8 billion. A recent wave of armed, sometimes fatal car jackings in the nation's suburbs, inner cities, and on the highways has raised fears that there are no safe havens from crime.

We have always regarded our home as our castle and safe refuge from crime. Likewise, our cars had been viewed as a reasonably safe place against intrusions. However, recent crime statistics clearly show that neither our home, cars, nor the streets are protected from criminal activity.

Statistics indicate that the typical burglar often lives in the neighborhood within a mile of the burglary. Although he is usually an amateur, he can easily break into most homes. The situation is likely to worsen unless you take some effective means to safeguard yourself and your home.

## Protecting Your Home

There are several practical crime fighting techniques you can implement to protect your home. You can start by inspecting all doors, windows, and other points of entry into your home. Your exterior doors should be solid core or metal and firmly attached to solid frames and to the house. All outside doors should have the hinges on the inside which are nonremovable. Those doors should also have deadbolt locks because these are difficult to pry or kick open. You should avoid having any breakable glass within three and one-half feet of the door locks. Use doors with unbreakable glass or which have a wide-angle peep hole to allow you to see visitors without having to open the door. If you have sliding doors, be sure that both panels are prevented from being lifted off the track. When the sliding doors are locked, use a rod to wedge the panels shut, in case the lock is picked or broken.

Securely lock your windows at night and when you are away from home. Consider putting shutters or metal grating on windows at ground level for added security. Also look at an alarm system for the windows and doors. Keep all trees and shrubs trimmed away from windows and doors so that they do not provide hidden cover for an intruder. Install good outdoor lighting at doors and windows. Motion sensitive lighting can be an inexpensive and effective crime-fighting technique.

If you are going away for an extended period, your house should appear as if someone is at home. Leave on an inside light and a radio. Have a neighbor keep an eye on your house and collect newspapers and mail. You can usually request that your post office and paper carrier hold your mail and newspapers until you return.

Use only your first initials and your last name for your mailbox and telephone listing if you are a woman living alone. Always verify the identity of repairmen, utility men, and other strangers before you let them into your home. Because senior citizens are greatly impacted by mail theft, you should consider having your paychecks, pension, and social security checks deposited directly into your bank account. Another crime deterrent is to mark your household items and other property to make them easier to trace.

Perhaps the most effective way to fight crime in your neighborhood is through a group of neighbors, organized as a community watch, helping each other. Through organization and communication with your neighbors, you can stop most crime in your community before it happens. And for those crimes you can't stop, you can help obtain convictions against criminals by thorough observations and testimony. Get to know the residents in your neighborhood and get involved in watching the activities on your block and in the community. Make a diagram showing every home in your immediate area and the name, address, and telephone number of the owners and residents. Tell them when you notice something unusual happening around their homes. Also report any suspicious behavior to the police.

Many people feel uncomfortable with firearms and are usually afraid to keep a gun around the house. Because of the alarming number of burglaries and other violent crimes, there may be situations where access to a gun at home can be advantageous. If you are comfortable and familiar with the use of a firearm, you may want to consider keeping a gun at home. There is plenty of merit in the philosophy for owning a gun that "it is better to have a gun and not need it, than to need one and not have it." If you own a gun, make sure that it is properly licensed and registered. Make sure that you handle and use it safely and keep it securely out of the reach of children.

### Preventing Crimes Against You And Your Car

Auto thefts and car jackings over the past year have startled everyone. You must be proactive in safeguarding your car and yourself to combat these dreaded violations. Lock your doors and roll your windows up while driving to keep someone from entering your car. Keep your car in gear while waiting at traffic lights and stop signs and observe everything that is happening around you. Always keep enough distance from the car in front of you to allow room to move your car if needed. Conceal your purse, wallet and other valuables from view, even while driving in your locked car.

Try to avoid traveling on dark, deserted streets. Although traveling on major streets and highways make take extra time, your life may depend on it. Refuse all hitch-hikers a ride, no matter how harmless they appear. Monitor the frequent routes you travel and identify some safe, public spots where you can get emergency assistance if necessary. Make note of the location of police stations, fire stations, government offices, hospitals, service stations, convenience stores, churches, and other places you can go to for help.

If someone tries to accost you or follow you, keep your doors locked and your windows up, use your emergency flashers and horn, and drive quickly and carefully to a safe public place. Do not drive home as this will only let the follower know where you live. If your car is bumped on the road and you are not comfortable getting out, motion to the other driver and drive to the nearest police station or safe place.

If your car breaks down on the road, again, try to make it to a service station or one of your safe places. Otherwise, get off the road to avoid being hit by another vehicle. You may have to drive on a flat tire to do this, but the tire is replaceable and your life is not. Turn on your emergency flashers and place flares or other emergency signals you have conspicuously near the car. Place a white cloth or handkerchief on your antenna or door handle. Call for help if there is a telephone or motorist call-box nearby. If not, get into your car, lock the doors and windows, and wait for help. If a stranger stops to help, remain in your locked car and ask the person to call the police or someone else for help. Likewise, if you see a motorist broken down on the highway, do not get out of your car because it could be a trap. Rather, get to a phone and call for help.

When parking your car, always leave it in a well-lit and well-travelled area. Check to make sure that you did not leave your keys in your car and that the doors are locked. Eighty percent of the stolen cars were left unlocked and 40 percent had the keys left in the ignition. Do not leave spare keys hidden in your car. Hide all valuables from view. Consider using an anti-theft device or alarm when your car is left unattended. When returning to your car, check carefully to make sure no one is hiding in your car before you get in. Exercise caution when returning home to be certain that there is no suspicious activity nearby. Blow your horn and have someone inside turn on lights or open the door for you.

It is not recommended that you carry a gun in your car or on your person, because it is generally prohibited in most states. However, you should consider carrying a canister of "Mace" or other attack repellant, or even a small knife. Don't be afraid to use these and other forms of self-defense in an attack, if you can do so without provoking harm to yourself. Retreating from an attacker and calling the police is always preferable to trying to conquer the attacker alone. Statistics indicate that you are less likely to suffer harm if you cooperate with an assailant rather than resisting. In any situation always try to remain calm and use common sense and caution.

Contact your local police for information on getting involved in or starting a neighborhood watch, self-defense techniques, and other crime prevention methods.

Remember also to be a wise consumer to protect yourself from becoming a victim of consumer fraud. See the discussion in chapter 8 beginning on page 130 for ways you can guard against the common crimes of consumer frauds against senior citizens.

# CHAPTER 10

# PLANNING FOR DISABILITY

## Appointing Someone to Manage Your Affairs

All of us are likely to have difficult times in our lives when we will need the help and trust of others. Finding someone who will care for you and manage your affairs if you become incapacitated or disabled is a very important task for you to accomplish. You can plan ahead for many of these situations by making a durable power of attorney, living will, or medical directive to explicitly state your choices.

A general power of attorney is basically a written document whereby you authorize someone else to act on your behalf. If you make a power of attorney, you are commonly referred to as the principal. The person to whom you have given the power of attorney to act on your behalf is referred to as your agent.

A power of attorney can be useful to you in a variety of situations. It can be useful if you are undergoing an operation or going away for an extended period of time. For almost anything that you can do for yourself, you can give a power of attorney to someone to act on your behalf. This includes the power to contract, buy and sell property, cash checks, make deposits and withdrawals, settle claims, file lawsuits, and almost anything else.

Your power of attorney serves as evidence to others that you have appointed someone to act on your behalf. It can also serve as an agreement between you and your agent regarding the business to be transacted under your power of attorney.

Although a general power of attorney normally terminates when you become incapacitated, you can make a durable power of attorney which will remain valid even if you later lose the capacity to contract and appoint an agent. Your durable power of attorney typically must be in writing signed by you, and it must contain language which shows that you intend your power of attorney to remain in effect even if you are disabled or incapacitated.

## Durable Power of Attorney

A durable power of attorney is essential if you plan to appoint someone to make decisions for you in the event that you are incapacitated. Remember, if you are seriously ill, unconscious, or lacking mental capacity, you will not be able to make decisions concerning your medical treatment and personal or business affairs. Unless you designate someone to act on your behalf by durable power of attorney or otherwise, a guardian may have to be appointed by the courts to make decisions for you. Appointment of a guardian is not only a lengthy and costly legal process, but it could result in the appointment of someone that you might not want to make choices for you.

Your power of attorney can be general to cover broad areas regarding your affairs, or it can be limited to specific acts or responsibilities. You do not give up control over your affairs when you execute a power of attorney, rather you maintain control by simply designating a person who has the authority to act for you under certain circumstances. For example, you can sign a "Health Care Power of Attorney" or "Medical Proxy" wherein you authorize someone to specifically make health care decisions for you in the event that you are unable to speak for yourself. You can usually revoke your power of attorney at any time.

## Living Wills and Medical Directives

In addition to appointing someone to make health care decisions for you, you can express your desire to refuse life-prolonging medical treatment in the event of terminal illness or injury. Your right to refuse treatment when you are unable to make decisions and have no chance for recovery can be carried out by making a "Living Will" (also referred to as a "Medical Directive").

A "Living Will" is not a will at all, but instructions to family members or doctors regarding the continuation or termination of medical life-support systems. You can execute a living will if you wish to avoid life-support systems which only prolong the dying process.

The States of Alabama, Alaska, Arizona, Arkansas, California, Colorado, Connecticut, Delaware, Florida, Georgia, Hawaii, Idaho, Illinois, Indiana, Iowa, Kansas, Louisiana, Maine, Maryland, Mississippi, Missouri, Montana, Nevada, New Hampshire, New Mexico, North Carolina, Oklahoma, Oregon, South Carolina, Tennessee, Texas, Utah, Vermont, Virginia, Washington, West Virginia, Wisconsin and Wyoming and the District of Columbia have adopted "living will," "death-with-dignity," or "right-to-die" laws which recognize the rights of terminally ill patients to stop life support. These laws are intended to protect doctors, hospitals, and others from civil and criminal liability, and to honor the wishes of patients who are dying from a terminal condition.

A typical death-with-dignity law provides that a terminally ill patient can request by conscious directive or living will that life-sustaining medical treatment be withheld or withdrawn. The hospital, staff, and family will be free from liability if such a request is honored. The laws also protect any insurance that the terminal patient may have, by providing that honoring a Living Will does not constitute suicide.

The requirements for making a living will are governed by the laws of your particular state. Generally, it is required that your living will be signed and dated by you when you are in a stable mental and physical condition. Typically, it must be witnessed by two or more people who are not your relatives, doctor or doctor's employees, beneficiaries, or creditors. You and your witnesses usually must be at least eighteen years of age. You should have the signatures notarized so that your living will is self-proving.

The living will document itself basically provides: if the situation should arise in which there is no reasonable expectation of recovery from terminal physical or mental disability, you request that you be allowed to die naturally, and not be kept alive by artificial means or extraordinary measures.

If you make a living will, be sure to give copies to your doctor and family so that they will know your wishes. If you change doctors, be sure your new doctor get a copy. Update and re-sign it periodically to show that it is still current.

Before your living will is honored, usually a determination of terminal illness or condition must be made by your attending physician and at least one other doctor. Some doctors or hospitals may be reluctant to honor your living will and terminate life support system, unless specifically requested by some authorized person at that time. For this reason, you should make a durable health care power of attorney or medical proxy a part of your living will, whereby you appoint someone to make medical decisions for you and carry out the directives of your living will.

Your choice of agent is very important in making a power of attorney, especially a health care power of attorney or medical proxy. You should appoint someone you trust and who will act in your best interest. Remember, the person you appoint will have great power over your affairs and personal care.

## Buying Private Health and Disability Insurance

In planning for disability, you also need to prepare for the financial burden of long-term illness and health care. Remember, Medicare pays for less than half of an older person's annual health care bills and less than 2 percent of nursing home costs. Medicaid covers only about 40 percent of nursing home expenses for those who meet low-income requirements. Yet, over the past decade, medical costs and the gaps in Medicare coverage have grown beyond anticipation. Insurance companies are now offering a variety of private health, long-term care, and disability insurance plans. You should review your needs and consider obtaining health and disability insurance if necessary.

Nearly three quarters of older Americans purchase Medicare supplemental insurance (Medigap) to fill gaps in their coverage. These Medigap policies, however, typically have limitations; insuring you against only that portion of your medical costs that are not covered by Medicare. Oftentimes the Medigap policies cover services only after

Medicare pays first. Therefore, if payment for a service is denied by Medicare, your Medigap insurance also may not pay.

Selecting a proper Medigap insurance plan can be difficult. Too often many seniors buy the wrong insurance and may end up paying too much and getting overlapping or inadequate protection.

There is a lot of misunderstanding about whether Medigap insurance covers nursing home care. Medigap insurance generally does not cover the care of senior citizens who can no longer care for themselves. Likewise, none of the costs for custodial care are covered by Medicare.

Medicare only covers the cost of skilled care in a nursing home for 100 days after your hospital stay. Your Medigap insurance could extend this period of coverage.

Do not let your fear of illness or disability push you to buy supplemental health insurance that is not right for you. Before you buy a Medigap policy, determine what you need in supplemental health insurance and examine the Medigap policy providing this coverage. Compare the premium, waiting periods, pre-existing condition clauses, exclusions, and benefits of several insurance plans and purchase the one that is most cost-effective and comprehensive for you. Go over the fine print with an attorney or some other able person you trust. Be certain that you fully understand the policy's coverage and limitations before you buy insurance.

Watch out for insurance policies that can cancel your coverage for any reason. Also be aware of policies that exclude coverage for a pre-existing condition.

The U.S. Senate Special Committee on Aging provides these helpful tips about buying supplemental health insurance:

- Identify Medicare's gap to determine what is important to you in a Medicare supplemental policy. Also consider such policy features as premiums, waiting periods, pre-existing condition exclusions, and maximum benefit clauses.

- Take into account any other coverage you have that continues beyond age sixty-five.

- Find out which doctors accept Medicare assignment and are participating physicians. Lists should be available at your nearest Social Security office or area agency on aging.

- Work with home town agents and companies that you know. A company must meet certain qualifications to do business in your state. In most states, agents must also be licensed by the state and must carry proof of licensing showing their name and the company they represent. Ask whether they belong to any professional organization so you can check their credentials.

- Talk with your friends who have had good experience with the Medigap policies.

- Investigate group insurance sold by legitimate organizations and associations. Some of the senior citizen or retired person organizations are "legitimate" and others are "gimmicks" set up as fronts to get your business. While some of these plans are good deals, others are expensive and not as good as individual plans.

- As a general rule, purchase one good comprehensive Medicare supplemental policy. There are some exceptions if you have an employer group policy that you can afford but which may have limited benefits. In this care, it may be advisable to have someone knowledgeable go over the options with you.

- Check for special circumstances for which the insurance company may eliminate coverage for a health condition you had before you bought the policy. A policy may refer to this as a "pre-existing condition."

- Beware of replacing existing coverage. Be suspicious of a suggestion that you give up any policy and buy a replacement. Replacement policies should meet the 1990 standards established by the National Association of Insurance Commissioners which prevent insurers replacing coverage from imposing any additional or new pre-existing condition, waiting, elimination, or probationary periods.

- Check your right to renew. Beware of policies that let the company refuse to renew your policy on an individual basis. Pursuant to 1990 standards established by the National Association of Insurance Commissioners policies must be guaranteed renewable.

- Remember, policies to supplement Medicare are neither sold nor serviced by state or federal governments. Do not be mislead into assuming such policies are government-sponsored.

- Do not pay cash for insurance. Write a check or money order payable to the company, not the agent. However, you should not pay for the annual premium until you have received the policy; a deposit should suffice (e.g., one month's premium).

- Keep the agent's and company's name(s), address(s), and telephone number(s). In case of problems you should be able to contact them easily.

- Take your time. The Medigap insurance market is highly competitive with many products to choose from. Do not let a short-term enrollment period pressure you. Most legitimate policies will not have limited enrollment periods. Some states prohibit special enrollment periods.

# CHAPTER 11

# HANDLING AGE DISCRIMINATION IN EMPLOYMENT

## Age Discrimination In Employment

As an older worker, you can be an invaluable resource, as you bring maturity, wisdom, and experience to the workplace. While you have a lot to offer, many work environments would rather avoid than welcome such resources if they come in an "older" package.

It is unlawful under the laws of many states as well as federal laws to discriminate in employment on the basis of age. These laws are designed to promote the employment of older persons based on their ability rather than age. Get to know your rights under the laws prohibiting age discrimination and how you can go about enforcing them.

## Your Rights Under the Federal Law

The Age Discrimination in Employment Act (ADEA) is a federal law that was established to promote the employment of older workers based on ability instead of age. Under ADEA, you are protected against arbitrary age discrimination if you are age forty or older and if your employer employs twenty or more persons in a business or in any activity affecting business.

In addition to private employers, ADEA applies to:

• employment agencies serving covered employers, even when they are acting on behalf of noncovered employers;

• labor unions with twenty-five or more members, or that maintain or operate a hiring hall supplying workers to covered employers. Under the law, labor unions are subject to the rules for employers with respect to the unions own employees;

• federal, state, and local governments.

ADEA applies to both applicants for employment and employees of any employer covered by the law. It also applies to U.S. citizens who are working in a foreign country for a U.S. employer or a foreign company controlled by a U.S. company. ADEA also applies to discrimination among those in the protected class which would favor younger class member. For example, an employer can not discriminate against a sixty-year-old employee in favor of one who is fifty years old.

Since the ADEA does not preempt or take the place of state or local laws banning age discrimination, a state's law that is more restrictive than the federal law must also be complied with by an employer. For example, if a state law protects persons under age forty or applies to employers with fewer than twenty employees, the employer must comply with the ADEA and the state law. You are generally required to pursue your remedies under state law before you can bring a lawsuit under the federal law.

You can find out your state's age discrimination requirements by contacting the state agency responsible for these laws. See the listing in the Appendix.

### Prohibited Employer Practices

According to the ADEA, it is illegal for an employer to fail or refuse to hire, or to discharge any individual because he or she is age forty or older, or to otherwise discriminate against any such individual as to compensation, terms, conditions, or privileges of employment. It is also illegal for an employer to segregate or classify employees so as to deprive any individual of employment opportunities, or to affect adversely his or her status as an employee because of age. Further, an employer cannot discriminate against an individual because he or she has opposed any unlawful practice or has made a charge, testified, assisted, or participated in any way in an investigation, proceeding, or suit under the law. Employers generally cannot justify age discrimination on the basis that an older workforce costs it more to do business.

Employment agencies are held to the same standards as employers. Therefore, they cannot fail or refuse to refer persons for employment or discriminate against them in other ways because of their age. Likewise, labor unions cannot discriminate by excluding or expelling members because of their age, and they cannot refuse to refer or otherwise discriminate against anyone because of age.

It is important to note that certain programs are exempt from ADEA if they are designed exclusively to provide employment for, or encourage employment of, individuals with special employment problems. This exemption would include programs under federal contracts or grants or those carried out by state public employment services.

Under the law, employers, agencies, and unions cannot print or publish a notice or ad that indicates a preference based on age. If the ad contains any such limitation or specification, it is discriminatory. Examples include references to "young," "boy," "girl," "age twenty-four-thirty-five," or similar statements which show an age preference. While employers' help wanted ads may use such terms as "high school graduates," college graduate," or other references to educational requirements, they should not use unlawful terms such as "recent high school graduates" or "recent college graduates" because these latter examples show an age preference. Job ads can state a minimum age of less than forty, such as "over twenty-two."

Under federal law, when you apply or interview for a job, you should know that an employer can ask you to state your age or date of birth on an application form or during an interview. However, you should be told that questions about your age will not be used for discriminatory purposes.

When reviewing employment applications, look for a legend on the form that states: "The Age Discrimination in Employment Act prohibits discrimination on the basis of age with respect to individuals who are at least forty years of age." While this statement does not guarantee that an employer will not discriminate against you, it at least shows that the employer is aware of the age discrimination laws.

## Proving Discrimination Based on Age

Proving age discrimination is not always easy. The simplest way to show age discrimination is by explicit evidence that the employer used the age of an applicant or employee as the basis for making an employment-related decision. However, age discrimination is rarely this overt and explicit. Nevertheless, you can establish age discrimination by reference to the treatment of others in similar circumstances, by showing a hostile environment to older employees, or by other circumstantial evidence of discriminatory intent. You can also show age discrimination by systemic policies that have greater negative effect on older employees.

The burden of proving age discrimination always falls on the person who is claiming discrimination. The employer may deny the discriminatory conduct or allege other explanations and justification for its action, but these can be rebutted with appropriate evidence. Age discrimination can exist even if age is not the only explanation for the employer's conduct. It is discriminatory if age is at least one of the bases of the employer's action.

The ADEA provides five defenses an employer, union, or employment agency can use against a claim of age discrimination. These defenses are discussed below and include a bona fide occupational qualification, a reasonable factor other than age, an employee benefit plan, discharge or discipline for good cause, and good faith reliance on a written regulation or court ruling:

- The bona fide occupational qualification defense allows age discrimination if age is a bona fide occupational qualification reasonably necessary to the normal operation of the particular business. The employer must demonstrate that the job qualifications it has established are reasonably necessary for its business operation.

The employer must also have a factual basis for concluding that substantially all of the people over the age limit can not perform the job, or that it is highly impractical to determine each individual's fitness. This defense is typically used in jobs involving police, fire fighters, pilots, and other public safety areas.

- Reasonable factors other than age can be a basis for employment decisions even if some forms of age discrimination result. These include physical fitness requirements; standards for the amount of production; validated tests which are a business necessity; and other factors such as misconduct, disrespect, inability to communicate, and the like.

- An employer generally can observe the terms of any bona fide employee benefit plan such as a retirement, pension, or insurance plan. This defense allows employers to reduce retirement, pension or insurance benefits to equalize the costs of these benefits between older and younger employees. However, no benefit plan can require an employee to retire before age seventy.

- An employer can also use as a defense to age discrimination that it acted in good faith and in conformance with any written administrative regulation, rule, or order.

### Do You Have to Retire at a Certain Age?

Prior to changes in the law in 1986, employers could mandate retirement of employees at a certain age. Now, as a result of the 1986 changes, mandatory retirements at any age has been abolished. However, there are three exceptions to the "no mandatory retirement" rule:

(1) an employee in a "bona fide executive or high policy-making position" who is immediately entitled to an employer-financed aggregate pension of at least $44,000 a year can be forced to retire at sixty-five;

(2) higher education institutions can require employees with contracts for unlimited tenure to retire at age seventy;

(3) firefighters and law enforcement officers can be forced to retire when they reach the retirement age in effect under applicable state or local law on March 3, 1983, or pursuant to a bona fide retirement plan that is not designed as a subterfuge to evade the law.

On December 31, 1993, the second and third exceptions above are scheduled to be repealed.

You can choose to retire at any age and can take early retirement if it is permitted by your employer's pension plan. With respect to a layoff or discharge, it would be discriminatory for your employer to lay you off or discharge you because of your eligibility for early retirement. If you are offered an incentive to take early retirement, your acceptance should be truly voluntary. In other words, it would be discriminatory for your employer to subtly (or overtly) demand that you take a voluntary retirement.

As long as you continue to work and until you retire, your employer must make full contributions to your retirement plan account. Prior to amendments to the pension laws in 1986, employers could stop making contributions when an employee reached "normal retirement age," (typically age sixty-five) and could exclude employees hired within five years of a pension plan's normal retirement age from plan participation. See chapter 4 for a thorough discussion of your rights under the pension laws.

## Physical Fitness and Other Requirements

Remember that an employer can require job applicants to meet reasonable standards of physical fitness or pass a bona fide physical examination if a particular job has certain physical requirements. Also, bona fide employment tests, which have been validated for specific jobs may be used, but they should be administered without discrimination based on age. An employer can also adhere to the terms of a bona fide seniority system. Further, an employer is not prevented from disciplining or discharging you for good cause, regardless of your age.

Where the safety of the public is concerned, courts have been more liberal in finding age to be a bona fide occupational qualification. Examples include upholding rules requiring commercial airline pilots to stop flying at age sixty and rules against hiring bus drivers past a certain age (thirty-five or forty). The arguments for such bona fide occupational qualifications center around the subtle effects of the aging process on fitness which cannot always be detected, and around the need for rules which support passenger safety.

ADEA bans discrimination against persons forty years of age and older, but it does not ban discrimination in favor of this protected age group. An employer can give additional benefits, for example, enhanced severance pay, to workers in the protected age group if the employer has a reasonable basis, because these benefits will counteract problems related to age bias.

## Employee Benefit Plans

ADEA, with amendments in 1990 by the Older Workers Benefit Protection Act (OWBPA), describes what your employer can and cannot do with respect to applying employee benefit plans to older workers. The employer is banned from age discrimination in the provision of employee benefits, unless it can show that it costs more to provide the same benefit to older employees. If age is shown to be a cost factor, benefits may be reduced for older workers in order to equalize the costs for older and younger workers.

The law also allows employers to offer voluntary early retirement incentive plans to the extent they are consistent with the "relevant purposes" of the ADEA. Under this rule, the following early retirement incentives would be within the law:

- incentives offering a flat dollar amount, a benefit based on length of service, or a percentage of salary;

- incentives providing flat-dollar increases in pension benefits; and

- incentives that add years of service or age.

With respect to health insurance benefits, your employer is required by law to offer all employees age sixty-five and over the same health insurance benefits that are available to younger employees. This requirement also covers employees' spouses age sixty-five and over.

## Enforcing Your Rights Against Age Discrimination

If your employer does not adhere to the ADEA, the Equal Opportunity Commission (EEOC) can investigate charges, issue guidelines, and enforce its provisions by legal proceedings. A lawsuit can be brought by the EEOC or by any aggrieved person within two years after the violation or within three years in cases of willful violation. If the government attempts conciliation and settlement, the time limits are suspended.

The process typically starts with you filing a complaint with the EEOC or designated state agency. Before you file an EEOC complaint, it is recommended that you first use any administrative mechanisms or forums your employer has established for handling charges of age discrimination. Contact your employer's EEOC representative, if any, or see your human resources representative. If you decide to file a complaint with the EEOC itself, here are some things you should do:

- Gather as much information as you can on the discriminatory practices, and how they have impacted you in earnings, promotions, work assignments, lay-offs, benefits, and other conditions of employment.

- Locate an EEOC office near you. Check local telephone listings for the nearest location.

- As an aggrieved or injured person, you must file your complaint with the EEOC within 180 days of the alleged discrimination. You can file your complaint within 300 days if the act occurred in a state with an age discrimination law to allow time to pursue your state law rights. You must then wait at least 60 days before bringing a lawsuit. Remember a lawsuit can be brought within two years after the violation or within three years in cases of willful violation.

If, as a result of your lawsuit against your employer, you recover back wages and the court finds the violation was willful, it will award you an additional sum called "liquidated damages" equal to the back wages. A "willful" violation is where your employer "knew or showed reckless disregard" of whether its conduct was prohibited by the ADEA.

Once your complaint has been filed with the EEOC, the following procedures apply:

- EEOC interviews you to obtain as much information as possible about the alleged discrimination. If all legal jurisdictional requirements are met, a charge is properly drafted and the investigative procedure is explained to you.

- EEOC notifies the employer about the charge. In investigating the charge to determine if discrimination occurred, EEOC requests information from the employer that addresses the issues directly affecting you as well as other potentially aggrieved persons. Any witnesses who have direct knowledge of the alleged discriminatory act will be interviewed. If the evidence shows there is no reasonable cause to believe discrimination occurred, both you and the employer will be notified. You may exercise the right to bring private court action.

- If the evidence shows there is reasonable cause to believe discrimination occurred, EEOC conciliates or attempts to persuade the employer to voluntarily eliminate and remedy the discrimination, following the standards of EEOC's Policy on Remedies and Relief for Individual Cases of Unlawful Discrimination.

- EEOC considers the case for litigation if conciliation fails. If litigation is approved by the Commission, EEOC will file a lawsuit in federal district court on your behalf and any other charging parties. Remember that you may initiate private civil action on your own in lieu of EEOC litigation.

As a general rule, the forms of relief that you may seek for age discrimination include:

- Back pay;

- Hiring, promotion, reinstatement, benefit restoration, front pay, and other affirmative relief;

- Actual pecuniary loss other than back pay;

- Liquidated damages;

- Compensatory damages for future monetary losses and mental anguish;

- Punitive damages when employer acts with malice or reckless disregard for federally protected rights;

- Posting a notice to all employees advising them of their rights under the laws EEOC enforces and their right to be free from retaliation;

- Corrective or preventive actions taken to cure the source of the identified discrimination and minimize the chance of its recurrence;

- Reasonable accommodation; or

- Stopping specific discriminatory practices.

### Recordkeeping Requirements For Your Employer, Union, and Employment Agency

Recordkeeping requirements are imposed by ADEA to ensure access to important employment records and information. Let us review the recordkeeping and record retention periods required for employers, unions, and employment agencies.

ADEA requires employers to keep, for three years, information on each employee regarding: name, address, date of birth, occupation, rate of pay, and compensation earned each week. If your employer keeps other employment or personnel records as a part of its business routine, it must keep the following data for one year, or ninety days in the case of temporary workers:

- Job applications, resumes, or other employment inquiries in answer to ads or notices, plus records about failure or refusal to hire.

- Records on promotion, demotion, transfer, selection for training, layoff, recall, or discharge of any employee.

- Job orders given to agencies or unions to recruit personnel for job openings.

- Test papers.

- Results of physical exams that are considered in connection with any personnel action.

- Ads or notices relating to job openings, promotions, training programs, or opportunities for overtime.

Your employer is required to keep copies of its benefit plans and seniority and merit systems for the full period that the plan is in effect plus one year after its termination. A memorandum can take the place of a nonwritten plan.

Your employer is not required to keep records in any particular order, but is required to keep them at the plant or office where you are employed or have applied—or at your company's central recordkeeping office. Records must be available for inspection by federal government representatives. If you want to see your file, contact your human resources representative for details on your employer's or state's access requirements and procedures.

Employment agencies are required to keep, for one year, records of placements, referrals, job orders, job applications or resumes, test papers that the agency considered in connection with referrals, advertisements, or notices about job openings.

Unions are required to keep current records which identify members by name, address, and date of birth. Additionally, unions must keep, for one year, a record of the name, address, and age of any applicant for membership.

By understanding your rights as an older employee under federal and state laws, you will be better prepared to recognize and defend against age discrimination. If you feel you have been a victim of age discrimination, analyze your case objectively and try to resolve the issue with your employer.

If you remain on the job be aware that any charge of age discrimination could lead to difficult relations with your supervisor and other coworkers. However, your employer is prohibited from retaliating against you for charging age discrimination. If the issue can not be resolved internally, consider filing an EEOC complaint within 180 days and taking other legal action if necessary. Age discrimination cases can be quite complex and will typically require the services of a good lawyer.

# CHAPTER 12

# MAKING YOUR WILL

## Should You Make a Will?

If you have not made a will at this point in your life, there are several good reasons why you should prepare one. Your will expresses your specific wishes as to how you want your property distributed and it eliminates speculation and confusion about how your estate will be given away. Also, it states who you want to handle your estate and can identify who you would want as guardian to any minor children. Equally important, your will provides a good inventory of your property and assets. Without this, it may be difficult for someone to identify and locate any real estate, bank accounts, safe deposit boxes, securities, or other personal property you may have in various places. Preparing your will is also good because it causes you to seriously consider the full extent of your property, family, and friends, and to plan your estate accordingly.

In earlier times a will was the most common means of handling the disposition of a person's estate. Today, however, if you want to create an estate plan, you have a variety of will substitutes and alternative to the traditional will. For example, you can hold property in joint tenancy with right of survivorship, whereby the property will automatically pass to the surviving co-owner upon your death. You can also put property into a living trust to have it transferred directly to named beneficiaries without having to go through probate. Even if you use one of the alternative estate planning methods, you should still prepare a will to cover any residual property and as a back-up in case the joint tenancy, living trust, or other alternative fails.

Before making your will, you should prepare a list of all of your real and personal property. This list should be complete with all your real estate, bank accounts, safe deposit boxes, stocks and bonds, automobiles, furniture, jewelry, artwork, and all other assets. It is also good to list any insurance policies you may have, even though insurance proceeds will generally be paid directly to the beneficiary named in the policy. You should also prepare a list of your children, spouse, other family members, friends, charities, and others which you would like to make beneficiaries in your will. Next, you should prepare a distribution plan which shows how you want your property distributed among your family, friends, and others. Identify someone that you would like to name as executor (male) or executrix (female) to carry out your wishes and the distribution of your estate. You should also identify an alternate person in the event that the first executor or executrix is unable to serve. With all the information you have just gathered, you can now prepare your will. You can prepare a simple will yourself using a standard will form. For a complex will an attorney may be required. Typical attorney's fees for preparing wills range from about $100-$300.

## Requirements for Making a Valid Will

A will is a legal document which is prepared with certain formalities and under which you direct what will happen to your property after your death. Your will is effective only upon your death and it can be modified or revoked by you at any time during your life. If you should die without leaving a will, your property will be distributed according to state law and will generally go to your spouse and children or other next of kin.

The formal requirements for making a valid will depend on your state law. However, most of the states have four general requirements for the formation of a valid will. First, there must be the necessary intent to make a will. This means that you must intend for the document and the words contained therein to operate as your will upon your death. Secondly, you must be of legal age and have the legal capacity to make a will. This means that you must have actual knowledge of the act that you are performing. You must also have an understanding of your property and your relationship to others at the time of making your will. Third, your will must be made free of fraud, duress, undue influence, and mistake. Fourth, your will must be executed in accordance with the formal requirements of your state law. This generally requires that your will be signed by you and by two disinterested witnesses in the presence of each other. Some states may require that the will be witnesses by three people. Therefore, it is recommended that you have at least three people sign your will as witnesses.

You must have the intent to make a will for your will to be valid. This is a question of fact which is determined from the circumstances surrounding the making of your will. Where your will is a sham or was executed as a joke, the required testamentary intent is lacking and your will is invalid. If you prepare a document or agreement which shows an intent to make a will in the future, this document or agreement is not a valid will. For your will to be valid, it must show your present intent to make a will.

For the required testamentary capacity to make a will, you must be of legal age and sound mental capacity. The legal age in most states is eighteen years. The sound mental capacity requires that you be able to (1) understand the relationship between you and the natural objects of your generosity, such as your spouse, children, and other family members; (2) understand the nature and extent of your property; and (3) understand that you are executing your will. The required mental capacity must exist at the time that you make your will. If you should later lose the required mental capacity, this does not affect the validity of an earlier will executed when you did have the required mental capacity.

Your capacity to make a will can be influenced by alcohol, drugs, medications, illness, and mental disease. To help avoid questions about your capacity to make a will, your will should contain an introductory clause declaring that you are of sound mind and body, have full testamentary intent and capacity, and voluntarily execute that document as your last will and testament. Your will should also include a witness attestation clause in which the witnesses declare that you are of sound mind and body and signed of your free will.

## Signing and Witnessing of Your Will

The valid execution of your will requires that it be signed by you. Your signature generally must appear at the end of the will. However, it is recommended that you sign at the end of each page to prevent fraud and substitution of pages. You should use your regular and complete signature, although any name or mark used by you and intended as your signature is generally acceptable. You should sign your will in the presence of the witnesses who will be attesting to it. If you are unable to sign your will, generally you can have another person sign for you. This must be done in your presence and in the presence of the witnesses and be at your specific direction.

It is required that your will be witnessed by two or three people, depending on state law. This usually requires that the witnesses observe your signing and also sign the will themselves in your presence and the presence of each other.

Who may be a witness to your will is also governed by your state law. Generally, any competent person who is of legal age can be a witness. Some states require that the witnesses not be beneficiaries under the will or lose their gift under the will if they act as witnesses. Therefore, it is recommended that your will be witnessed by disinterested witnesses who will not be beneficiaries under your will.

Your will should contain a witness attestation clause which declares that the will was signed and published in their presence and that you were of sound mind and body and acting from your free will at that time. This witness attestation clause may be useful in preventing challenges to your will that might be based on arguments that you lacked testamentary intent and capacity. Your witnesses should include their addresses along with their signatures so they will be easier to find, if necessary.

Your will can be "self-proving" if your signature and those of your witnesses are notarized. If your will is "self-proving," the signatures are presumed to be valid and authentic. This would make it difficult for someone to challenge your will by claiming that the signatures are not genuine. For this reason, it is recommended that you and your witnesses sign the will before a notary and have it notarized.

## What Should Your Will Provide?

Generally, there are no required provisions for including in a will. Everyone's will is unique in that it contains instructions on how each maker would like to have his or her property given away. Make sure that your will expresses your particular wishes and desires.

Your will should contain a declaration that you are of sound mind and body and free will, that you have full testamentary intent and capacity, and that you voluntarily make your will. Also include your current domicile.

Your will should also include a clause expressly revoking any previous wills or codicils executed by you. A codicil is an amendment to a will which does not revoke it, but merely modifies it. Your new will should always be intended to supersede any earlier wills or codicils and a revocation clause would make your intentions clear.

An executor or executrix should be appointed under your will to handle your estate. Most people name their spouse, attorney or a close friend, and provide that no bond be required to carry out his or her duties under the will. You should direct your executor or executrix to pay all of your just debts and other expenses of the administration of your estate. These debts and expenses are usually paid directly from the assets of your estate before any distribution is made to your beneficiaries.

Your will should contain provisions for gifts to your beneficiaries. In the simplest form these can be gifts of specific property to named individuals. You may also make gifts to members of a class, such as your children, brothers or sisters, and the like. Care must be taken to make certain that any gift will vest within twenty-one years after the life of some specific person. For complicated will and trust provisions you should consult an attorney.

In many states, your surviving spouse may be entitled to a certain minimum portion (usually from one quarter to one half) of your estate regardless of what your will provides. Thus, you may need to indicate in your will whether any bequest or devise to your spouse is in lieu of, or in addition to, any minimum portion mandated by state law.

Likewise, some states provide that a child who is not mentioned or provided for in your will may be entitled to a share of your estate. Similar provisions may apply to children born after execution of your will. For these reasons, your state laws should be checked for specific provisions of testamentary gifts to children. It is recommended that all your children be acknowledged and mentioned in your will, even if you do not leave them anything or only leave a small token gift.

Be sure to include a residuary clause in your will wherein you give the remainder of your estate. This provision is important in case you have omitted to give away any of your property, or if any of your other gifts should fail for any reason.

Depending on your particular circumstances, you may want to include additional provisions in your will, such as a guardianship clause, trust clause for your minor children, a simultaneous death clause, or predeceased clause in case a beneficiary should predecease you.

The guardianship clause nominates someone whom you would like to act as guardian of your minor children. The trust clause provides the terms and conditions as to how a gift to your minor children will be held and distributed. In the trust clause, you should appoint a trustee and give instructions as to how the trustee should distribute the gifts. The simultaneous death clause provides that, if you and a beneficiary should die together, the gift to that beneficiary will pass through your estate rather than the estate of the beneficiary. The predeceased clause provides that, if beneficiaries should die before you, their gifts will pass to their lawful descendants who survive you. Otherwise the gifts become part of your residuary estate. You may also want to include a pledge of your body or organs in your will.

You can revoke your will at any time before your death. You can revoke your will by tearing, canceling, burning, or otherwise destroying it with the intent of revoking it. Your will can also be revoked by making a new will. Your new will can revoke the old one by explicit language of revocation or by conflicting provisions. The best ways of revoking a will are to execute a new will which expressly revokes the old one, or to cancel or otherwise revoke the will in the presence of witnesses.

## Planning for Probate

Many people think of probate as a complex, costly, and time-consuming process. Anxiety about the probate process has caused a lot of people to look at alternatives to probate, such as setting up a living trust or holding joint property or other nonprobate assets. However, in some cases probate can be simple and relatively inexpensive, particularly with small estates of about $50,000 or less. It may be important to review your particular situation, and your estate planning options, with a qualified attorney or estate planner to make sure that you make the best choices.

Probate is the legal process by which your estate is settled and the property of your estate distributed. In general, this process involves settling all of your accounts and debts, paying any applicable estate and inheritance taxes, and distributing your property to your beneficiaries or heirs.

Probate proceedings are generally held in the probate court in the county and state where you resided on the date of your death. If you do not leave a will, your estate will be administered and distributed according to the law of inheritance of your state. If you have prepared a will, it will be offered for probate and your estate will be administered according to your will.

Your will has no real effect until it has been probated. The procedures for probate of a will vary for each state, but they generally require the filing of a petition or application for probate with the probate court. Your will can be offered for probate by anyone who has an interest in your estate. If no will is involved, a petition for the appointment of an administrator and administration of your estate would have to be filed.

Obviously, you will not be handling the probate of your own estate after your death. Unless you make other very specific arrangements, someone will have to go through some form of probate of your estate. As you grow older, it is also likely that you will have to probate the estate of a deceased family member or friend.

The procedures for probating an estate are governed by the law of the state where the decedent was domiciled. If real estate is located in other states, supplementary probate proceedings may also be required in those states to settle title to any real estate.

Generally a sworn petition or application for probate is filed in the probate court of the county where the decedent had his or her last domicile. The petition or application may be filed by the executor or executrix, a beneficiary, an heir, a creditor, or anyone with a claim against or interest in the estate. The petition or application should include a copy of any will, the decedent's death certificate, and a list of decedent's surviving spouse, next of kin, and heirs at law known to the petitioner or applicant. Hearings are scheduled by the court to settle claims and approve the disposition of the estate assets. The petitioner/applicant is usually required to publish notice of the probate hearing in the newspaper and send notice to any person known to have an interest in the decedent's estate.

There are usually several types of probate proceedings, such as court supervised, informal, and small estate administration. In supervised probate the court oversees nearly all of the probate proceedings, imposes significant reporting requirements, and requires court approval for selling or disposing of estate property. Supervised probate can be time-consuming and expensive, and is typically required for large estates or where there is conflict between the heirs or beneficiaries.

Informal or unsupervised probate requires little court involvement and can be specified in the decedent's will or agreed to by the heirs and beneficiaries. They are less costly and less time-consuming than the supervised probate, and can usually be handled by you without the necessity of hiring a lawyer. In many cases the probate clerk's office or registrar of wills may be willing to provide guidance in handling these probate matters.

Small estate administration is probably the best probate process in terms of costs, time, and simplicity. It is available when the value of the estate is comparatively small. Be sure to check the law in your state for the estate value limits for small estate administration. Small estate probate can usually be accomplished in one to three months, compared to a year or longer for supervised probate.

Although the procedures vary from state to state, other steps in the probate process involve:

• having the court officially confirm the executor or executrix named in the will, or appointing an administrator if there is no will;

• notifying heirs, beneficiaries, creditors, and other affected parties about the probate proceeding;

- preparing an inventory and appraisal of the estate property and debts, and filing this with the probate court;

- paying the creditors, taxes and other expenses associated with probating or administering the estate;

- preparing a final accounting of the value of the estate, which shows all assets, debts, taxes, and other expenses, and filing this with the probate court;

- distributing the remainder of the estate property to beneficiaries according to the will, or to the heirs according to state law if there is no will; and

- closing the estate by filing an affidavit that the estate business is finished or obtaining a court order that the estate is closed.

Although a vast majority of probate cases are routine and uncomplicated, the services of an experienced attorney may be needed in a complex probate. Typical attorney's fees in probate cases range from about 3 percent to about 7 percent of the value of the decedent's estate. The executor, executrix or other administrator is generally paid a fee for administering the estate in the range of about 3 percent to about 5 percent of the value of the estate. These legal and administrative fees are usually paid out of the proceeds of the decedent's estate.

Probate is not required if you pass away leaving only property which is classified as "nonprobate property." Nonprobate property includes property that you own in trust, property owned jointly with a right of survivorship, and life insurance and pension benefits which are paid to someone else as beneficiary.

### Using a Living Trust as an Alternative to Probate

A living or "inter vivos" trust can be used to avoid a lot of the expenses, time, and procedures of probating your estate. Basically, a living trust is the establishment of a separate legal entity during your lifetime to hold, manage, and distribute property according to the terms of a trust agreement.

A living trust can serve important functions in planning your estate for both probate and tax purposes. If you retain the right to revoke the trust, your estate must pay federal estate taxes on the trust assets. Also, income that the revocable trust earns will be taxable to you even if this income is paid to someone else. Federal estate taxes can be avoided by making the trust irrevocable or revocable only upon the occurrence of an event outside of your control.

A trust is established when you transfer real estate or personal property to someone to act as trustee pursuant to a trust agreement. A valid trust requires that title to the trust property actually be transferred to the trust. This is generally done by transferring the property to the trustee with a designation such as "to Carl Battle, trustee." The requirements as to who can serve as a trustee are governed by the laws of your specific state. Generally, any person or entity that is capable of contracting can serve as trustee. The trustee usually is a bank, an insurance company, a certified public accountant, an attorney, or any other person competent in business affairs. In many states, you can be the maker (or "settlor") of the trust and also serve as trustee, provided that you are not the only beneficiary.

Assets that you transfer to a living trust are generally not included in your estate for probate purposes. Instead, the assets of your living trust are distributed by your trustee according to the terms of your trust agreement. Therefore, it is important that your trust provide for the disposition of trust property and income after your death, particularly if you are the trustee or the initial life beneficiary. If you are the trustee, it is also important that you have appointed an alternate trustee in case of your death so that the trust provisions can be carried out.

Any property can be transferred to your living trust, whether it is real or personal property. The trust agreement can also provide for additional property to be added to the trust in the future. Your living trust can also be coordinated with your will to avoid probate by providing that any property that would be probated shall be transferred to your living trust upon your death. The trust property should be handled separately from and not commingled with your individual property or the trust may be invalidated as a sham.

There are many tax and estate issues that may arise in setting up a trust. Complicated and difficult trust arrangement may require the assistance of an attorney or tax specialist. Typical legal fees for establishing a simple trust range from about $300 to $1,000, depending on location and complexity.

CHAPTER **13**

# TAX GUIDANCE FOR OLDER AMERICANS

## Obtaining Federal Tax Information

The Internal Revenue Service (IRS) and the U.S. Senate Special Committee on Aging have compiled a variety of publications to assist older Americans in preparing their federal income tax returns. Much of the information in this chapter is drawn from these publications and further explained to assure that you claim every legitimate income tax credit, exemption, and deduction due you as a senior taxpayer. Keep in mind that the tax laws are constantly changing and you need to keep informed of changes that may impact you as a senior citizen. For complex tax issues you may need the assistance of a knowledgeable tax attorney or accountant.

The IRS has prepared many free publications to help answer your tax questions. In addition to the general publication 17, *Your Federal Income Tax*, publications are available on specific topics, such as:

  1  *Your Rights as a Taxpayer*

505 *Tax Withholding and Estimated Tax*

524 *Credit for the Elderly or the Disabled*

525 *Taxable and Nontaxable Income*

530 *Tax Information for Homeowners*

554 *Tax Information for Older Americans*

575 *Pension and Annuity Income (Including Simplified General Rule)*

596 *Earned Income Credit*

721 *Comprehensive Tax Guide to U.S. Civil Service Retirement Benefits*

907 *Tax Information for Persons with Handicaps or Disabilities*

910 *Guide to Free Tax Services*

915 *Social Security Benefits and Equivalent Railroad Retirement Benefits*

Any IRS publication can be ordered by mail, using the order form in your tax package or by calling IRS toll-free at 1-800-829-3676. They also may be found at public libraries, post offices, and some banks.

There are other special IRS programs offering free assistance to you. Through the Tax Counseling for the Elderly (TCE) program, IRS-trained volunteers assist individuals age sixty or older with their tax returns at neighborhood locations in many areas. In addition, certain Volunteer Income Tax Assistance (VITA) aides have been trained to help older Americans with their tax returns. VITA assistance is also available to persons who cannot afford professional tax help as well as to military, individuals with disabilities, and non-English-speaking individuals. To find your nearest location, call the IRS toll-free number, 1-800-829-1040.

Private Tax Return Preparers: The law requires a paid preparer to sign the return and to complete the "paid preparers use only" section at the bottom of the form, just below your signature. You are responsible for the accuracy of every item entered on your return. If you pay someone to prepare the return for you and there is a mistake, the IRS will ask you, and not the preparer, to pay any back taxes, interest, and/or penalties. Therefore, you should be careful to choose someone who understands tax matters and who will prepare a complete and accurate return. You should also know how to locate this person in the future if the IRS has a question about your return.

### Your Filing Status

In general, your filing status depends on whether you are considered single or married on the last day of your tax year. If you file a calendar-year return, your last day generally is December 31. Each filing status has a different tax rate. If more than one filing status applied to you, choose the one that gives you the lowest tax.

Each of the five filing statuses are explained below:

**Single:** Generally, you are considered single if you were never married or you were divorced as of December 31 of the tax year. You are also considered single if you were legally separated, according to your state law, under a decree of divorce or a decree of separate maintenance.

**Married filing a joint return:** Generally, you are married if you were legally married as of December 31, even if you did not live with your spouse during the tax year. You are also considered married if your spouse died in the tax year and you did not remarry in that year. You may file a joint return even if only one spouse had all the income.

**Married filing a separate return:** If you are married, you can choose to file separate tax returns. After the due date of the return, however, you may not choose to file separate returns if you first filed a joint return for that year. You must provide your spouse's full name and Social Security number in the box provided for it on your tax return. Generally, you report only your own income, exemptions, deductions, and credits.

**Head of household:** If you were unmarried or considered unmarried as of December 31 of the tax year, and you provide more than half the cost of keeping up a home (that was the main home) for yourself and your unmarried child (regardless of his/her age or whether he/she was financially dependent on you) for more than six months, you may be eligible to file as head of household. You may also be able to file as head of household if you are entitled to claim other relatives such as your mother or father, or your married child as dependents.

**Qualifying widow(er) with dependent child:** If your spouse died and you remained unmarried during the tax year, you may be able to continue to pay taxes at the lower joint tax rates if: (1) your dependent child lived with you for the entire year, except for temporary absences; (2) you paid more than one-half of the costs of keeping up your home; and (3) you were entitled to file a joint return with your spouse for the year your spouse died.

## Do You Have to File a Tax Return?

The tax laws and regulations specify who must file a federal tax return based on gross income and filing status. The filing deadline is April 15 of the year following the tax year, unless you request an extension by the April 15 date. Tax returns which are postmarked after April 15 may be subject to penalties and interest.

The filing requirements based on filing status and gross income for the tax year 1992 are given below:

| Filing status | Gross income |
|---|---|
| Single: | |
|     Under age 65.................................. | over $5,900 |
|     Age 65 or older............................. | over $6,800 |
| | |
| Married Filing Joint Return: | |
|     Both spouses under age 65......... | over $10,600 |
|     One spouse age 65 or older........ | over $11,300 |
|     Both spouses age 65 or older...... | over $12,000 |
|     Not living with spouse at the end | |
|       of year (or on date spouse died) | over $ 2,300 |
| | |
| Married Filing Separate Return............ | over $ 2,300 |
| | |
| Head of Household: | |
|     Under age 65.................................. | over $7,550 |
|     Age 65 or older............................. | over $8,450 |
| | |
| Qualifying Widow(er): | |
|     Under age 65.................................. | over $8,300 |
|     Age 65 or older............................. | over $9,000 |

If you were self-employed and your net earnings were at least $400, then you must file a return to pay Social Security and Medicare taxes. This rule applies regardless of your age, whether or not you are receiving Social Security benefits, and even if you do not otherwise have to file a federal tax return. You are self-employed if you carry on a trade or business as a sole proprietor, a member of a partnership, or an independent contractor. This includes certain part-time work that you do at home or in addition to your regular job.

Even if you are not required to file a tax return, you should do so if you want to claim a refund for any taxes withheld. You should also file to get a refund of the earned income credit if you are eligible for the credit. If you do not file, you will not get a refund.

## Claiming Exemptions and Dependents

You are allowed a deduction for each exemption that you claim on your tax return. The personal exemption amount for tax year 1992 is $2,300. You can claim yourself, your spouse, your minor children, or any other relative or member of your household, if all five dependency tests are met for that individual. However, you may not take an additional exemption if you are age 65 or older or blind. Instead, you are allowed a higher standard deduction amount if you qualify. The amount of your exemption will be reduced or phased out beginning at an adjusted gross income of $100,000.

There are five tests to determine whether someone is your dependent: relationship, married person, citizen or resident, income, and support tests. Each dependent must meet all five of the following tests.

**Test 1: Relationship.** Your dependent must be either your relative or someone who lived in your home as a member of your household all year. Any relationships established by marriage are not treated as ended by divorce or death. The relationship must not violate local law.

The following are considered your relatives:

• Your child. Your child includes your son, daughter, stepchild, adopted child; a child who lived in your home as a family member if placed with you by an authorized placement agency for legal adoption; and a foster child (any child who lived in your home as a family member for the whole year).

• Your grandchild, great-grandchild, etc.

• Your son-in-law, daughter-in-law.

- Your parent, grandparent, stepparent, parent-in-law.

- Your brother, sister, stepbrother, stepsister, brother-in-law, sister-in-law, half brother, half sister.

- If related by blood, your aunt, uncle, nephew, niece.

**Test 2: Married person.** Your married dependent cannot file a joint return. However, if neither the dependent nor the dependent's spouse is required to file, but they file a joint return to get a refund of all taxes withheld, you may claim him or her if the other four tests are met.

**Test 3: Citizen or resident.** The dependent must be either a U.S. citizen or resident alien, or a resident of Canada or Mexico, or your adopted child who is not a U.S. citizen but who lived with you all year in a foreign country.

**Test 4: Income.** Generally, the dependent's gross income must be less than $2,150. Gross income does not include nontaxable income, such as welfare benefits or nontaxable, Social Security benefits.

If your dependent was permanently and totally disabled and had income from services performed at a sheltered workshop school, that income is generally not included for purposes of the income test.

Special rules for your dependent child: Your dependent who is your child does not have to meet this income test if either your child was under nineteen at the end of the tax year, or your child was under age twenty-four at the end of the tax year and qualifies as a student.

**Test 5: Support.** The general rule is that you had to provide over half the dependent's support during the tax year. If you file a joint return, support can come from either spouse.

Support includes food, a place to live, clothing, medical and dental care, and education. Support also includes such items as a car and furniture, but only if they are given to the dependent solely for his or her own use or benefit. In figuring total support, use the actual cost of these items. However, you should figure the cost of a place to live at its fair rental value. In figuring support, you must include money used by the dependent for his or her own support, even if this money was not taxable. Examples are Social Security and welfare benefits, gifts, and savings.

Support does not include such items as income tax, Social Security and Medicare taxes, life insurance premiums, scholarship and fellowship grants, or funeral expenses.

## What is Taxable Income?

Generally, you must include in gross income everything you receive in payment for personal services. In addition to wages, salaries, commissions, tips and fees, this includes other forms of compensation, such as fringe benefits and payments for certain expenses you incur.

You must report income in the form of goods or services at the fair market value of the goods or services you received. Income of particular interest to older Americans includes interest, dividends, gain from the sale of a main home, pensions and annuities, distributions from IRAs, Social Security and equivalent Railroad Retirement benefits, and gambling and lottery winning.

### Interest

You must report all your taxable interest income, even if it is $400 or less. If your total interest is more than $400 or you are claiming the exclusion of interest from Series EE U.S. Savings Bonds issued after 1989, you must first fill in Schedule B (Form 1040) or Schedule 1 (Form 1040A).

After 1990, all or part of the interest from certain Series EE U.S. savings bonds issued after 1989 to an individual age 24 or older can be excluded from income if you pay qualified higher education expenses during the year you redeem the bonds. Qualified higher education expenses are tuition and required fees at a college or eligible vocational school for the bonds' owner or the owner's spouse or dependent.

Interest earned on notes or bonds issued by a state or local government may not be taxable. You must show on your tax return any tax-exempt interest you received or accrued during the tax year. This is an information-reporting requirement and does not convert tax-exempt interest to taxable interest.

**Note:** Although interest earned on your IRA is generally not taxed in the year earned, it is not "tax-exempt interest." Do not report this interest on you tax return as "tax exempt."

Each payer of interest should send you a Form 1099-INT or a Form 1099-OID. A copy of the form is also sent to IRS. Be sure to provide the payer of interest with your correct Social Security number and include all of this income on your return. Otherwise, the payer may withhold 20 percent of your interest and you may be subject to penalties.

### Dividends

Dividends are distributions of money, stock, or other property that corporations pay to shareholders. You must report all your ordinary dividends, even if it is $400 or less. If your total is more than $400, you must fill in Schedule B (Form 1040) or Schedule 1 (Form 1040A).

Each payer of dividends should send you a Form 1099-DIV. A copy of the form is also sent to IRS. Be sure to provide the payer of dividends with your correct Social Security number and include all of the taxable income on your return. Otherwise, the payer may withhold 20 percent of your dividends and you may be subject to penalties. For more information on dividends and interest income, see IRS Publication 550.

### Sale of Your Main Home

If you sold your main home during the year, you must report the sale or exchange of your home on Form 2119, "Sale of Your Home." You may be able either to postpone paying tax on some or all of the gain or to exclude the gain from your taxable income. In either case, you must use Form 2119 to inform IRS that you meet certain qualifications. If you are unable to either postpone the tax on the gain or to exclude the gain from gross income, then the taxable gain for the sale is reported on Schedule D, "Capital Gains and Losses." You cannot deduct a loss on the sale of your home. The loss has no effect on the basis of your new home.

**Postponement of Gain.** If, within two years before or two years after the date of sale, you purchase (or build) and live in another main home that costs at least as much as the adjusted sale price of the old home, your entire gain on the sale is postponed at the time of the sale or exchange. You need not use the same funds received for the sale of your old home to buy or build your new home. The tax on the gain is postponed, not forgiven. Any gain not taxed in the year of sale is subtracted from the cost of your new home, giving you a lower basis in the new home.

**Exclusion of Gain.** Special rules apply to the sale of a main home by persons age fifty-five or older. If (1) you were age fifty-five or older on the date of the sale or exchange of your main home, (2) you owned and lived in the home for at least three years of the five-year period ending on the date of the sale or exchange, and (3) you or your spouse (depending on your marital status on the date of the sale) have never excluded gain on the sale or exchange of a home after July 26, 1978; then you may elect to exclude up to $125,000 ($62,500 if you are married filing separately) of the gain from gross income whether or not you purchase a new home.

In the case of a jointly owned home, both you and your spouse will meet the age, ownership, and use tests if:

- You hold the home either as joint tenants, tenants by the entirety, or as community property on the date of the sale or exchange;

- You file a joint return of the tax year in which you sell the home; and

- Either of you is fifty-five or older on the date of the sale and has owned and lived in the property as a main home for the required time before the sale or exchange.

If the home is not jointly owned, the spouse who owns the property must meet the age, ownership, and use tests. The other spouse must join in making the choice.

If you become physically or mentally unable to care for yourself and live in a nursing home or a state-licensed facility, you will be considered to have lived in your home as your main home during your stay in the facility if you have owned and lived in your home as your main home for a total of at least one year during the five-year period. This exception applies only to sales after September 30, 1988.

For more complete information, get IRS Publication 523, *Tax Information on Selling Your Home.*

### Pensions and Annuities

You should receive a Form 1099-R showing the amount of your pension or annuity. Be sure to attach Form 1099-R to your return if any federal income tax was withheld. Your pension or annuity payments are fully taxable if you did not contribute to the cost of your pension or annuity. Fully taxable pensions and annuities also include military retirement pay shown on form 1099R and any taxable Railroad Retirement benefits shown in Form RRB-1099-R.

If your pension or annuity is not fully taxable and your Form 1099-R does not show the taxable part, you must use the General Rule to figure the taxable part. The General Rule is explained in Publication 939, *Pension General Rule (Nonsimplified Method)*. But, if your annuity starting date was after July 1, 1986, you may be able to use the Simplified General Rule as explained in Publication 575, *Pension and Annuity Income (Including Simplified General Rule)*. If your pension is civil service, you should get Publication 721, *Comprehensive Tax Guide to U.S. Civil Service Retirement Benefits*.

If you receive a lump-sum payment, you may be eligible to lower the taxes due on it by using Form 4972, *Tax on Lump-Sum Distributions*. For details, get Form 4972.

### Distributions From Individual Retirement Arrangements (IRAs):

Distributions from an IRA, whether from principal or earnings, are generally fully taxable when received. See Publication 590, *Individual Retirement Arrangements (IRA's),* for exceptions to this general rule, including rollovers and timely withdrawals of excess contributions. If you made nondeductible contributions to your IRA, you may have a cost basis in your IRA. The part representing a return of your nondeductible contributions is not taxed when distributed to you. A 10-percent tax in addition to the regular income tax applies to any distributions before age fifty-nine and one half, except in certain cases such as the death or disability of the IRA owner. You must withdraw the entire balance in your IRA or begin distributions by April 1 of the calendar year following the year in which you become age seventy and one half to avoid substantial additional taxes. The required minimum distributions for any later year after your seventy and one half year must be made by December 31 of that year. For example, you reached seventy and one half in 1992. By April 1, 1993, you must withdraw the minimum required distribution for 1992. You must also withdraw the 1993 minimum required distribution by December 31, 1993. Both distributions are taxable in the year received.

### Social Security and Railroad Retirement

Generally, you will owe taxes on some (but never more than half) of your Social Security and equivalent Railroad Retirement benefits if your total income (including half of your benefits) exceeds $25,000 for single and married persons (who live apart all year) filing a separate return or $32,000 for married couples who file a joint return. Married couples who live together but file separate tax returns must include part of their benefits in taxable income, regardless of the rest of their income.

**Social Security:** You should receive Form SSA-1099, Social Security Benefit Statement, if you received benefits in the tax year. This form will show any deductions made by Social Security from your total benefits, such as Medicare premiums, repayments of prior-year over-payments, etc. If you do not receive an SSA-1099 by early February or you believe the statement to be incorrect, you should call the SSA toll-free number, 1-800-234-5772.

To estimate quickly whether you must include any of your Social Security benefits in taxable income, add up your income from all sources including any tax-exempt interest you may have received and one-half of your net benefits.

If your total income is $25,000 or less and you are a single person, or a married person filing separately and did not live with your spouse at any time during the year ($32,000 for married couples filing a joint return), then none of your benefits will be included.

If your total income exceeds $25,000 and you are a single person or a married person filing separately and did not live with your spouse at any time during the year ($32,000 for married couples filing a joint return), then some of your benefits will be included. You will need to figure the taxable part of your benefits.

If you have any income and you are a married person who lived together with your spouse during the year and files a separate tax return, then some of your benefits will be includable in taxable income. For more information, get Publication 915, *Social Security Benefits and Equivalent Railroad Retirement Benefits.*

**Railroad Retirement Benefits:** A Railroad Retirement benefit is comprised of up to four different parts. Before 1984, only the supplemental annuity was taxable. Beginning in 1984, the other three parts became taxable but each in a different way. Only the Social Security equivalent portion of tier I benefits is taxed in the same manner as Social Security benefits. Tier II and the non-Social Security equivalent portion of tier I benefits are fully taxable after they exceed your contributions which were deducted during your career. Vested dual benefits are also fully taxable.

The Railroad Retirement Board will send each beneficiary a Form RRB-1099. If you receive both Social Security benefits and Railroad Retirement benefits, you should use the Railroad Retirement worksheet. More complete information can be found in Publication 575, *Pension and Annuity Income (Including Simplified General Rule)*.

### Nontaxable Income

Generally gifts and inheritances you receive are not taxable to you; the person making the gift/bequest already paid taxes, if any, on the income used to purchase the gift or to build the estate. However, if you later receive income such as interest, dividends, or rents from such property, that income is taxable to you. Department of Veterans Affairs (VA) payments and/or insurance proceeds paid at the death of the insured are usually tax free.

## Adjustments to Your Income

Once you have figured your total income, you may "adjust" it downward with any of six major adjustments to arrive at adjusted gross income. You do not have to itemize to take these adjustments to income. Employee business expenses are no longer an adjustment to income (but they are an itemized deduction on Schedule A) except for certain performing artists and handicapped employees.

**Individual Retirement Arrangements:** An IRA is a personal savings plan that lets you set aside money for your retirement. You may be able to deduct contributions you make to an IRA in whole, or in part, depending on your circumstances. Earnings and gains on your IRA generally are not taxed until they are distributed to you. Generally, you can contribute up to the lesser of your taxable compensation, or $2,000. If you (or your spouse) were covered at any time during the year by an employer's retirement plan, your deduction may be limited. If your deduction is limited, you can still make nondeductible contributions up to your remaining contribution limit. If you file a joint return with your spouse (who did not work during the year), you may be eligible to contribute up to $2,250 into two separate IRAs (one for you and one for your spouse, a spousal IRA). You can divide the contribution between the two accounts in any way except that neither account can be credited with more than $2,000. See Publication 590 for more information.

If you were age seventy and one half or older by the end of the tax year, you cannot deduct any contributions made to your IRA or treat them as nondeductible contributions.

**Keogh Plans:** You must have net earnings from self-employment to claim a deduction for payments to a Keogh (H.R. 10) plan. For information on Keogh plans, see Publication 560, *Retirement Plans for the Self-Employed*.

**One-Half of Self-Employment Tax:** If you had income from self-employment and you owe self-employment tax, you may deduct one-half of that tax. But you will first need to complete Schedule SE to figure your deduction.

**Other Adjustments to Income:** In addition, you may be eligible to take certain other adjustments to income. They include self-employed health insurance, penalty on early withdrawal of savings, alimony paid, and jury duty pay given to your employers.

## The Standard Deduction

The standard deduction reduced the need for many taxpayers to itemize their deductions. The standard deduction, which depends on your filing status (explained earlier) and whether you are age sixty-five or older or blind, is figured separately. Once you have figured your standard deduction amount, you should then decide which gives you a higher tax benefit—taking the standard deduction or itemizing your deductions on Schedule A of Form 1040.

If you are age sixty-five or older or blind in the tax year, you are entitled to a higher standard deduction amount than taxpayers under sixty-five and not blind. If you are totally blind, attach a statement to this effect to your return. If you are partially blind, you must submit with your return each year a certified statement from an eye physician or registered optometrist.

For the 1992 tax year, the standard deduction is $3,600 for single taxpayers; $3,000 for married filing separate taxpayers; $5,250 for head-of-household taxpayers; and $6,000 for qualifying widows and widowers, and married-filing-jointly taxpayers.

## Itemized Deductions

If your itemized deductions total more than your standard deduction, it will usually save you taxes to itemize. Use Schedule A (Form 1040) to itemize your deductions. These deductions can include:

**Medical and Dental Expenses:** Medical and dental expenses are payments you make for the diagnosis, treatment, or prevention of disease. They also include payments for treatment affecting any part or function of the body. Expenses for transportation to get medical care are included in medical expenses. Payments for insurance (including Medicare premiums) that provides medical care for you, your spouse, and dependents are included in medical expenses. Unreimbursed expenses are deductible to the extent they are more than 7.5 percent of your adjusted gross income. Expenses may be deducted only in the year you paid them. If you charge medical expenses on your credit card, deduct the expenses in the year the charge is made.

**Taxes:** Deductions can be taken for any real estate, personal property, and state, local, or foreign income taxes you paid during the tax year.

**Home Mortgage Interest:** Generally, home mortgage interest is any interest you pay on a loan secured by your home (main home or a second home). These loans include a:

(1) Mortgage to buy your home,

(2) Second mortgage,

(3) Line of credit, and

(4) Home equity loan.

In most cases, you will be able to deduct all of your home mortgage interest. Whether it is all deductible depends on the date you took out the mortgage, the amount of the mortgage, and your use of its proceeds. Get publication 936 for more information on home mortgage interest.

Beginning in 1991, you can no longer deduct personal interest. Personal interest is any that is not home mortgage interest, investment interest, or business interest. Personal interest includes interest you pay on car loans, installment purchases, credit cards, and personal loans.

**Charitable Contributions:** A charitable contribution is a contribution or gift to, or for the use of, a qualified organization. Any organization can tell you if it is a qualified organization. To deduct your contributions, you must make them in cash or other property before the end of your tax year.

**Casualty or Theft Losses:** You may deduct casualty losses, such as those that result from a tornado, flood, storm, fire, or auto accident (provided it was not caused by a willful act or willful negligence), or theft losses. Your casualty loss deduction is generally the lesser of (1) the decrease in fair market value of the property as a result of the casualty or theft, or (2) your adjusted basis in the property before the casualty or theft. This amount must be reduced by any insurance or other reimbursement you receive.

Your nonbusiness casualty or theft losses are deductible only to the extent that your total losses during the year exceed 10 percent of your adjusted gross income after reducing each separate casualty or theft by $100. You must use Form 4684 to figure your casualty or theft loss.

You may not deduct a casualty or theft loss that is covered by insurance unless you filed a timely insurance claim for reimbursement. However, even if you did not file an insurance claim, you may deduct the part of the loss not covered by insurance. For more information, see Publication 547, *Nonbusiness Disasters, Casualties, and Thefts*.

Miscellaneous Deductions: Miscellaneous deductions (such as professional dues, educational expenses, uniforms and other expenses) can be taken to the extent that they exceed 2 percent of your adjusted gross income. For more information, see Publication 529.

## Tax Credits

Tax credits are beneficial because they directly reduce the tax you owe. You can generally take a credit for child and dependent care expenses, if you paid someone to care for your disabled spouse, disabled dependent or child under age thirteen so you could work or look for work. See Publication 503 for more information on the *Child and Dependent Care Credit*.

You may be able to claim the credit for the elderly and the disabled if you are: (1) age sixty-five or over, or (2) under age sixty-five and retired on a permanent and total disability for which you received taxable disability benefits in the tax year, and under the mandatory retirement age. See Publication 524 if you want more information on the *Credit for the Elderly and Disabled*.

The Earned Income Credit may be available to you if you have a qualifying child living with you and meet certain earnings and income requirements. See Publication 596 for more information on the *Earned Income Credit*.

## Estate and Gift Taxes

You generally do not have to pay tax on any cash or property you receive as a gift or inheritance. Likewise, any gift or inheritance you pass on is generally tax-free to the recipient. If you make a gift of more than $10,000 ($20,000 for married couples) to any one individual in the same year, you—but not the recipient—may be required to pay a gift tax. Remember, no taxes are paid on gifts between spouses, regardless of the amount.

For decedents who died during 1992, no federal estate tax, nor any estate tax return, is due if the value of the decedent's gross estate is $600,000 or less.

For more information, get Publication 448, *Federal Estate and Gift Taxes*.

CHAPTER **14**

# VACATIONING AT HOME AND ABROAD

## Planning for Your Vacation

Whether you retire at age fifty-five or sixty-five the odds are that you have probably put off traveling to some parts of the United States or the world until that time many call the "golden years." Even if you have not yet reached your "golden years," the fact that children are on their own provides more freedom for many to give into that urge to "see some of the world before I die."

Travel can be immensely rewarding and fun. Yet, we all know people whose well-thought-out vacation turned into a nightmare because of accommodations that were less than optimal or whose vacation was overcome by unexpected events. In this chapter is included some general advice on vacations and foreign travel as a way of helping you insure that your trip is pleasurable and carefree. Most would agree that a little forethought can go a long way towards best positioning yourself to recover financially and emotionally should some unforeseen events ruin your vacation, or to avoid these problems in the first place.

There is a lot you can do to prepare for your trip. The first thing is to learn something about the places or countries you plan to visit. There are several good sources of information and they include:

- travel agents who can provide brochures and tourist information,

- local bookstores and public libraries,

- tourist information offices located in many large cities,

- airlines which may also have maps and brochures on the countries they serve,

- foreign embassies or consulates in many major cities. Look for their addresses in your local telephone directory or in the library.

The next step is to make travel, lodging, and other necessary arrangements for your vacation. Although you can try to handle these arrangements yourself, it is usually more expedient and more relaxing to deal with a reputable travel agent. Most trips and vacations you take will involve arrangements for services and accommodations that you simply can not inspect before paying for them. Also, it may not be easy for you to evaluate and compare travel and vacation options without the assistance of an experienced travel agent.

Planning a good vacation takes time. Be sure to allow yourself and your travel agent enough time to make reservations, submit payments, and receive any necessary tickets, vouchers or other documents. Talk to your travel agent as early as possible to begin making plans. Let the agent know what you plan to spend and what your expectations are.

With over 20,000 members in 125 countries, the American Society of Travel Agents (ASTA) is the oldest and perhaps the most influential travel trade association in the world. ASTA includes travel agencies, airlines, hotels, rail roads, cruise lines, tour operators, car rental companies, and travel schools. Because these travel agents are required to adhere to a code of ethics, you should consider using ASTA agents, or members of similar travel industry trade groups. For further information on ASTA and participating members contact:

American Society of Travel Agents, Inc.
1101 King Street
Alexandria, VA 22314
Phone (703) 739-2782

### Selecting a Packaged Tour

Unless you are visiting relatives, a packaged tour may be the solution to organizing a vacation. Here are some basic guidelines for selecting a reliable tour program and for choosing the right tour for you.

These days packaged tours come in many different "flavors," despite their image of being overly regimented and lacking in adventure or sophistication. Now you can select vacations that range from the most meticulously preplanned escorted tour to the free-wheeling spontaneity of a fly/drive holiday. Overall, package tours are appealing because they offer greater savings for many, and the peace of mind that comes from knowing that their vacation was planned by professionals.

One good thing to look for initially is whether your tour company is a member of the United States Tours Operators Association (USTOA). According to the association's code, the member's brochures must be clear and accurate. Membership requires companies to have been in business at least three years, carry a minimum of $1 million professional liability insurance and participate in the association's $5 Million Consumer Protection Plan. This plan protects you against financial loss resulting from bankruptcy or insolvency of active tour operators. Usually when you see the USTOA symbol in a tour brochure, it is meant to be your assurance of good value for your money, reliability, and integrity in tourism.

When choosing a tour, the most important step is to decide what kind of travel operator will provide the experience and services that you want. When reading a tour brochure, be sure you understand what is and what is not included. It's what you don't know and don't expect that can be irritating and disappointing during your trip.

Always pay close attention to the price quoted. For example, is the price all inclusive or is it for the land arrangements only? Several other factors may add to the tour price, such as optional excursions, service charges, taxes, weekend air surcharges, and peak season supplements.

Pay attention to the day-to-day itineraries featured in most tour brochures because they are a guide to what you can expect to see and do on the tour. If you are considering an escorted tour, distinguish between the cities and sites that you will simply be driving through and those you will be spending time in. Make sure you are comfortable with the amount of time spent at each location, or the amount of time spent on a bus or walking. Also, is there enough free time for shopping and other activities you want to do? When it comes to sleeping arrangements note the descriptions and ratings of the hotel featured. Keep in mind that hotel ratings in other countries may not always reflect American standards. In other words, a "deluxe" hotel in one country could differ in size, style, and degree of luxury from a similarly rated hotel in another country.

Be sure to look for the section of the brochure outlining the "conditions." This very important section usually covers details about reservations, cancellations, refunds, and availability of insurance. Other items typically covered include meals, accommodations, air transportation, sight-seeing, baggage allowance, health information, and things not included in the tour price. Go over this information carefully before reaching a decision.

Before selecting a tour operator you should find out how long the company has been in business under the same ownership, and if it was recently merged or sold, who and how experienced are the new owners. Also, how long have they been operating tours to your area or interest? You should consider purchasing default insurance that will pay if your tour operator does not perform.

## Traveling by Air

Newspaper, radio, and television advertise discount and special-rate airline tickets almost every day. The variety of air service available ranges from super premium service where a limousine picks you up at your door, to no-frills, low-cost service where you carry your own bags.

Your travel agent is a good source of information about air fares, schedules, baggage limits, and other features. In addition, travel agencies can sometimes obtain discount tickets to popular destinations. Check with your travel agent, even if the airlines are sold out.

You may have to be flexible in your travel plans in order to get the lowest fare. There may be complicated conditions you have to meet to qualify for a discount.

When making airline travel arrangements, always ask about fees or penalties for changing or canceling your reservation. Find out if there is a cut-off date for making and changing reservations without having to pay more.

Some airlines will not increase the price of your ticket after it has been issued and paid for. However, simply holding a reservation without a ticket does not guarantee the ticket price. Other airlines may reserve the right to increase your ticket price anytime before your departure. Be sure to find out which price increase policy applies to your tickets.

Your airline ticket will show the flight numbers, dates and departure times and the status of your reservation. If the "status" box is marked "OK," this means that your are confirmed. Otherwise your reservation is not certain and you may only be wait-listed.

You should reconfirm your reservation before you start your trip. Oftentimes airline flight schedules will change. On international flights, most airlines require that you reconfirm your departing and return reservations at least seventy-two hours before each flight or your reservation may be canceled.

Airlines do not guarantee their flight schedules because many things can go wrong, such as bad weather, air traffic delays, and mechanical problems. If your flight is canceled, some airlines will reschedule you on the first available flight to your destination at no additional charge.

Most airlines over-book their flights and some passengers are "bumped." If you are bumped involuntarily, you are generally entitled to be compensated. The amount depends on the price of your ticket and the length of time you are delayed.

If you are bumped involuntarily and the airline arranges substitute transportation that is scheduled to get you to your destination (including later connections) within one hour of your original scheduled arrival time, there is no compensation. If the airline arranges substitute transportation that is scheduled to arrive at your destination more than one hour but less than two hours (four hours on international flights) after your original arrival time, the airline must pay you an amount equal to the one-way fare to your final destination, with a $200 maximum. If the substitute transportation is scheduled to get you to your destination more than two hours later (four hours internationally), or if the airline does not make any substitute travel arrangements for you, the compensation doubles (200% of the fare, $400 maximum). You always get to keep your original ticket, and you can use it on another flight or have it refunded. The denied boarding compensation is essentially a payment for your inconvenience.

To qualify for compensation for being bumped, you must have a confirmed reservation, meet the ticketing or check-in deadline, and be departing from some place within the United States. No compensation is due to you for scheduled flights of sixty or less passengers, flights where a smaller plane is substituted for the original one, or flights which are chartered.

At check-in, the airline will put baggage destination tags on your luggage and give you the stubs to use as claim checks. Each tag has a three-letter code and flight number that show the baggage sorters on which plane and to which airport your luggage is supposed to go. Double-check the tag and flight number before your bags go down the conveyor belt. Also, make sure that you have put your name and address on each of your bags. Be sure all of the tabs from previous trips are removed from your bags, since they may confuse busy baggage handlers. Don't lose your claim checks — they are your only proof that you really did check bags with the airline.

If your suitcase arrives smashed or torn, the airline will usually pay for repairs. If it can not be fixed, they will negotiate a settlement to pay you its depreciated value. The same holds true for clothing packed inside. Report external damage in writing before you leave the airport.

If your bags are delayed, lost or damaged on a domestic flight, the airline may invoke a $1250 ceiling on the amount of money they will pay you. When your luggage and its contents are worth more than that, you may want to purchase "excess valuation," if available, from the airline as you check in. This will increase the carrier's potential liability. The airline may refuse to sell excess valuation on some items that are especially valuable or breakable, such as antiques, musical instruments, jewelry, manuscripts, negotiable securities, and cash.

On international trips, the liability limits are set by a treaty called the Warsaw Convention. Unless you buy excess valuation, the liability limits are 250 French gold francs for each kilo (a kilo is equal to about 2.2 pounds) of checked baggage, and the airlines have a formula for converting this limit into U.S. dollars.

The disclosure statement on the back of your ticket explains your rights and responsibilities. However, some airlines do not put all of the contract terms on the ticket, but may elect to incorporate terms by reference into a separate contract of carriage which you can inspect or request a copy of.

## Traveling Outside the United States

If you are planning a trip outside of the United States, you should check for travel advisories before finalizing your destination. The U.S. State Department issues travel advisories to alert U.S. citizens to conditions overseas that may affect them adversely. There are three types of travel advisories, including:

(1) Warning recommends deferral of travel to all or part of a country.

(2) Caution advises about unusual security conditions, including the potential for unexpected detention, unstable political conditions, or serious health problems. It is not intended to deter travel to a country.

(3) Notice provides information on situations that do not present a broad scale risk, but which could result in inconvenience or difficulty for Americans traveling abroad. Travel advisories are posted at U.S. Passport agencies and are distributed to the travel and airline industry.

Travel document requirements vary from country to country but for most you will need a passport or other proof of citizenship, plus a visa or a tourist card. You may also need evidence that you have enough money for your trip and have ongoing or return transportation tickets.

All U.S. citizens need a passport to depart or enter the United States. The only exceptions are short term travel between the U.S. and Mexico, Canada, and some countries in the Caribbean. Even if you are not required to have a passport to visit a country, U.S. Immigration requires you to prove your U.S. citizenship and identity when you reenter the United States. Make certain that you take adequate documentation to pass through U.S. Immigration upon your return. A passport is best, but other documents useful to prove citizenship include a certified copy of your birth certificate, a certificate of naturalization, a certificate of citizenship or a report of birth abroad of a citizen of the United States. To prove your identity either a valid driver's license or a government identification card that includes a photo or a physical description is typically adequate.   If you already have a passport please pay attention to the expiration date. Certain countries will not permit you to enter and will not give you a visa if the remaining validity is less than six months. And if you return to the United States with an expired passport, you are subject to a passport waiver fee of $100 at the port of entry.

All persons must have their own passport, so family members are not permitted to be included in each others' passports. For your first passport, you must appear in person with a completed from at a U.S. passport agency, federal or state court, or post office authorized to accept passport applications. You should be able to find the addresses of passport acceptance facilities in your area in the government listings of your local telephone book.

Since the flow of applications and the necessary processing time is unpredictable, you should apply for your passport several months in advance of your planned departure. Passport agencies may, however, expedite issuance in cases of genuine documented emergencies.

Be sure to safeguard your passport. Its loss could cause you unnecessary travel complications as well as significant expense. Just in case you have to replace it, photocopy the date page of your passport and keep it in a separate place from your valuables. In addition, leave the passport number, date, and place of issuance with a relative or friend in the United States.

In many cases you will need a visa from a country you plan to visit. A visa is an endorsement or stamp placed in your passport by a foreign government that permits you to visit that country for a specified purpose and a limited time. An example would be a three-month tourist visa. It is advisable to obtain visas before you leave the U.S., because you will not be able to obtain visas for some countries once you have departed. Apply directly to the embassy or consulate of each country you plan to visit. You will have to fill out a form, submit pictures, and surrender your passport where the visa will be stamped, so be prepared to wait a few weeks and apply early.

## Medical Requirements in Foreign Countries

Some countries may also require medical vaccinations. The consulate would be a good place to check. A letter from your doctor, describing preexisting medical problems, including information on prescription medicines you take, may come in handy for customs processing. You should also have the generic names of the drugs and leave them in their original, labeled containers. If you have allergies, reactions to certain medicines, or any other unique medical problems, consider wearing a medical alert bracelet or carrying a similar warning.

If you become seriously ill or injured overseas, obtaining medical treatment and hospital care can be costly. The Social Security/Medicare program does not cover hospital and medical services outside the United States. Before you leave the U.S. learn what medical services your health insurance will cover abroad.

If your health insurance policy does not cover you abroad, you should purchase a temporary health policy that does. There are several short term health and emergency assistance policies designed for travelers. For further information contact your travel or insurance agent. Consider a plan that covers bringing you home for treatment as well, because that can cost as much as $5,000, depending on your location and condition.

### Protecting Your Valuables

Safeguard your money while traveling. Nothing can take the fun out of sight-seeing faster than a stolen wallet. The first rule is: Do not carry large amounts of cash. Take most of your money in traveler's checks and remember to record the serial number, denomination, date, and location of the issuing bank. Keep this information in a safe place separate from your valuables. Record the numbers of the credit cards you take with you and keep the list separate from the cards. Leave all unnecessary credit cards at home.

Before departing, you may wish to purchase small amounts of foreign currency to use for buses, taxis, phones, or tips when you first arrive. You can purchase foreign currency at some banks, foreign exchange firms, or windows and vending machines at many international airports.

If you intend to drive overseas, check with the embassy or consulate of the countries you will visit to learn of their driver's license, road permit, and auto insurance requirements. Many countries do not recognize a U.S. driver's license. Most, however, accept an international driver's permit. The local automobile association can provide you with one but you must be at least eighteen, have two passport-sized photos, and have a valid U.S. license. Some countries require road permits instead of tolls to use their divided highways and will fine drivers without a permit.

Leave a detailed itinerary (with names, addresses, and phone numbers of persons and places you will be visiting with relatives or friends in the U.S.) so you can be reached in an emergency. Remember to also include a photocopy of your passport information.

Your trip overseas can provide you with many wonderful memories. However, there are a few things to keep in mind while you are seeing the sights and shopping. Have a reasonable amount of cash with you, but not more than you will need for a day or two. Convert your traveler's checks to a local currency as you use them, rather than all at once. If you must take jewelry or other valuables, use hotel security vaults to store them.

Your passport is the most valuable document you will carry abroad. It confirms your U.S. citizenship. Guard it carefully. Do not use it as collateral for a loan or lend it to anyone. You will probably need it when you pick up mail or check into hotels, embassies, or consulates. It is a good idea to pack an "emergency kit" to help you get a replacement passport in case yours is lost or stolen. To make a kit, obtain the date-page photocopy; write down the addresses and telephone numbers of the U.S. embassies and consulates in the countries you plan to visit; and put this information, along with two-passport-sized photographs, in a place separate from your passport.

While on the streets and in restaurants guard against theft. Coat pockets, handbags, and hip pockets are particularly susceptible to theft. Thieves will use all kinds of ploys to divert your attention just long enough to pick your pocket and grab your purse or wallet. These ploys include creating a disturbance, spilling something on your clothing, and many others. Consider not carrying a purse or wallet when going on to crowded streets. Women who carry a shoulder bag should keep it tucked under the arm and held securely. Men should put their wallets in their front trouser pockets or use money belts. Be especially cautious in a large crowd in the subway, marketplace, or even at a festival.

## Buying Merchandise In Foreign Countries

When shopping beware of purchasing souvenirs made from endangered wildlife. These species and products made from them are prohibited either by U.S. or foreign laws from import into the United States. These prohibited products include ivory, furs from spotted cats or marine animals, products from sea turtles, feathers from wild birds, many live and stuffed birds, most crocodile and caiman leather, and most coral and coral jewelry. Your wildlife souvenirs could be confiscated by the government inspectors, and you could face other penalties for attempting to bring them into the United States.

Be cautious of buying glazed ceramic ware abroad. It is possible to suffer lead poisoning if you consume food or beverages that are stored or served in improperly glazed ceramics. The U.S. Food and Drug Administration recommends that ceramic tableware purchased abroad be tested for lead release by a commercial laboratory on your return or be used for decorative purposes only.

For you antique lovers, some countries consider antiques to be national treasures and the "inalienable property of the nation." In these and other countries, customs authorities will seize illegally purchased antiques without compensation and may also levy fines on the purchaser. If you have questions about purchasing antiques, the country's tourist office can guide you.

Keep all receipts for items you buy overseas. They will be helpful in making your U.S. Customs declaration when you return.


## Obeying Foreign Laws and Regulations

While abroad, you are subject to the laws and regulations of your host country and are not protected by the U.S. Constitution and laws. Try to avoid areas of unrest and disturbance. Deal only with authorized outlets when exchanging money or buying airline tickets and travelers checks. Do not deliver a package for anyone unless you know the person well and are certain the package does not contain drugs or other contraband. And keep in mind that many countries have stiff penalties for drug violations and strictly enforce drug laws. If you should be detained by local authorities, ask to talk to a U.S. consular officer.

Under international agreements and practice, you have a right to contact an American consul. Although U.S. consuls cannot act as your attorney or get you out of jail, they can provide you with a list of local attorneys and inform you of your rights under local laws.

Should you encounter serious legal, medical, or financial difficulties while abroad, contact the nearest U.S. embassy or consulate for assistance. Consular officers cannot cash checks, lend money, or act as travel agents. However, in an emergency, they can help you get in touch with your family back home to inform them on how to wire funds to you and to let them know your situation. In the case of a death abroad, consular officials will contact the next of kin in the U.S. and will explain the local requirements. It is a worthwhile precaution to have insurance that covers the cost of local burial or shipment of remains home. Otherwise, this cost must be borne by next of kin and can be extremely expensive.

While traveling you should register at the consular section of the nearest U.S. embassy or consulate:

- if you find yourself in a country or area that is experiencing civil unrest, has an unstable political climate, or is undergoing a natural disaster, such as an earthquake or hurricane.

- if you plan to go to a country where there are no U.S. officials. In such cases, register in an adjacent country, leave an itinerary and ask about what third country may represent U.S. interests there.

- if you plan to stay in a country for longer than one month.

### Returning To The United States

On your return trip home reconfirm your reservation at least seventy-two hours before departure. Whenever possible, obtain a written confirmation. If you do it by phone, record the time, day, and the agent's name who took the call. Some countries levy an airport departure tax on travelers that can be $50 or more. Ask the airline or travel agent for details, and make certain you have enough money at the end of your trip to be able to get on the plane.

Have your passport ready when you go through immigration and customs. Also have your receipts handy in case you need to support your customs declaration. You should pack your baggage in a way to make inspection easier. For example, pack the articles you acquired abroad separately. U.S. Customs generally allows each U.S. citizen to bring back $400 worth of merchandise duty free. The next $1000 worth of items brought back for personal use or gifts is subject to duty at a flat rate of 10 percent. For many countries in the Caribbean and Central America the duty-free exemption is $600. And for the U.S. Virgin Islands, American Samoa and Guam the exemption is $1,200.

There is no limit on the amount of money or negotiable instruments which can be brought into or taken out of the United States. However, any amount over $10,000 must be reported to the U.S. Customs when you depart or enter the country. Do not bring home any fresh fruit or vegetables because they may be confiscated.

If you encounter problems during your trip with the tour operator, airlines, hotel, or others, try to resolve it on the spot rather than wait. If your complaint does not get resolved immediately, at least you will have registered your grievance. Keep notes that include the names of the people with whom you speak and the date, time, and location of your conversations. Keep all receipts if you have to spend money to resolve a problem. If your baggage is lost or delayed, file a claim immediately to protect your rights. Be sure to obtain and retain a copy of the claim.

Should you have to pursue a complaint after returning from your trip, first review the materials you were given by the travel agent or supplier. If you are satisfied that your complaint has merit, write a letter to the firm that you feel is responsible. Outline the nature of your complaint, as well as the steps you feel should be taken to rectify the problem. Include copies of supporting documentation. You should also seek the assistance of your travel agent, who will often pursue the matter for you. If you are unable to get satisfactory response to you complaint, you should contact a Better Business Bureau, government consumer affairs office, American Society of Travel Agents, Unites States Tour Operators Association, or a lawyer if necessary.

Travel during your senior years can be one of your most enjoyable and enriching pastimes. To ensure against problems, do your home work, plan early and follow the guidelines discussed earlier in this chapter.

Bon Voyage!

# APPENDIX

SOURCE:

CONSUMER'S RESOURCE HANDBOOK
U.S. OFFICE OF CONSUMER AFFAIRS

## Better Business Bureaus

Better Business Bureaus (BBBs) are non-profit organizations sponsored by local businesses. BBBs offer a variety of consumer services. For example, they can provide consumer education materials, answer consumer questions, mediate and arbitrate complaints, and provide general information on companies' consumer complaint records.

Each BBB has its own policy about reporting information. It might or might not tell you the nature of the complaint against a business, but all will tell you if a complaint has been registered. Many of the BBBs accept written complaints and will contact a firm on your behalf. BBBs do not judge or rate individual products or brands, handle complaints concerning the prices of goods or services, or give legal advice. However, many bureaus do offer binding arbitration, a form of dispute resolution, to those who ask for it. If you need help with a consumer question or complaint, call your local BBB to ask about their services.

This list includes the local BBBs in the United States.

### National Headquarters:

Council of Better Business Bureaus, Inc.
4200 Wilson Boulevard
Arlington, VA 22203
(703) 276-0100

# Local Bureaus

## Alabama

P.O. Box 55268
Birmingham, AL 35255-5268
(205) 558-2222

118 Woodburn Street
Dothan, AL 36301
(205) 792-3084

P.O. Box 383
Huntsville, AL 35801
(205) 522-1640

707 Van Antwerp Building
Mobile, AL 36104
(205) 262-5606

## Alaska

3380 C Street, Suite 103
Anchorage, AK 99503
(907) 562-0704

## Arizona

4428 North 12th Street
Phoenix, AZ 85014-4585
(602) 264-1721

50 West Drachman Street, Suite 103
Tucson, AZ 85705
(602) 622-7651 (inquiries)
(602) 622-7654 (complaints)

## Arkansas

1415 S. University
Little Rock, AR 72204
(501) 664-7274

## California

705 Eighteenth Street
Bakersfield, CA 93301-4882
(805) 322-2074

P.O. Box 970
Colton, CA 92324-0522
(714) 825-7280

6101 Ball Rd., Suite 309
Cypress, CA 90630
(714) 527-0680

1398 West Indianapolis, Suite 102
Fresno, CA 93705
(209) 222-8111

494 Alvarado Street, Suite C
Monterey, CA 93940
(408) 372-3149

510 16th Street
Oakland, CA 94612
(415) 839-5900

400 S Street
Sacramento, CA 95814
(916) 443-6843

3111 Camino Del Rio, North, Suite 600
San Diego, CA 92108-1729
(619) 281-6422

33 New Montgomery St. Tower
San Francisco, CA 94105
(415) 243-9999

1505 Meridian Avenue
San Jose, CA 95125
(408) 978-8700

P.O. Box 294
San Mateo, CA 94401
(415) 696-1240

P.O. Box 746
Santa Barbara, CA 93102
(805) 963-8657

300 B Street
Santa Rosa, CA 95401
(707) 577-0300

1111 North Center Street
Stockton, CA 95202-1383
(209) 948-4880,4881

## Colorado

P.O. Box 7970
Colorado Springs, CO 80933
(719) 636-1155

1780 South Bellaire, Suite 700
Denver, CO 80222
(303) 758-2100 *(inquiries)*
(303) 758-2212 *(complaints)*

1730 S. College Ave., Suite 303
Fort Collins, CO 80525
(303) 484-1348

119 West 6th Street, Suite 203
Pueblo, CO 81003-3119
(719) 542-6464

## Connecticut

2345 Black Rock Turnpike
Fairfield, CT 06430
(302) 374-6161

2090 Silas Deane Highway
Rocky Hill, CT 06067-2311
(203) 529-3575

100 South Turnpike Road
Wallingford, CT 06492-4395
(203) 269-2700 *(inquiries)*
(203) 269-4457 *(complaints)*

## Delaware

2055 Limestone Road, Suite 200
Wilmington, DE 19808
(302) 996-9200

## District of Columbia

1012 14th Street, N.W.
Washington, DC 20005-3410
(202) 393-8000

## Florida

P.O. Box 7950
Clearwater, FL 34618-7950
(813) 535-5522

2976-E Cleveland Avenue
Fort Myers, FL 33901
(813) 334-7331

3100 University Blvd., South, Suite 239
Jacksonville, FL 32216
(904) 721-2288

2605 Maitland Center Parkway
Maitland, FL 32751-7147
(407) 660-9500

16291 Northwest 57th Avenue
Miami, FL 33014-6709
(305) 625-0307 *(inquiries for Dade County)*
(305) 625-1302 *(complaints for Dade County)*
(305) 542-2803 *(inquiries for Broward County)*
(305) 527-1643 *(complaints for Broward County)*

P.O. Box 1511
Pensacola, FL 32597-1511
(904) 433-6111

1950 SE Port St. Lucie Blvd., Suite 211
Port St. Lucie, FL 34952
(407) 878-2010
(407) 337-2083 *(Martin County)*

2247 Palm Beach Lakes Blvd., Suite 211
West Palm Beach, FL 33409
(407) 686-2200

## Georgia

1319-B Dawson Road
Albany, GA 31707
1 (800) 868-4222 *(toll free)*

100 Edgewood Avenue, Suite 1012
Atlanta, GA 30303
(404) 688-4910

P.O. Box 2085
Augusta, GA 30903
(404) 722-1574

P.O. Box 2587
Columbus, GA 31902
(404) 324-0712

1765 Shurling Drive
Macon, GA 31211
(912) 742-7999

P.O. Box 13856
Savannah, GA 31416-0956
(912) 354-7521

## Hawaii

1600 Kapiolani Boulevard, Suite 714
Honolulu, HI 96814
(808) 942-96814

## Idaho

1333 West Jefferson
Boise, ID 83702
(208) 342-4649
(208) 467-5547 *(Canyon County)*

545 Shoup Avenue, Suite 210
Idaho Falls, ID 83402
(208) 523-9754

## Illinois

211 W. Wacker Drive
Chicago, IL 60606
(312) 444-1188 *(inquiries)*
(312) 346-3313 *(complaints)*

3024 West Lake
Peoria, IL 61615
(309) 688-3741

810 East State Street, 3rd Floor
Rockford, IL 61104
(815) 963-2222

## Indiana

P.O. Box 405
Elkhart, IN 46515-0405
(219) 262-8996

4004 Morgan Avenue, Suite 201
Evansville, IN 47715
(812) 473-0202

1203 Webster Street
Fort Wayne, IN 46802
(219) 423-4433

4231 Cleveland Street
Gary, IN 46408
(219) 980-1511

Victoria Centre
22 East Washington Street, Suite 200
Indianapolis, IN 46204
(317) 488-2222
1 (800) 552-4631 *(toll free in IN)*

Consumer Education Council *(non-BBB)*
BSW WB 150
Muncie, IN 47306
(317) 285-5668

52303 Emmons Road, Suite 9
South Bend, IN 46637
(219) 277-9121

## Iowa

852 Middle Road, Suite 290
Bettendorf, IA 52722-4100
(319) 355-6344

615 Insurance Exchange Building
Des Moines, IA 50309
(515) 243-8137

318 Badgerow Building
Sioux City, IA 51101
(712) 252-4501

## Kansas

501 Jefferson, Suite 24
Topeka, KS 66607-1190
(913) 232-0454

300 Kaufman Building
Wichita, KS 67202
(316) 263-3146

## Kentucky

311 West Short Street
Lexington, KY 40507
(606) 259-1008

844 South 4th Street
Louisville, KY 40203-2186
(502) 583-6546

## Louisiana

1605 Murray St., Suite 117
Alexandria, LA 71301
(318) 473-4494

2055 Wooddale Boulevard
Baton Rouge, LA 70806-1519
(504) 926-3010

501 East Main Street
Houma, LA 70360
(504) 868-3456

P.O. Box 30297
Lafayette, LA 70593-0297
(318) 981-3497

P.O. Box 1681
Lake Charles, LA 70602
(318) 433-1633

141 De Siard Street, Suite 808
Monroe, LA 71210-7380
(318) 387-4600, 8421

1539 Jackson Avenue
New Orleans, LA 70170-3400
(504) 581-6222

1401 North Market Street
Shreveport, LA 71107-6525
(318) 221-8352

## Maine

812 Stevens Avenue
Portland, ME 04103
(207) 878-2715

## Maryland

2100 Huntingdon Avenue
Baltimore, MD 21211-3215
(301) 347-3990

## Massachusetts

20 Park Plaza, Suite 820
Boston, MA 02116-4404
(617) 426-9000
1 (800) 422-2811 *(toll-free in MA)*

293 Bridge Street, Suite 320
Springfield, MA 01103
(413) 734-3114

P.O. Box 379
Worcester, MA 01601
(508) 755-2548

## Michigan

620 Trust Building
Grand Rapids, MI 49503
(616) 774-8236

30555 Southfield Road, Suite 200
Southfield, MI 48076-7751
(313) 644-1012 *(inquiries)*
(313) 644-9136 *(complaints)*
(313) 644-9152 *(Auto Line)*
(800) 955-5100 *(toll-free nationwide auto line)*

## Minnesota

2706 Gannon Road
St. Paul, MN 55116
(612) 699-1111

## Mississippi

460 Briarwood Drive, Suite 340
Jackson, MS 39206-3088
(601) 956-8282
1 (800) 274-7222 *(toll free in MS)*
(601) 957-2886 *(automotive complaints only)*

## Missouri

306 East 12th Street, Suite 1024
Kansas City, MO 64106-2418
(816) 421-7800

5100 Oakland Avenue, Suite 200
St. Louis, MO 63110
(314) 531-3300

205 Park Central East, Suite 509
Springfield, MO 65806
(417) 863-9231

## Nebraska

719 North 48th Street
Lincoln, NE 68504-3491
(402) 467-3033

## Nevada

1022 E. Sahara Avenue
Las Vegas, NV 89104-1515
(702) 735-6900, 1969

P.O. Box 21269
Reno, NV 89515-1269
(702) 322-0657

## New Hampshire

410 South Main Street
Concord, NH 03301
(603) 224-1991

## New Jersey

494 Broad Street
Newark, NJ 07102
(201) 642-INFO

2 Forest Avenue
Paramus, NJ 07652
(201) 845-4044

1721 Route 37
East Toms River, NJ 08753-8239
(201) 270-5577

1700 Whitehorse
Hamilton Square, Suite D-5
Trenton, NJ 08690
(609) 588-0808 *(Mercer County)*

P.O. Box 303
Westmont, NJ 08108-0303
(609) 854-8467

## New Mexico

4600-A Montgomery NE.
Suite 200
Albuquerque, NM 87109
(505) 884-0500
1 (800) 445-1461*(toll-free in NM)*

308 North Locke
Farmington, NM 87401
(505) 326-6501

2407 W. Picacho, Suite B-2
Las Cruces, NM 88005
(505) 524-3130

## New York

346 Delaware Avenue
Buffalo, NY 14202
(716) 856-7180

266 Main Street
Farmingdale, NY 11735
(516) 420-0500
1 (800) 955-5100
*(toll-free Auto Line)*

257 Park Avenue South
New York, NY 10010
(900) 463-6222 *($.85 per minute)*

1122 Sibley Tower
Rochester, NY 14604-1084
(716) 546-6776

847 James Street, Suite 200
Syracuse, NY 13203
(315) 479-6635

1211 Route 9
Wappingers Falls, NY 12590
(914) 297-6550
1 (800) 955-5100 *(toll-free Auto line)*

30 Glenn Street
White Plains, NY 10603
(914) 428-1230, 1231
1 (800) 955-5100 *(toll-free Auto Line)*

## North Carolina

801 BB&T Building
Asheville, NC 28801
(704) 253-2392

1130 East Third Street, Suite 400
Charlotte, NC 28204-2626
(704) 332-7151

3608 West Friendly Avenue
Greensboro, NC 27410
(919) 852-4240, 4241, 4242

P.O. Box 1882
Hickory, NC 28603
(704) 464-0372

3120 Poplarwood Court, Suite 101
Raleigh, NC 27604-1080
(919) 872-9240

2110 Cloverdale Avenue, Suite 2-B
Winston-Salem, NC 27103
(919) 725-8348

## Ohio

222 West Market Street
Akron, OH 44303-2111
(216) 253-4590

1434 Cleveland Avenue, NW
Canton, OH 44703
(216) 454-9401

898 Walnut Street
Cincinnati, OH 45202
(513) 421-3015

2217 East 9th St., Suite 200
Cleveland, OH 44115-1299
(216) 241-7678

527 South High Street
Columbus, OH 43215
(614) 221-6336

40 West Fourth Street
Suite 1250
Dayton, OH 45402
(513) 222-5825
1 (800) 521-8357
*(toll free in OH)*

P.O. Box 269
Lima, OH 45802
(419) 223-7010

130 West 2nd Street
Mansfield, OH 44902-1915
(419) 522-1700

425 Jefferson Avenue
Suite 909
Toledo, OH 43604-1055
(419) 241-6276

345 N. Market, Suite 202
Wooster, OH 44691
(216) 263-6444

P.O. Box 1495
Youngstown, OH 44501-1495
(216) 744-3111

## Oklahoma

17 South Dewey
Oklahoma City, OK 73102
(405) 239-6860 *(inquiries)*
(405) 239-6081 *(inquiries)*
(405) 239-6083 *(complaints)*

6711 S. Yale, Suite 230
Tulsa, OK 74136-3327
(918) 492-1266

## Oregon

610 S.W. Adler St., Suite 615
Portland, OR 97205
(503) 226-3981
1 (800) 488-4166 *(toll-free in OR)*

## Pennsylvania

528 North New Street
Bethlehem, PA 18018
(215) 866-8780

6 Marion Court
Lancaster, PA 17602
(717) 291-1151
(717) 232-2800 *(Harrisburg)*
(717) 846-2700 *(York County)*
(717) 394-9318 *(Auto Line)*

P.O. Box 2297
Philadelphia, PA 19103-0297
(215) 496-1000

610 Smithfield Street
Pittsburgh, PA 15222
(412) 456-2700

P.O. Box 993
Scranton, PA 18501
(717) 342-9129, 655-0445

## Puerto Rico

Condominium Olimpo Plaza, Suite 208
1002 Munoz Rivera Avenue
Rio Piedras, PR 00927
(809) 756-5400, 767-0446

## Rhode Island

Bureau Park
P.O. Box 1300
Warwick, RI 02887-1300
(401) 785-1212 *(inquiries)*
(401) 785-1213 *(complaints)*

## South Carolina

1830 Bull Street
Columbia, SC 29201
(803) 254-2525

311 Pettigru Street
Greenville, SC 29601
(803) 242-5052

1310-G Azalea Court
Myrtle Beach, SC 29577
(803) 297-8667

## Tennessee

P.O. Box 1178 TCAS
Blountville, TN 37617
(615) 323-6311

1010 Market Street, Suite 200
Chattanooga, TN 37402-2614
(615) 266-6144 *(also serves Whitfield and Murray counties in GA)*
(615) 479-6096 *(Bradley County only)*

900 East Hill Avenue, Suite 165
Knoxville, TN 37915-2525
(615) 522-2552

P.O. Box 750704
Memphis, TN 38175-0704
(901) 795-8771

Sovron Plaza, Suite 1830
Nashville, TN 37239
(615) 254-5872

## Texas

3300 S. 14th St., Suite 307
Abilene, TX 79605
(915) 691-1533

P.O. Box 1905
Amarillo, TX 79105-1905
(806) 379-6222

708 Colorado, Suite 720
Austin, TX 78701-3028
(512) 476-1616

P.O. Box 2988
Beaumont, TX 77704-2988
(409) 835-5348

202 Varisco Building
Bryan, TX 77803
(409) 823-8148, 8149

4535 S. Padre Island Drive, Suite 28
Corpus Christi, TX 78411
(512) 854-2892

2001 Bryan Street, Suite 850
Dallas, TX 75201
(214) 220-2000
1 (800) 442-1456 *(toll-free in TX)*

5160 Montana, Lower Level
El Paso, TX 79903
(915) 772-2727

512 Main Street, Suite 807
Fort Worth, TX 76102
(817) 332-7585

2707 North Loop West, Suite 900
Houston, TX 77008
(713) 868-9500

P.O. Box 1178
Lubbock, TX 79408-1178
(806) 763-0459

P.O. Box 60206
Midland, TX 79711-0206
1 (800) 592-4433
 *(toll-free in 915 area code)*

P.O. Box 3366
San Angelo, TX 76902-3366
(915) 949-2989

1800 Northeast Loop 410, Suite 400
San Antonio, TX 78217
(512) 828-9441

P.O. Box 6652
Tyler, TX 75711-6652
(903) 581-5704

P.O. Box 7203
Waco, TX 76714-7203
(817) 772-7530

P.O. Box 69
Weslaco, TX 78596-0069
(512) 968-3678

1106 Brook Street
Wichita Falls, TX 76301-5079
(817) 723-5526

## Utah

1588 South Main Street
Salt Lake City, UT 84115
(801) 487-4656

## Virginia

4022B Plank Road
Fredericksburg, VA 22407
(703) 786-8497

3608 Tidewater Drive
Norfolk, VA 23509-1499
(804) 627-5651

701 East Franklin Street
Suite 712
Richmond, VA 23219
(804) 648-0016

31 W. Campbell Avenue
Roanoke, VA 24011-1301
(703) 342-3455

## Washington

127 West Canal Drive
Kennewick, WA 99336-3819
(509) 582-0222

2200 Sixth Avenue, Suite 828
Seattle, WA 98121-1857
(206) 448-8888
(206) 448-6222
*(24-hour business reporting system)*

South 176 Stevens
Spokane, WA 99204-1393
(509) 747-1155

P.O. Box 1274
Tacoma, WA 98401-1274
(206) 383-5561

P.O. Box 1584
Yakima, WA 98907-1584
(509) 248-1326

## Wisconsin

740 North Plankinton Avenue
Milwaukee, WI 53203
(414) 273-1600 *(inquiries)*
(414) 273-0123 *(complaints)*

## Wyoming

BBB/Idaho Falls *(serves Teton, Park and Lincoln counties in Wyoming)*
545 Shoup Avenue, Suite 210
Idaho Falls, ID 83402
(208) 523-9754

BBB-Fort Collins
*(serves all other Wyoming Counties)*
1730 South College Avenue, Suite 303
Fort Collins, CO 80525
1 (800) 873-3222 *(toll-free in WY)*

## State Government Consumer Protection Offices

## Alabama

Consumer Protection Division
Office of Attorney General
11 South Union Street
Montgomery, AL 36130
(205) 242-7334
1 (800) 392-5658 (toll-free in AL)

## Arizona

Consumer Protection
Office of the Attorney General
1275 West Washington Street, Room 259
Phoenix, AZ 85007
(602) 542-3702
(602) 542-5763
(consumer information and complaints)
1 (800) 352-8431 (toll-free in AZ)

Consumer Protection
Office of the Attorney General
402 West Congress Street, Suite 315
Tucson, AZ 85701
(602) 628-6504

## Arkansas

Consumer Protection Division
Office of Attorney General
200 Tower Building
323 Center Street
Little Rock, AR 72201
1 (800) 482-8982

## California

California Dept of Consumer Affairs
400 R Street, Suite 1040
Sacramento, CA 95814
(916) 445-0660 *(complaint assistance)*
(916) 445-1254 *(consumer information)*
(916) 522-1799 *(TDD)*
1 (800) 344-9940 *(toll-free in CA)*

Office of Attorney General
Public Inquiry Unit
P.O. Box 944255
Sacramento, CA 94244-2550
(916) 322-3360
1 (800) 952-5225 *(toll-free in CA)*
1 (800) 952-5548 *(toll-free TDD in CA)*

Bureau of Automotive Repair
California Dept of Consumer Affairs
10240 Systems Parkway
Sacramento, CA 95827
(916) 366-5100
(800) 952-5210 *(toll-free in CA-auto repair only)*

## Colorado

Consumer Protection Unit
Office of Attorney General
110 16th Street, 10th Floor
Denver, CO 80202
(303) 620-4500

Consumer and Food Specialist
Department of Agriculture
700 Kipling Street, Suite 4000
Lakewood, CO 80215-5894
(303) 239-4114

## Delaware

Division of Consumer Affairs
Department of Community Affairs
820 North French Street, 4th Floor
Wilmington, DE 19801
(302) 577-3250

Economic Crime & Consumer Protection
Office of Attorney General
820 North French Street
Wilmington, DE 19801
(302) 577-3250

## District of Columbia

Department of Consumer and
Regulatory Affairs
614 H Street, N.W.
Washington, DC 20001
(202) 727-7000

## Florida

Department of Agriculture and
Consumer Services
Division of Consumer Services
218 Mayo Building
Tallahassee, FL 32399
(904) 488-2226
(800) 327-3382 *(toll-free information and education in FL)*
(800) 321-5366 *(toll-free lemon law in FL)*

Consumer Litigation Section
The Capitol
Tallahassee, FL 32399-1050
(904) 488-9105

Consumer Division
Office of Attorney General
4000 Hollywood Boulevard
Suite 505 South
Hollywood, FL 33021
(305) 985-4780

## Georgia

Governors Office of Consumer Affairs
2 Martin Luther King, Jr. Drive, S.E.
Plaza Level—East Tower
Atlanta, GA 30334
(404) 651-8600
(404) 656-3790
1 (800) 869-1123 *(toll-free in GA)*

## Hawaii

Office of Consumer Protection
Department of Commerce and
Consumer Affairs
828 Fort St. Mall, Suite 2000B
P.O. Box 3767
Honolulu, HI 96812-3767
(808) 586-2630

## Idaho

Office of the Attorney General
Consumer Protection Unit
Statehouse, Room 113A
Boise, ID 83720-1000
(208) 334-2424
1 (800) 432-3545 *(toll-free in ID)*

## Illinois

Governor's Office of Citizen's Assistance
222 South College
Springfield, IL 62706
(217) 782-0244
1 (800) 642-3112 *(toll-free in IL)*

Consumer Protection Division
Office of Attorney General
100 West Randolph, 12th Floor
Chicago, IL 60601
(312) 814-3580
(312) 793-2852 *(TDD)*

Department of Citizen Rights
100 West Randolph, 13th Floor
Chicago, IL 60601
(312) 814-3289

## Indiana

Consumer Protection Division
Office of Attorney General
219 State House
Indianapolis, IN 46204
(317) 232-6330
1 (800) 382-5516
*(toll-free in IN)*

## Iowa

Consumer Protection Division
Office of Attorney General
1300 East Walnut Street, 2nd Floor
Des Moines, IA 50319
(515) 261-5926

## Kansas

Consumer Protection Division
Office of Attorney General
301 West 10th
Kansas Judicial Center
Topeka, KS 66612-1597
(913) 296-3751
1 (800) 432-2310 *(toll-free in KS)*

## Kentucky

Consumer Protection Division
Office of Attorney General
209 Saint Clair Street
Frankfort, KY 40601-1875
1 (800) 432-9257 *(toll-free in KY)*

## Louisiana

Consumer Protection Section
Office of Attorney General
State Capitol Building
P.O. Box 94005
Baton Rouge, LA 70804-9005
(504) 342-7373

## Maine

Superintendent
Bureau of Consumer Credit Protection
State House Station No. 35
Augusta, ME 04333-0035
(207) 582-8718
1 (800) 332-8529 *(toll-free)*

Consumer and Antitrust Division
Office of Attorney General
State House Station No. 6
Augusta, ME 04333
(207) 289-3716 *(9 A.M.-1 P.M.)*

## Maryland

Consumer Protection Division
Office of Attorney General
200 St. Paul Place
Baltimore, MD 21202-2021
(301) 528-8662
1 (800) 969-5766 *(toll-free)*

## Massachusetts

Consumer Protection Division
Department of Attorney General
131 Tremont Street
Boston, MA 02111
(617) 727-8400

## Michigan

Consumer Protection Division
Office of Attorney General
P.O. Box 30213
Lansing, MI 48909
(517) 373-1140

Michigan Consumers Council
414 Hollister Building
106 West Allegan Street
Lansing, MI 48933
(517) 373-0947

## Minnesota

Office of Consumer Services
Office of Attorney General
117 University Avenue
St. Paul, MN 55155
(612) 296-2331

## Mississippi

Consumer Protection Division
Office of Attorney General
P.O. Box 22947
Jackson, MS 39225-2947
(601) 354-6018

## Missouri

Office of the Attorney General
Consumer Complaints or Problems
P.O. Box 899
Jefferson City, MO 65102
(314) 751-3321
1 (800) 392-8222 *(toll-free in MO)*

## Montana

Consumer Affairs Unit
Department of Commerce
1424 Ninth Avenue
Helena, MT 59620
(406) 444-4312

## Nebraska

Consumer Protection Division
Department of Justice
2115 State Capitol
P.O. Box 98920
Lincoln, NE 68509
(402) 471-2682

## Nevada

Commissioner of Consumer Affairs
Department of Commerce
State Mail Room Complex
Las Vegas, NV 89158
(702) 486-7355
1 (800) 992-0900 *(toll-free in NV)*

## New Hampshire

Consumer Protection & Antitrust Bureau
Office of Attorney General
State House Annex
Concord, NH 03301
(603) 271-3641

## New Jersey

Divison of Consumer Affairs
P.O. Box 45027
Newark, NJ 07101
(201) 648-4010

Department of the Public Advocate
CN 850, Justice Complex
Trenton, NJ 08625
(609) 292-7087
1 (800) 792-8600 *(toll-free in NJ)*

## New Mexico

Consumer Protection Division
Office of Attorney General
P.O. Drawer 1508
Santa Fe, NM 87504
(505) 827-6060
1 (800) 432-2070 *(toll-free in NM)*

## New York

New York State Consumer
Protection Board
99 Washington Avenue
Albany, NY 12210-2891
(518) 474-8583

Bureau of Consumer Frauds & Protection
Office of Attorney General
State Capitol
Albany, NY 12224
(518) 474-5481

## North Carolina

Consumer Protection Section
Office of Attorney General
Raney Building
P.O. Box 629
Raleigh, NC 27602
(919) 733-7741

## Ohio

Consumer Frauds and Crimes Section
Office of Attorney General
20 East Broad Street
State Office Tower, 25th Floor
Columbus, OH 43266-0410
(614) 466-4986 *(complaints)*
1 (800) 282-0515 *(toll-free in OH)*

## Oklahoma

Office of Attorney General
420 West Main, Suite 550
Oklahoma City, OK 73102
(405) 521-4274

Department of Consumer Credit
4545 Lincoln Blvd., Suite 104
Oklahoma City, OK 73105-3408
(405) 521-3653

## Oregon

Financial Fraud Section
Department of Justice
Justice Building
Salem, OR 97310
(503) 378-4320

## Pennsylvania

Bureau of Consumer Protection
Office of Attorney General
Strawberry Square, 14th Floor
Harrisburg, PA 17120
(717) 787-9707
1 (800) 441-2555 *(toll-free in PA)*

## Puerto Rico

Department of Consumer Affairs (DACO)
Minillas Station, P.O. Box 41059
Santurce, PR 00940
(809) 721-0940

Department of Justice
P.O. Box 192
San Juan, PR 00902
(809) 721-2900

## Rhode Island

Consumer Protection Division
Department of Attorney General
72 Pine Street
Providence, RI 02903
(401) 277-2104
1 (800) 852-7776 (toll-free in RI)

Rhode Island Consumers' Council
365 Broadway
Providence, RI 02909
(401) 277-2764

## South Carolina

Consumer Fraud and Antitrust Section
Office of Attorney General
P.O. Box 11549
Columbia, SC 29211
(803) 734-3970

Department of Consumer Affairs
P.O. Box 5757
Columbia, SC 29250-5757
(803) 734-9452
1 (800) 922-1594 *(toll-free in SC)*

## South Dakota

Division of Consumer Affairs
Office of Attorney General
500 East Capitol, State Capitol Building
Pierre, SC 57501-5070
(605) 773-4400

## Tennessee

Antitrust & Consumer Protection Div.
Office of Attorney General
450 James Robertson Parkway
Nashville, TN 37243-0485
(615) 741-2672

Division of Consumer Affairs
Department of Commerce and
Insurance
500 James Robertson Parkway
5th Floor
Nashville, TN 37243-0600
(615) 741-4737
1 (800) 342-8385
*(toll-free in TN)*

## Texas

Assistant Attorney General and Chief
Consumer Protection Division
Office of Attorney General
P.O. Box 12548
Austin, TX 78711
(512) 463-2070

## Utah

Division of Consumer Protection
Department of Commerce
160 East 3rd South
P.O. Box 45802
Salt Lake City, UT 84145-0802
(801) 530-6601

## Vermont

Public Protection Division
Office of Attorney General
109 State Street
Montpelier, VT 05609-1001
(802) 828-3171

## Virginia

Antitrust and Consumer
Litigation Section
Office of Attorney General
Supreme Court Building
101 North Eighth Street
Richmond, VA 23219
(804) 786-2116
1 (800) 451-1525 *(toll-free in VA)*

Division of Consumer Affairs
Department of Agriculture and
Consumer Services
Room 101, Washington Building
1100 Bank Street
P.O. Box 1163
Richmond, VA 23219
(804) 786-2042

## Washington

Consumer and Business
Fair Practices Division
Office of the Attorney General
111 Olympia Avenue, NE
Olympia, WA 98501
(206) 753-6210

## West Virginia

Consumer Protection Division
Office of Attorney General
812 Quarrier Street, 6th Floor
Charleston, WV 25301
(304) 348-8986
1 (800) 368-8808 *(toll-free in WV)*

## Wisconsin

Division of Trade & Consumer Protection
Department of Agriculture, Trade
and Consumer Protection
801 West Badger Road
P.O. Box 8911
Madison, WI 53708
(608) 266-9836
1 (800) 422-7128 *(toll-free in WI)*

## Wyoming

Office of Attorney General
123 Capital Building
Cheyenne, WY 82002
(307) 777-7874

# Selected Federal Agencies

**Commission on Civil Rights**
1121 Vermont Avenue, N.W., Suite 800
Washington, DC 20425
1 (800) 552-6843
*(toll-free complaint referral outside DC)*
(202) 376-8512 *(complaint referral in DC)*

**Commodity Futures Trading
Commission (CFTC)**
2033 K Street, N.W.
Washington, DC 20581
(202) 254-3067 *(complaints only)*
(202) 254-8630 *(information)*

**Consumer Information Center (CIC)**
Pueblo, CO 81009
*You can obtain a free* Consumer
Information Catalog *by writing to
the above address or by calling*
(719) 948-4000.

**Department of Agriculture
Agricultural Marketing Service**
Washington, DC 20250
(202) 447-8998

**Department of Agriculture
Cooperative Extension Service**
Washington, DC 20250
(202) 447-3029

**Department of Agriculture
Inspector General's Hotline**
Office of the Inspector General
P.O. Box 23399
Washington, DC 20026
1 (800) 424-9121 *(toll-free)*

**Department of Agriculture
Office of the Consumer Advisor**
Washington, DC 20250
(202) 382-9681

**Department of Commerce
Office of Consumer Affairs**
Room 5718
Washington, DC 20230
(202) 377-5001

Department of Defense
Office of National Ombudsman
National Committee for Employer
Support of the Guard and Reserve
1555 Wilson Boulevard, Suite 200
Arlington, VA 22209-2405
(703) 696-1400
1 (800) 336-4590 *(toll-free outside DC metropolitan area) Provides assistance with employer/employee problems for members of the Guard and Reserve and their employers.*

Department of Education
Clearinghouse on Disability Information
OSERS
Room 330 C Street, S.W.
Washington, DC 20202-2524
(202) 732-1241

Department of Education
Federal Student Financial Aid Programs
Public Documents Distribution Center
31451 United Avenue
Pueblo, CO 81009-8109
(202) 708-8391

Department of Energy
Office of Consumer & Public Liaison
Washington, DC 20585
(202) 586-5373

Department of Health & Human Services
AIDS Hotline
*(Acquired Immune Deficiency Syndrome)*
1 (800) 342-AIDS *(toll-free)*

Department of Health & Human Services
Cancer Hotline
1(800) 4-CANCER *(toll-free)*

Food and Drug Administration (FDA)
*Look in your telephone directory
under "U.S. Government, Health and
Human Services Department,
Food and Drug Administration"*

Department of Health & Human Services
Consumer Affairs and Information Staff
Food and Drug Administration
(HFE-88)
5600 Fishers Lane, Room 16085
Rockville, MD 20857
(301) 443-3170

Department of Health & Human Services
Division of Beneficiary Services
Health Care Financing Administration
(HCFA)
6325 Security Boulevard
Baltimore, MD 21207
1 (800) 638-6833 *(toll free)*

Department of Health & Human Services
Inspector General's Hotline
HHS/OIG/Hotline
P.O. Box 17303
Baltimore, MD 21203-7303
1 (800) 368-5779 *(toll-free)*

Department of Health & Human Services
National Health Information Center
P.O. Box 1133
Washington, DC 20013-1133
(301) 565-4167 *(Washington Metro Area)*
1 (800) 336-4797 *(toll-free)*

Department of Health & Human Services
Office of Prepaid Health Care
Operations and Oversight
HCFA
Washington, DC 20201
(202) 619-3555

Department of Health & Human Services
Second Surgical Opinion Program
Washington, DC 20201
1 (800) 838-6833 *(toll-free outside DC)*

Department of Health & Human Services
Social Security Administration
1 (800) SSA-1213 *(toll-free)*

Department of Housing and
Urban Development
HUD Fraud Hotline
(202) 708-4200
1 (800) 347-3735  *(toll-free outside DC)*

Department of Housing and
Urban Development
Interstate Land Sales Registration Division
Room 9158
Washington, DC 20410
(202) 708-2210

Department of Housing and
Urban Development
Office of Fair Housing and
Equal Opportunity
Room 5100
Washington, DC 20410
1 (800) 424-8590  *(toll-free outside DC)*

Department of the Interior
Consumer Affairs Administrator
Office of the Secretary
Washington, DC 20240
(202) 208-5521

Department of the Interior
National Park Service
Washington, DC 20240
(202) 208-4917

Department of Justice
Antitrust Division
Washington, DC 20530
(202) 514-2401

Department of Justice
Civil Rights Division
*Look in your telephone directory under
"U.S. Government, Justice Department,
Civil Rights Division." If it does not ap-
pear, call the appropriate FIC number
or contact:*

Civil Rights Division
Department of Justice
Washington, DC 20530
(202) 514-2151

Department of Justice
Federal Bureau of Investigation (FBI)
*Look inside the front cover of your telephone
directory for the number of the nearest FBI
office. If it does not appear, look under
"U.S. Government, Federal Bureau of
Investigation." You may also contact:*

Federal Bureau of Investigation
Washington, DC 20535
(202) 324-3000

Department of Justice
Immigration and Naturalization Service
*Look in your telephone directory under
"U.S. Government, Justice Department,
Immigration and Naturalization Ser-
vice" or contact:*

Immigration & Naturalization Service
425 I Street, N.W.
Washington, DC 20536
(202) 514-4316
Department of Labor
Coordinator of Consumer Affairs
Washington, DC 20210
(202) 523-6060 *(general inquiries)*

Department of Labor
Employment & Training
Administration
*Look in your telephone directory under
"U.S. Government, Labor Department,
Employment & Training
Administration" or contact:*

Employment & Training
Administration
Director, Office of Public Affairs
Washington, DC 20210
(202) 523-6871

Department of Labor
Employment Standards
Administration
Office of Public Affairs
Washington, DC 20210
(202) 523-8743

Department of Labor
Occupational Safety and
Health Administration (OSHA)
*Look in your telephone directory under
"U.S. Government, Labor Department,
Occupational Safety and Health Administra-
tion" or contact:*

Occupational Safety and
Health Administration
Office of Information and
Consumer Affairs
Washington, DC 20210
(202) 523-8151

Department of Labor
Office of Labor-Management Standards
Washington, DC 20210
(202) 523-7343

Department of Labor
Pension and Welfare Benefits
Administration
Office of Program Services
Washington, DC 20210
(202) 523-8776

Department of Labor
Women's Bureau
The Work and Family Clearinghouse
Washington, DC 20210
1 (800) 827-5335 *(toll-free)*

Department of State
Overseas Citizen Services
Washington, DC 20520
(202) 647-3666 *(non-emergencies)*
(202) 647-5225 *(emergencies)*

Department of State
Passport Services
Washington Passport Agency
1425 K Street, N.W.
Washington, DC 20524
(202) 647-0518

Department of State
Visa Services
Washington, DC 20520
(202) 647-0510

Department of Transportation (DOT)
Air Safety:
Federal Aviation Administration (FAA)
Community and Consumer
Liaison Division
FAA (APA-200)
Washington, DC 20591
(202) 267-3479, 8592
1 (800) FAA-SURE *(toll-free outside DC)*

Airline Service Complaints:
Office of Intergovernmental
and Consumer Affairs (I-25)
Department of Transportation
Washington, DC 20590
(202) 366-2220

Auto Safety Hotline:
National Highway Traffic
Safety Administration (NHTSA)
(NEF-11)
Department of Transportation
Washington, DC 20690
(202) 366-0123

Department of the Treasury
Comptroller of the Currency
*The Comptroller of the Currency handles
complaints about national banks, i.e., banks
that have the word "National" in their
names or the initials "N.A." after their
names. For assistance, look in your telephone directory under "U.S. Government,*

*Treasury Department, Comptroller of the Currency" or contact:*

Comptroller of the Currency
Director, Compliance Policy
250 E Street, S.W.
Washington, DC 20219
(202) 874-4820

**Department of the Treasury
Internal Revenue Service (IRS)**
*Look in your telephone directory under "U.S. Government, Treasury Department, Internal Revenue Service."*

**Department of the Treasury
Office of Thrift Supervision**
*(formerly Federal Home Loan Bank Board)*
*The Office of Thrift Supervision handles complaints about savings and loan associations and savings banks.*
*For assistance contact:*

**Office of Thrift Supervision
Consumer Affairs**
1700 G Street, N.W.
Washington, DC 20552
(202) 906-6237
1 (800) 842-6929 *(toll-free outside DC)*

**Department of the Treasury
United States Savings Bonds Division
Office of Public Affairs**
Washington, DC 20220
(202) 634-5389
1 (800) US-BONDS

**Department of Veterans' Affairs (VA)**
*For information about VA medical care or benefits, write, call, or visit your nearest VA facility. Your telephone directory will list a VA medical center or regional office under "U.S. Government, Department of Veterans' Affairs," or under "U.S. Government, Veterans' Administration." You may also contact the offices listed below.*

*For information about benefits:*

Veterans' Benefits Administration (27)
Department of Veterans' Affairs
810 Vermont Avenue, N.W.
Washington, DC 20420
(202) 233-2576

*For information about medical care:*

Veterans' Health Administration (184C)
810 Vermont Avenue, N.W.
Washington, DC 20420
(202) 535-7208

*For consumer information or general assistance:*

Consumer Affairs Service
Department of Veterans Affairs
810 Vermont Avenue, N.W.
Washington, DC 20420
(202) 535-8962

**Equal Employment Opportunity Commission**
*Look in your telephone directory under "U.S. Government, Equal Employment Opportunity Commission" or contact:*

Office of Communications and
Legislative Affairs
Equal Employment Opportunity
Commission
1801 L Street, N.W.
Washington, DC 20507
(202) 663-4900
1 (800) USA-EEOC *(toll-free)*

**Federal Communications Commission (FCC)**
*Complaints about telephone systems:*
Common Carrier Bureau
Informal Complaints Branch
Federal Communications Commission
1919 M Street, N.W., Room 6202
Washington, DC 20554
(202) 632-7553

*General Information:*
Consumer Assistance and
Small Business Office
Federal Communications Commission
1919 M Street, N.W., Room 254
Washington, DC 20554
(202) 632-7000

*Complaints about radio or television:*
Mass Media Bureau
Complaints and investigations
Federal Communications Commission
2025 M Street, N.W., Room 8210
Washington, DC 20554
(202) 632-7048

**Federal Deposit Insurance Corporation**
*FDIC handles questions about deposit in-
surance coverage and complaints about
FDIC-insured state banks which are not
members of the Federal Reserve System. For
assistance, look in your telephone directory
under "U.S. Government, Federal Deposit Insurance Corporation" or contact:*

Office of Consumer Affairs
Federal Deposit Insurance Corporation
550 17th Street, N.W.
Washington, DC 20429
(202) 898-3536
1 (800) 424-5588 *(toll-free outside DC)*

**Federal Reserve System**
*The Board of Governors handles consumer
complaints about state-chartered banks and
trust companies which are members of the
Federal Reserve System. For assistance, look
in your telephone directory under "U.S.
Government, Federal Reserve System,
Board of Governors," or "Federal Reserve
Bank" or contact:*
Board of Governors of the
Federal Reserve System
Division of Consumer and
Community Affairs
Washington, DC 20551
(202) 452-3946

**Federal Trade Commission (FTC)**
*Look in your telephone directory under
"U.S. Government, Federal Trade
Commission" or contact:*
Correspondence Branch
Federal Trade Commission
Washington, DC 20580

Public Reference Section
Federal Trade Commission
6th & Pennsylvania Ave., N.W., Rm 130
Washington, DC 20580
(202) 326-2222 *(publications)*

**Government Printing Office (GPO)**
Government Publications:
Publications Service Section
Government Printing Office
Washington, DC 20402
(202) 275-3050

**Interstate Commerce Commission**
Office of Compliance and
Consumer Assistance
Washington, DC 20423
(202) 275-7148

**National Credit Union Administration**
*Look in your telephone directory under
"U.S. Government, National Credit Union
Administration" or contact:*
National Credit Union Administration
1776 G Street, N.W.
Washington, DC 20456
(202) 682-9640

**National Labor Relations Board**
Office of the Executive Secretary
1717 Pennsylvania Ave., N.W., Rm 701
Washington, DC 20570
(202) 254-9430

**Pension Benefit Guaranty Corporation**
2020 K Street, N.W.
Washington, DC 20006-1860
(202) 778-8800

Postal Rate Commission
Consumer Advocate
Postal Rate Commission
1333 H Street, N.W., Suite 300
Washington, DC 20268
(202) 789-6830

President's Committee on Employment
of People with Disabilities
1111 20th Street, N.W., Suite 636
Washington, DC 20036-3470
(202) 653-5044

Railroad Retirement Board
844 Rush Street
Chicago, IL 60611
(312) 751-4500

Securities and Exchange Commission
(SEC)
Office of Filings, Information,
and Consumer Services
450 5th Street, N.W.
(Mail Stop 2-6)
Washington, DC 20549
(202) 272-7440
*(investor complaints)*
(202) 272-5624
*(SEC Information Line- general topics and
sources of assistance)*

Small Business Administration (SBA)
Office of Consumer Affairs
409 Third Street, N.W.
Washington, DC 20416
(202) 205-6948
*(complaints only)*
1 (800) U-ASK-SBA
*(toll-free information)*

U.S. Consumer Product Safety
Commission (CPSC)
*To report a hazardous product or a product-
related injury, or to inquire about product
recalls, call or write:*

U.S. Consumer Product
Safety Commission
Product Safety Hotline
Washington, DC 20207
*(complaints only)*
1 (800) 638-CPSC *(toll-free)*

United States Postal Service
*If you experience difficulty when order mer-
chandise or conducting business transactions through the mail, or suspect that you
have been the victim of a mail fraud or misrepresentation scheme, contact your post-
master or local postal inspector. Look in
your telephone directory under "U.S. Government, Postal Service U.S." for these
local listings or contact:*

Chief Postal Inspector
United States Postal Service
Washington, DC 20260-2100
(202) 268-4267

*For consumer convenience, all post offices
and letter carriers have postage-free consumer service cards available for reporting
mail problems and submitting comments
and suggestions. If the problem cannot be
resolved using the Consumer Service Card
or through direct contact with the local post
office, write or call:*

Consumer Advocate
United States Postal Service
Washington, DC 20260-6720
(202) 268-2284

# State Agencies on Aging

The offices listed in this section coordinate services for older Americans. They provide information on services, programs, and opportunities for these consumers.

## Alabama

Commission on Aging
136 Catoma Street
Montgomery, AL 36130
(205) 242-5743
1 (800) 243-5463
*(toll-free in AL)*

## Alaska

Older Alaskans Commission
P.O. Box C
Juneau, AK 99811-0209

## Arizona

Aging and Adult Administration
1400 West Washington, 950A
Phoenix, AZ 85007
(602) 542-4446

## Arkansas

Office of Aging and Adult Services
Department of Human Services
P.O. Box 1437
Little Rock, AR 72203-1437
(501) 682-2441
1 (800) 482-8040
*(toll-free in AR)*

## California

Department of Aging
1600 K Street
Sacramento, CA 95814
(916) 322-5290
1 (800) 231-4024
*(toll-free in CA)*

## Colorado

Colorado Department of
Social Services
1575 Sherman Street
Denver, CO 80203-1714
(303) 866-5700

## Connecticut

Department on Aging
175 Main Street
Hartford, CT 06106
(302) 566-3238
1 (800) 443-9946 *(toll-free in CT)*

## Delaware

Department of Health and
Social Services
Division of Aging
1908 North DuPont Highway
New Castle, DE 19720
(302) 421-6791
1 (800) 223-9074 *(toll-free in DE)*

## District of Columbia

D.C. Office on Aging
1424 K Street, N.W., 2nd Floor
Washington, DC 20005
(202) 724-5623

## Florida

Aging and Adult Services
1321 Winewood Boulevard
Room 323
Tallahassee, FL 32399-0700
(904) 488-8922

## Georgia

Office of Aging
878 Peachtree Street, N.E.Suite 632
Atlanta, GA 30309
(404) 894-5333

## Hawaii

Executive Office on Aging
335 Merchant Street, Room 241
Honolulu, HI 98613
(808) 548-2593
1 (800) 468-4644 *(toll-free in HI)*

## Idaho

Idaho Office on Aging
Statehouse, Room 108
Boise, ID 83720
(208) 334-3833

## Illinois

Department on Aging
421 East Capitol Avenue
Springfield, IL 62701
(217) 785-2870
1 (800) 252-8966 *(toll-free voice TDD)*

## Indiana

Aging/In-Home Care
Services Division
Department of Human Services
P.O. Box 7083
Indianapolis, IN 46207-7083
(317) 232-7020
1 (800) 622-4972 *(toll-free in IN)*

## Iowa

Department of Elder Affairs
914 Grand Avenue, Suite 236
Des Moines,IA 50319
(515) 281-5187
1 (800) 532-3213 *(toll-free in IA)*

## Kansas

Department on Aging
Docking State Office Building, Rm 122 S
915 Southwest Harrison Street
Topeka, KS 66612-1500
(913) 296-4986
1 (800) 432-3535 *(toll-free in KS)*

## Kentucky

Division for Aging Services
Department for Social Services
275 East Main Street, 6th Floor West
Frankfort, KY 40621
(502) 564-6930
1 (800) 372-2991 *(toll-free in KY)*

## Louisiana

Governor's Office of Elder Affairs
P.O. Box 80374
Baton Rouge, LA 70898
(504) 925-1700

## Maine

Bureau of Elder and Adult Service
35 Anthony Avenue
Statehouse, Station 11
Augusta, ME 04333-0011
(207) 626-5335

## Maryland

Office on Aging
301 West Preston Street, 10th Floor
Baltimore, MD 21201
(301) 225-1100
1 (800) 243-3425 *(toll-free in MD)*

## Massachusetts

Executive Office of Elder Affairs
38 Chauncy Street
Boston, MA 02111
(617) 727-7750
1 (800) 882-2003 *(toll-free in MA)*

## Michigan

Office of Services to the Aging
P.O. Box 30026
Lansing, MI 48909
(517) 373-8230

## Minnesota

Minnesota Board on Aging
444 Lafayette Road
St. Paul, MN 55155-3843
1 (800) 652-9747 *(toll-free in MN)*

## Mississippi

Divison of Aging and
Adult Services
421 West Pascagoula Street
Jackson, MS 39203
(601) 949-2070
1 (800) 453-6347 *(toll-free in MS)*

## Missouri

Division of Aging
P.O. Box 1337
Jefferson City, MO 65102
(314) 751-8535
1 (800) 392-0210
*(toll-free in MO)*

## Montana

Coordinator of Aging Services
Governor's Office
State Capitol
Helena, MT 59620
(406) 444-4204
1 (800) 332-2272 *(toll-free in MT)*

## Nebraska

Nebraska Department on Aging
State Office Building
P.O. Box 95044
Lincoln, NB 68509
(402) 471-2306

## Nevada

Division for Aging Services
Department of Human Resources
340 North 11th Street
Las Vegas, NV 89158
(702) 486-3545

## New Hampshire

Division of Elderly and
Adult Services
6 Hazen Drive
Concord, NH 03301
(603) 271-4680
1 (800) 351-1888
*(toll-free in NH)*

## New Jersey

Division on Aging
Department of Community Affairs
101 South Broad Street, CN 807
Trenton, NJ 08625
(609) 292-4833
1 (800) 792-8820
*(toll-free in NJ)*

## New Mexico

State Agency on Aging
224 East Palace Avenue
4th Floor
Santa Fe, NM 87501
1 (800) 432-2080
*(toll-free in NM)*

## New York

New York State Office
for the Aging
Agency Building 2, ESP
Albany, NY 12223
(518) 474-5731
1 (800) 342-9871
*(toll-free in NY)*

### North Carolina

Division on Aging
Department of Human Resources
Caller Box No. 2953
693 Palmer Drive
Raleigh, NC 27626-0531
(919) 733-3983
1 (800) 662-7030
*(toll-free in NC)*

### North Dakota

Aging Services
Department of Human Services
600 East Boulevard
Bismarck, ND 58505
(701) 224-2310
1 (800) 472-2622
*(toll-free in ND)*

### Ohio

Ohio Department of Aging
50 West Broad Street, 9th Floor
Columbus, OH 43266-0501
(614) 466-5500
1 (800) 282-1206
*(toll-free in OH)*

### Oklahoma

Special Unit on Aging
P.O. Box 25352
Oklahoma City, OK 73125
(405) 521-2281

### Oregon

Senior Services Division
Department of Human Resources
State of Oregon
313 Public Service Building
Salem, OR 97310
(503) 378-4728
1 (800) 232-3020
*(toll-free in Or)*

### Pennsylvania

Department of Aging
231 State Street
Harrisburg, PA 17101
(717) 783-1549

### Puerto Rico

Office of Elder Affairs
Call Box 563
Old San Juan
Station, PR 00902
(809) 721-4560

### Rhode Island

Department of Elderly Affairs
160 Pine Street
Providence, RI 02903
(401) 277-2880
1 (800) 322-2880
(toll-free in RI)

### South Carolina

South Carolina Commission
on Aging
400 Arbor Lake Drive
Suite B-500
Columbia, SC 29223
(803) 735-0210
1 (800) 868-9095
(toll-free)

### South Dakota

Office of Adult Services and Aging
700 Governors Drive
Pierre, SD 57501
(605) 773-3656

### Tennessee

Commission on Aging
706 Church Street, Suite 201
Nashville, TN 37243-0860
(615) 741-2056

## Texas

Texas Department on Aging
P.O. Box 12786, Capitol Station
Austin, TX 78711
(512) 444-2727
1 (800) 252-9240 *(toll-free in TX)*

## Utah

Division of Aging and Adult Services
P.O. Box 45500
Salt Lake City, UT 84145-0500
(801) 538-3910

## Vermont

Department of Aging
and Disabilities
103 South Main Street
Waterbury, VT 05671-2301
(802) 241-2400

## Virginia

Department for the Aging
700 East Franklin Street
10th Floor
Richmond, VA 23219
(804) 225-2271
1 (800) 552-4464 *(toll-free in VA)*

## Washington

Aging and Adult Services
Administration
OB-44A
Olympia, WA 98504
(206) 493-2509
1 (800) 422-3263
*(toll-free in WA)*

## West Virginia

Commission on Aging
State Capitol
Charleston, WV 25305
(304) 348-3317

## Wisconsin

Bureau on Aging
P.O. Box 7851
Madison, WI 53707
(608) 266-2536

## Wyoming

Division on Aging
139 Hathaway Building
Cheyenne, WY 82002-0480
(307) 777-7986
1 (800) 442-2766
*(toll free in WY)*

## Sources of Assistance in Employment Areas

### National Offices

U.S. Equal Employment
Opportunity Commission
Washington, DC 20507

Civil Rights Division
U.S. Department of Health and
Human Services
Washington, DC 20201

Social Security Administration
U.S. Department of Health and
Human Services
Baltimore, MD 21235

Occupational Safety and Health
Administration
U.S. Department of Labor
Washington, DC 20210
Office of Pension & Welfare
Benefit Program
U.S. Department of Labor
Washington, DC 20210

Office of Federal Contract
Compliance Programs
Employment Standards Administration
U.S. Department of Labor
Washington, DC 20210

Office of Workers' Compensation
Programs
Employment Standards Administration
U.S. Department of Labor
Washington, DC 20210

Federal Trade Commission
Washington, DC 20580

Pension Benefit Guaranty Corp.
2020 K Street, NW
Washington, DC 20006
Office of Labor Management Standards
U.S. Department of Labor
Washington, DC 20210

Internal Revenue Service
U.S. Department of the Treasury
Washington, DC 20224

Office of Revenue Sharing
U.S. Department of the Treasury
Washington, DC 20226

Women's Bureau
Office of the Secretary
U.S. Department of Labor
Washington, Dc 20210

Wage and Hour Division
Employment Standards Administration
U.S. Department of Labor
Washington, DC 20210

## State Agencies

**Alabama**
Department of Industrial Relations
Industrial Relations Building
Montgomery, AL 36130

**Alaska**
Department of Labor
P.O. Box 1149
Juneau, AK 99802

Alaska State Commission for
Human Rights
800 "A" Street, Suite 202
Anchorage, AK 99501

**Arizona**
Department of Labor
800 W. Washington Ave.
P.O. Box 19070
Phoenix, AZ 85005

Arizona Civil Rights Division
1275 W. Washington
Phoenix, AZ 85007

**Arkansas**
Department of Labor
1022 High Street
Little Rock, AR 72202

**California**
Department of Industrial Relations
525 Golden Gate Avenue
P.O. Box 603
San Francisco, CA 94101

Department of Fair Employment and
Housing
1201 I Street
Sacramento, CA 95814

**Colorado**
Department of Labor and Employment
251 East 12th Avenue
Denver, CO 80203

Colorado Civil Rights Commission
1525 Sherman, Room 600C
Denver, CO 80203

**Connecticut**
Labor Department
200 Folly Brook Boulevard
Wethersfield, CT 06109

Commission on Human Rights and
Opportunities
90 Washington Street
Hartford, CT 06101

**District of Columbia**
DC Dept of Employment Services
500 C Street, NW
Washington, DC 20001

Commission on Human Rights
District Building
Washington, DC 20004

**Florida**
Department of Labor and
Employment Security
Berkeley Building
2590 Executive Center Circle East
Tallahassee, FL 32301

Commission on Human Relations
325 John Knox Road
Suite 240, Building F
Tallahassee, FL 32303

**Georgia**
Department of Labor
State Labor Building
254 Washington Street, SW
Atlanta, GA 30334

**Guam**
Department of Labor
Government of Guam
Box 23548, GMF
Guam, M.I. 96921

**Hawaii**
Department of Labor and
Industrial Relations
830 Punchbowl Street
Honolulu, HI 96813

Dept. of Labor and Industrial Relations
Labor Law Enforcement
888 Mililani Street, Room 401
Honolulu, HI 96813
P.O. Box 1149
Juneau, AK 99802

**Idaho**
Dept. of Labor and Industrial Services
Room 400, Statehouse Mail
317 Main Street
Boise, ID 83720

Commission on Human Rights
450 W. State Street, 1st Floor
Boise, ID 83720

**Illinois**
Department of Labor
1 West Old Capitol Plaza
Springfield, IL 62701-1217

Department of Human Rights
100 West Randolph Street
Chicago, IL 60601

**Indiana**
Department of Labor
Room 1013, State Office Building
100 North Senate Avenue
Indianapolis, IN 46204

Civil Rights Commission
32 West Washington Street
Indianapolis, IN 26204-3526

**Iowa**
Division of Labor
1000 East Grand Avenue
Des Moines, IA 50319

Civil Rights Commission
211 East Maple Street
c/o State Mailroom
Des Moines, IA 50319

**Kansas**
Department of Human Resources
401 Topeka Avenue
Topeka, KS 66603

Commission on Civil Rights
214 Southwest 6th Street
Liberty Building, 5th Floor
Topeka, KS 66603

**Kentucky**
Labor Cabinet
U.S. 127 South Building
Frankfort, KY 40601

Commission on Human Rights
823 Capitol Plaza Tower
Frankfort, KY 40601

**Louisiana**
Department of Labor
1045 State Land & Natural Resources
Bldg.
P.O. Box 44094
Baton Rouge, LA 70804

**Maine**
Department of Labor
20 Union Street
Augusta, ME 04330

Human Rights Commission
State House—Station 51
Augusta, ME 04330

**Maryland**
Division of Labor and Industry
501 St. Paul Place
Baltimore, MD 21202

Commission on Human Relations
20 East Franklin Street
Baltimore, MD 21202

**Massachusetts**
Department of Labor and Industries
State Office Building
100 Cambridge Street
Boston, MA 02202

Commission Against Discrimination
1 Ashburton Place, Suite 601
Boston, MA 02108

**Michigan**
Department of Labor
Leonard Plaza Building
309 North Washington
P.O. Box 30015
Lansing, MI 48909

Department of Civil Rights
303 W. Kalamazoo
Lansing, MI 48913

**Minnesota**
Department of Labor and Industry
444 Lafayette Road
St. Paul, MN 55101

Department of Human Rights
5th Floor Bremer Tower
7th Place and Minnesota Street
St. Paul, MN 55101

**Mississippi**
Workmen's Compensation Commission
P.O. Box 5300
Jackson, MS 39216

**Missouri**
Dept. of Labor and Industrial Relations
1904 Missouri Boulevard
P.O. Box 599
Jefferson City, MO 65102

Commission on Human Rights
315 Ellis Boulevard
P.O. Box 1129
Jefferson City, MO 65102-1129

**Montana**
Department of Labor and Industry
P.O. Box 1728
Helena, MT 59624

Human Rights Commission
1236 6th Avenue
P.O. Box 1728
Helena, MT 59624

**Nebraska**
Labor Commission
505 S. 16th Street
Box 94600, State House Station
Lincoln, NE 68509

Equal Opportunity Commission
301 Centennial Mall, South
P.O. Box 94934
Lincoln, NE 68509-4934

**Nevada**
Labor Commission
505 East King Street, Room 602
Carson City, NV 89710

Equal Rights Commission
1515 E. Tropicana
Las Vegas, NV 89158

**New Hampshire**
Department of Labor
19 Pillsbury Street
Concord, NH 03301

Commission for Human Rights
61 South Spring Street
Concord, NH 03301

**New Jersey**
Department of Labor
P.O. Box CN 110
Trenton, NJ 08625

Division of Civil Rights
1100 Raymond Boulevard
Newark, NJ 07102

**New Mexico**
Labor Department
P.O. Box 1928
Albuquerque, NM 07102

Human Rights Commission
930 Baca Street, Suite A
Santa Fe, NM 87501

**New York**
Department of Labor
State Campus Building 12
Albany, NY 12240

Division of Human Rights
55 West 125 Street
New York, NY 10047

**North Carolina**
Department of Labor
Labor Building
214 West Jones Street
Raleigh, NC 27603

**North Dakota**
Department of Labor
State Capitol, 5th Floor
Bismark, ND 58505

**Ohio**
Department of Industrial Relations
2323 W. 5th Avenue
Columbus, OH 43215

Civil Rights Commission
220 Parsons Avenue
Columbus, OH 43215

**Oklahoma**
Department of Labor
1315 N. Broadway Place
Oklahoma City, OK 73103-4817

Human Rights Commission
Room 311, Jim Thorpe Building
2101 North Lincoln Boulevard
Oklahoma City, OK 73105

**Oregon**
Bureau of Labor and Industries
State Office Building
1400 SW Fifth
Portland, OR 97201

**Pennsylvania**
Department of Labor and Industry
1700 Labor and Industry Building
7th & Forster Streets
Harrisburg, PA 17120

Human Relations Commission
101 South Second Street, Suite 300
P.O. Box 3145
Harrisburg, PA 17105

**Puerto Rico**
Department of Labor and
Human Resources
505 Munoz Rivera Avenue
G.P.O. Box 3088
Hato Rey, PR 00918

**Rhode Island**
Department of Labor
220 Elmwood Avenue
Providence, RI 02907

Commission for Human Rights
10 Abbott Park Place
Providence, RI 02903-3768

**South Carolina**
Department of Labor
3600 Forest Drive
P.O. Box 11329
Columbia, SC 29211

Human Affairs Commission
Post Office Drawer 11300
Columbia, SC 29211

**South Dakota**
Department of Labor
700 Governors Drive
Pierre, SD 57501

Division of Human Rights
Pierre, SD 57501-5070

**Tennessee**
Department of Labor
501 Union Building
Nashville, TN 37219

Commission for Human Development
208 Tennessee Building
535 Church Street
Nashville, TN 37219

**Texas**
Department of Labor and Standards
P.O. Box 12157, Capitol Station
Austin, TX 78711

Commission on Human Rights
P.O. Box 13493, Capitol Station
Austin, TX 78711

**Utah**
Industrial Commission
160 East 300 South
P.O. Box 5800
Salt Lake City, UT 84110-5800

Anti-Discrimination Division
160 East 300 South
P.O. Box 5800
Salt Lake City, UT 84110-5800

**Vermont**
Department of Labor and Industry
State Office Building
Montpelier, VT 05602

**Virginia**
Department of Labor and Industry
P.O. Box 12064
Richmond, VA 23241

Human Rights Council
 Office of the Secretary of Administration
P.O. Box 1475
Richmond, VA 23241

**Virgin Islands**
Department of Labor
P.O. Box 890
Christiansted, St. Croix 00820

**Washington**
Department of Labor and Industries
General Administration Building
Olympia, WA 98504

Human Rights Commission
402 Evergreen Plaza Building
FJ-41
Olympia, WA 98504

**West Virginia**
Department of Labor
Capitol Complex
1800 Washington Street, East
Charleston, WV 25305

Human Rights Commission
215 Professional Building
1036 Quarrier Street
Charleston, WV 25301

**Wisconsin**
Department of Industry, Labor and Human Relations
210 East Washington Avenue
P.O. Box 7946
Madison, WI 53707

Equal rights Division
P.O. Box 8928
Madison, WI 53708

**Wyoming**
Department of Labor and Statistics
Herschler Building
Cheyenne, WY 82002

Fair Employment Commission
Herschler Building
Cheyenne, WY 82002

# EEOC Offices

EEOC has twenty-three district, one field, seventeen area and nine local offices. District offices are full service units which investigate charges and systemic cases and conduct litigation. Area offices investigate charges, including charges for potential litigation. Local offices investigate charges but forward cases to district offices for litigation development. The field office investigates charges and systemic cases and conducts litigation. It reports directly to headquarters.

## Area Offices

| | | |
|---|---|---|
| Albuquerque, NM | Little Rock, AR | Pittsburgh, PA |
| Boston, MA | Louisville, KY | Raleigh, NC |
| Cincinnati, OH | Nashville, TN | Richmond, VA |
| El Paso, TX | Newark, NJ | San Diego, CA |
| Jackson, MS | Norfolk, VA | Tampa, FL |
| Kansas City, MO | Oklahoma City, OK | |

## Local Offices

| | | |
|---|---|---|
| Buffalo, NY | Greenville, SC | Oakland, CA |
| Fresno, CA | Honolulu, HI | San Jose, CA |
| Greensboro, NC | Minneapolis, MN | Savannah, Ga |

## Field Office

Washington, DC

## District Offices

| | | |
|---|---|---|
| Atlanta, GA | Detroit, MI | New York, NY |
| Baltimore, MD | Houston, TX | Philadelphia, PA |
| Birmingham, AL | Indianapolis, IN | Phoenix, AZ |
| Charlotte, NC | Los Angeles, CA | San Antonio, TX |
| Chicago, IL | Memphis, TN | San Francisco, CA |
| Cleveland, OH | Miami, FL | Seattle, WA |
| Dallas, TX | Milwaukee, WI | St. Louis, MO |
| Denver, CO | New Orleans, LA | |

# U.S Government Bookstores Locations

The U.S. Government Printing Office (GPO) operates bookstores throughout the country where you can browse through the shelves and purchase books. The bookstores can order any government book currently offered for sale and have it sent directly to you. All of GPO's bookstores accept VISA, MasterCard and Superintendent of Documents deposit account orders.

**Atlanta**
275 Peachtree Street, NE
Room 110
PO Box 56445
Atlanta, GA 30343
Tel: (404) 331-6947
Fax: (404) 331-1787

**Birmingham**
O'Neill Building
2021 Third Ave., North
Birmingham, AL 35203
Tel: (205) 731-1056
Tel: (205) 731-3444

**Boston**
Thomas P. O'Neill Building
Room 169
10 Causeway Street
Boston, MA 02222
Tel: (617) 720-4180
Fax: (617) 720-5753

**Chicago**
One Congress Center
401 South State St., Ste 124
Chicago, IL 60605
Tel: (312) 353-5133
Fax: (312) 353-1590

**Cleveland**
Room 1653, Federal Building
1240 E. 9th Street
Cleveland, OH 44199
Tel: (216) 522-4922
Fax: (216) 522-4714

**Columbus**
Room 207, Federal Bldg.
200 N. High Street
Columbus, OH 44199
Tel: (614) 469-6956
Fax: (614) 469-5374

**Dallas**
Room IC46, Federal Building
1100 Commerce Street
Dallas, TX 75242
Tel: (214) 767-0076
Tel: (214) 767-3239

**Denver**
Room 117, Federal Building
1961 Stout Street
Denver, CO 80294
Tel: (303) 844-3964
Fax: (303) 844-4000

**Detroit**
Suite 160, Federal Building
Detroit, MI 48226
Tel: (313) 226-7816
Fax: (313) 226-4698

**Houston**
Texas Crude Building
801 Travis Street, Suite 120
Houston, TX 77002
Tel: (713) 228-1187
Fax: (713) 228-1186

**Jacksonville**
100 West Bay Street
Suite 100
Jacksonville, FL 32202
Tel: (904) 353-0569
Fax: (904) 353-1280

**Kansas City**
120 Bannister Mall
5600 E. Bannister Road
Kansas City, MO 64137
Tel: (816) 765-2256
Tel: (816) 767-8233

**Laurel**
U.S. Gov't Printing Office
Warehouse Sales Outlet
8660 Cherry Lane
Laurel, MD 20707
Tel: (301) 953-7974
Tel: (301) 792-0262
Fax: (301) 498-9107

**Los Angeles**
ARCO Plaza, C-Level
505 South Flower St.
Los Angeles, CA 90071
Tel: (213) 239-9844
Fax: (213) 239-9848

**Milwaukee**
Room 190, Federal Bldg.
517 E. Wisconsin Avenue
Milwaukee, WI 53202
Tel: (414) 297-1304
Fax: (414) 297-1300

## U.S Government Bookstores Locations (continued)

**New York**
Room 110, Federal Building
26 Federal Plaza
New York, NY
Tel: (212) 264-3825
Fax: (212) 264-9318

**Philadelphia**
Robert Morris Building
100 North 17th Street
Philadelphia, PA 19103
Tel: (215) 597-0677
Fax: (215) 597-4548

**Pittsburgh**
Room 118, Federal Building
1000 Liberty Avenue
Pittsburgh, PA 15222
Tel: (412( 644-2721
Fax: (412) 644-4547

**Portland**
1305 SW First Avenue
Portland, OR 97201-58010
Tel: (503) 221-6217
Tel: (503) 225-0563

**Pueblo**
World Savings Building
720 North Main Street
Pueblo, CO 81003
Tel: (719) 544-3142
Fax: (719) 544-6719

**San Francisco**
Room 1023, Federal Building
450 Golden Gate Avenue
San Francisco, CA 94102
Tel: (415) 252-5334
Fax: (415) 252-5339

**Seattle**
Room 194, Federal Building
915 Second Avenue
Seattle, WA 98174
Tel: (206) 553-4270
Fax: (206) 553-6717

**Washington, D.C.**
U.S. Gov't Printing Office
710 N. Capitol Street, NW
Washington, DC 20401
Tel: (202) 512-0132
Fax: (202) 512-1355

1510 H. Street, NW
Washington, DC 20401
Tel: (202) 653-5075
Fax: (202) 376-5055

## Other Organizations

American Association of
Retired Persons
1909 K Street, N.W.
Washington, D.C. 20049

American Society of Travel
Agents, Inc.
1101 King Street
Alexandria, VA 22314
(703) 739-2782

Consumer Federation of
America
Suite 604
1424 Street, N.W.
Washington, D.C. 20036

Direct Marketing Association
6 East 43rd Street
New York, N.Y. 10017
(212) 689-4977

Direct Selling Association
Suite 60
1730 M Street, N.W.
Washington, D.C. 20036

Institute of Certified
Financial Planners
Suite 301
7600 E. Eastman Avenue,
Denver, Colorado 80231
(303) 751-7600

International Association for
Financial Planning
2 Concourse Parkway, Suite 800
Atlanta, Georgia 30328
(404) 395-1605

National Association of
Personal Financial Advisors
1130 Lake Cook Rd, Suite 105
Buffalo Grove, Illinois 60089
1-800-366-2732

National Foundation for
Consumer Credit
8611 Second Avenue, Suite 100
Silver Spring, Maryland 20910
(301) 589-5600

# INDEX

# ALLWORTH PRESS BOOKS

**Allworth Press publishes quality books to help individuals and small businesses. Titles include:**

**Legal-Wise:** Self-Help Legal Forms for Everyone
*by Carl Battle* (208 pages, 8½" X 11", $16.95)

**Business and Legal Forms for Authors and Self-Publishers**
*by Tad Crawford* (176 pages, 8⅞" X 11", $15.95)

**Business and Legal Forms for Fine Artists**
*by Tad Crawford* (128 pages, 8⅞" X 11", $12.95)

**Business and Legal Forms for Graphic Designers**
*by Tad Crawford and Eva Doman Bruck* (208 pages, 8½" X 11", $19.95)

**Business and Legal Forms for Illustrators**
*by Tad Crawford* (160 pages, 8⅞" X 11", $15.95)

**Business and Legal Forms for Photographers**
*by Tad Crawford* (192 pages, 8½" X 11", $18.95)

**Legal Guide for the Visual Artist**
*by Tad Crawford* (224 pages, 7" X 12", $18.95)

**Careers By Design**
*by Roz Goldfarb* (224 pages, 6¾" X 10", $16.95)

**How to Sell Your Photographs and Illustrations**
*by Elliott and Barbara Gordon* (128 pages, 8" X 10", $16.95)

**The Business of Being an Artist**
*by Dan Grant* (224 pages, 6" X 9", $16.95)

**On Becoming an Artist**
*by Dan Grant* (192 pages, 6" X 9", $12.95)

**The Family Legal Companion**
*by Thomas Hauser* (256 pages, 6" X 9", $16.95)

**How to Shoot Stock Photos that Sell**
*by Michal Heron* (192 pages, 8" X 10", $16.95)

**The Photographer's Organizer**
*by Michal Heron* (192 pages, 28" X 10", $16.95)

# ALLWORTH PRESS BOOKS

**Stock Photo Forms**
*by Michal Heron* (32 pages, 8½" X 11", $8.95)

**Accepted:** Your Guide to Finding the Right College —and How to Pay for It
*by Stuart Kahan* (128 pages, 6¾" X 10", $10.95)

**The Photographer's Assistant**
*by John Kieffer* (208 pages, 6¾" X 10", $16.95)

**Licensing Art & Design**
*by Caryn R. Leland* (272 pages, 6" X 9", $18 .95)

**Travel Photography:** A Complete Guide to How to Shoot and Sell
*by Susan McCartney* (384 pages,6¾" X 10", $22.95)

**The Graphic Designer's Basic Guide to the MacIntosh**
*by Michael Meyerowitz and Sam Sanchez* (144 pages, 8" X 10", $19.95)

**Hers:** The Wise Woman's Guide to Starting a Business on $2,000 or Less
*by Carol Milano* (208 pages, 6" X 9", $12.95)

**The Artist's Complete Health and Safety Guide**
*by Monona Rossol* (328 pages, 6" X 9", $16.95)

**Stage Fright**
*by Monona Rossol* (144 pages, 6" X 9", $12.95)

**The Unemployment Survival Handbook**
by Nina Schuyler (144 pages, 6"X9", $9.95)

**Electronic Design and Publishing: Business Practices**
*by Liane Sebastian* (112 pages, 6¾" X 10", $19.95)

**Overexposure:** Health Hazards in Photography
*by Susan Shaw and Monona Rossol* (320 pages, 6¾" X 10", $18.95)

**Caring for Your Art**
*by Jill Snyder* (176 pages, 6" X 9", $14.95)

**Make It Legal**
*by Lee Wilson* (272 pages, 6" X 9", $18 .95)

---

Please write to request our free catalog.
If you wish to order a book, send your check or money order to:
**Allworth Press, 10 East 23rd Street, Suite 400, New York, New York 10010**
To pay for shipping and handling, include $3 for the first book ordered and $1 for each additional
book($7 plus $1 if the order is from Canada). New York State residents must add sales tax.